ASEAN Law and Regional Integration

Since the passage of the ASEAN Charter in 2008, ASEAN has transformed itself from a loose economic cooperation, into a formal intergovernmental organization designed to create an "ASEAN Community" forged together in three pillar communities – the ASEAN Political-Security Community, ASEAN Economic Community, and ASEAN Socio-Cultural Community. Forty years of pre-Charter ASEAN practices, coupled with over ten years of post-Charter ASEAN practices thus far, has witnessed the conclusion of hundreds of legally binding regional treaties and similarly binding international instruments in all areas of economic, political-security, and socio-cultural concerns for Southeast Asia to achieve ASEAN's rule of law-based development objective. Pre-Charter and post-Charter ASEAN Law is variably implemented under a hybrid governance system that depends heavily on ASEAN Member State national implementation alongside ASEAN's evolving regional institutions. The result is not a model of deep integration as in the case of the European Union, but a particular paradigm of horizontal embeddedness of ASEAN Law – in all its norms and operational practices – contingent on the capacities and compliance of national government bureaucracies in Southeast Asia.

This edited collection is a concise authoritative volume covering the practical, doctrinal, legal, and policy aspects of the new regime of ASEAN Law and its consequences for realizing rule of law-based development in Southeast Asia's emerging single market and production base. Drawing together contributions from a range of key thinkers in the field, the editors present the legal and policy-making issues implicated in the practical implementation of Southeast Asia's single market and its regime for the free movement of goods, services, foreign investment, and cross-border labor. The book also examines the nature of regional law-making under ASEAN before and after the commencement of regional integration in 2015, the nature of ASEAN's economic regulators, as well as the evolving structure for enforcement and harmonization of "ASEAN Law" through the array of Southeast Asian national courts, arbitral tribunals, and incipient mechanisms for inter-State, intra-regional, and individual-State conflict management and dispute resolution.

This book is highly relevant to students, scholars, and policy-makers with an interest in ASEAN Law and regional policy, and to Southeast Asian studies in general.

Diane A. Desierto is tenured Associate Professor of Human Rights Law and Global Affairs at the University of Notre Dame Keough School of Global Affairs; Professor of International Law at the Philippines Judicial Academy; and Faculty Fellow at the Klau Center for Civil and Human Rights, the Kellogg Institute of International Studies, Liu Institute for Asia and Asian Studies, and the ND Initiative for Global Development at the University of Notre Dame (Notre Dame, USA).

David Cohen is Director, Center for Human Rights and International Justice, WSD Handa Professor in Human Rights and International Justice, and Professor of Classics, Stanford University.

ASEAN Law and Regional Integration

Governance and the Rule of Law in Southeast Asia's Single Market

Edited by Diane A. Desierto and David Cohen

Routledge
Taylor & Francis Group
LONDON AND NEW YORK

First published 2021
by Routledge
2 Park Square, Milton Park, Abingdon, Oxon OX14 4RN

and by Routledge
52 Vanderbilt Avenue, New York, NY 10017

Routledge is an imprint of the Taylor & Francis Group, an informa business

British Library Cataloguing-in-Publication Data
A catalogue record for this book is available from the British Library

Library of Congress Cataloging-in-Publication Data
Names: Desierto, Diane A., editor. | Cohen, David (David J.), editor.
Title: ASEAN law and regional integration: governance and the rule of law in Southeast Asia's single market / edited by Diane A. Desierto and David J. Cohen.
Description: New York: Routledge, 2021. |
Includes bibliographical references and index.
Identifiers: LCCN 2020031059 (print) | LCCN 2020031060 (ebook) |
ISBN 9781138934917 (hardback) | ISBN 9781315267401 (ebook)
Subjects: LCSH: ASEAN. | Law and economic development–Southeast Asia. |
Rule of law–Southeast Asia. | Southeast Asia–Economic integration. |
Corporate governance–Law and legislation–Southeast Asia.
Classification: LCC KNE171 .A84 2021 (print) |
LCC KNE171 (ebook) | DDC 341.24/73–dc23
LC record available at https://lccn.loc.gov/2020031059
LC ebook record available at https://lccn.loc.gov/2020031060

ISBN: 978-1-138-93491-7 (hbk)
ISBN: 978-1-315-26740-1 (ebk)

Typeset in Galliard
by Newgen Publishing UK

Contents

Contributors

Lead editor and author

Prof. Dr. Diane A. Desierto is tenured Associate Professor of Human Rights Law and Global Affairs at the Keough School of Global Affairs, University of Notre Dame (Notre Dame, Indiana, USA), where she is also Faculty Fellow at the University of Notre Dame's Klau Center for Civil and Human Rights; the Kellogg Institute for International Studies; the Liu Institute for Asia and Asian Studies; and the Notre Dame Initiative for Global Development. At Notre Dame, she teaches graduate students in global affairs; JSD, LLM, and JD law students; and undergraduates in various interdisciplinary courses in international law, human rights, and global affairs; as well as in focused seminars in her specialist areas (international economic law and development, international human rights and humanitarian law, international dispute settlement, maritime security, and ASEAN Law). She is also Professor of International Law at the Philippine Judicial Academy of the Supreme Court of the Philippines; External Faculty Fellow at Stanford University's Handa Center for Human Rights and International Justice; and External Executive Director of the University of the Philippines College of Law's LLM Graduate Program at the Bonifacio Global City campus.

Professor Desierto is active as International Counsel at the Permanent Court of Arbitration, the International Criminal Court, the Human Rights Committee, and Philippine appellate courts; listed arbitrator of the British Virgin Islands Arbitration Centre (BVIAC); Drafting Team Member of the Hague Business and Human Rights Arbitration Rules; Academic Forum Member for the UNCITRAL Working Group on ISDS Reform; Co-Chair of the Oxford Investment Claims Summer Academy, and Academic Council Member of the Institute of Transnational Arbitration. She serves frequently as Resource Expert for the Association of Southeast Asian Nations (ASEAN), the European Union External Action Service, the US Agency for International Development (USAID), and currently serves as Expert for the United Nations Intergovernmental Working Group tasked to draft the new treaty on the right to development. She is a Scientific Advisory Board Member of the *European Journal of International Law* and Editor for *EJIL:Talk!*, Editorial Board

Member for both the *Indonesian Journal of International and Comparative Law* and *Integrated Bar of the Philippines Law Journal.* Professor Desierto received her doctorate (JSD) and master of laws (LLM) from Yale Law School, and her first law degree (JD cum laude and class salutatorian) and undergraduate degree in economics (BSc Economics summa cum laude and class valedictorian) from the University of the Philippines. Before joining Notre Dame, Professor Desierto taught in the University of the Philippines, Peking University STL, University of Hawaii Richardson School of Law, and was a former law clerk at the International Court of Justice, Director of Studies at the Hague Academy of International Law, and held various senior fellowships in Berlin, Singapore, Stanford CASBS, the Max Planck Institute for Comparative Public Law and International Law, among others.

Co-editor and author

Prof. Dr. David Cohen is Director, Center for Human Rights and International Justice, WSD Handa Professor in Human Rights and International Justice, Professor of Classics, Stanford University. He is a leading expert in the fields of human rights, international law, and transitional justice. Cohen taught at UC Berkeley from 1979–2012 as the Ancker Distinguished Professor for the Humanities, and served as the founding Director of the Berkeley War Crimes Studies Center, which moved to Stanford in 2013 and became the WSD Handa Center for Human Rights and International Justice.

Cohen's research into war crimes tribunals began in the mid-1990s with a project to collect the records of the national war crimes programs conducted in approximately 20 countries in Europe and Asia after WWII. Since 2001, Cohen's work has largely focused on contemporary tribunals and transitional justice initiatives. Cohen has led justice sector reform initiatives and tribunal monitoring programs in Indonesia, East Timor, Sierra Leone, Bangladesh, Rwanda, and Cambodia. At the regional level, Cohen has worked closely with the ASEAN Secretariat and the USAID Technical Facility to the ASEAN Secretariat in forming and leading an expert group to create a Human Rights Resource Center for ASEAN. Cohen serves as the Advisor to the Executive Director and the Governing Board of the Resource Center and leads the Center's research projects.

Professor Cohen received his JD at UCLA's School of Law, his PhD in Classics and Ancient History from Cambridge University, and an Honorary Doctorate in Law from the University of Zurich.

Contributing authors

Dr. Timothy Buehrer is Principal Associate at Nathan Inc., a private international economic and analytics consulting firm that works with governments around the world. He attained his JD from Harvard Law School and his PhD and MPP from Harvard Kennedy School of Government. An economist and lawyer, Dr. Buehrer advises governments on a wide range of economic policy issues with a focus on macroeconomics, private sector development, logistics, and trade. His experience in directing complex policy-reform initiatives has earned him recognition at USAID and among governments worldwide as a trusted advisor, capable manager, and intellectual leader. He is also a lawyer with experience in regulatory reform and legislative drafting. As Chief of Party for the USAID and State Department's ASEAN Connectivity through Trade and Investment (ACTI) project, Dr. Buehrer supports the Association of Southeast Asian Nations' economic integration efforts. The project works closely with US companies that are active in the region to promote trade and investment reforms and expand opportunities for small and medium enterprises. Since the 1980s, he has also led or held senior roles in projects in Africa and the Middle East, Southeast Asia, and Micronesia. In addition, he has offered consulting services Eastern Europe and South Asia, and East Asia. He has written extensively on inflation, monetary policy, trade, regulatory reform, and investment.

Professor Pasha L. Hsieh is Associate Professor of Law and Lee Kong Chian Fellow at the Singapore Management University School of Law. He holds Juris Doctor and LLM degrees from the University of Pennsylvania Law School, where he was a Senior Editor of the *University of Pennsylvania Law Review*. Prior to joining academia, he served as Legal Affairs Officer at the WTO Appellate Body Secretariat and as Associate at Shearman & Sterling LLP. He has been the Managing Editor of the *Chinese (Taiwan) Yearbook of International Law and Affairs* since 2006. Hsieh's teaching and research focus on public international law, international economic law, and Asian legal studies. He is particularly interested in the roles of ASEAN and China in international law and cross-Taiwan Strait relations, and has published articles in the *Journal of International Economic Law*, the *Journal of World Trade*, the *Cornell International Law Journal*, and the *Northwestern Journal of International Law and Business*. His work has been cited by the Federal Supreme Court of Switzerland, the European Parliament, and the OECD. Hsieh was awarded SMU's Lee Foundation Fellowship for Research Excellence in 2010 and received the Most Outstanding Legal Studies Teacher Award in 2015. He was elected Co-Chair of the Law in the Pacific Rim Region Interest Group of the American Society of International Law (ASIL) and co-convened the International Law Association-ASIL Asia-Pacific Research Forum in 2019.

Dr. Michelle Staggs Kelsall joined SOAS as Lecturer in International Law in July 2018. She holds a combined Bachelors in Media and Communications and Law (with Honors) from Macquarie University (Australia), a Masters in Public International Law (with Distinction) from the LSE and a PhD from the University of Nottingham. Prior to joining SOAS, Michelle worked for several years as a Human Rights Officer for the Office of the United Nations High Commissioner for Human Rights as well as in leadership positions for not-for-profit centers undertaking applied research in Southeast Asia and West Africa (Sierra Leone). This included leading trial monitoring programs and conducting training for judges and lawyers working at UN-assisted international criminal tribunals in Sierra Leone and Cambodia. Most recently, she was Deputy Director of the Human Rights Resource Centre (for ASEAN) where she oversaw all of the Centre's research, training, and outreach initiatives, including leading multi-country human rights studies with teams of researchers across all ten countries in ASEAN.

In keeping with her background, Michelle's research has a strong empirical focus. She is particularly interested in how international law is understood, interpreted, and reconstituted in the Global South, particularly in Asia (Southeast Asia). Her work adopts an interdisciplinary approach and draws on the social sciences and humanities to consider the intersections between public/private, global/local and domestic/international (amongst others). Michelle's current thematic focus is on the emergence of Business & Human Rights at the turn of the millennium. This includes considering the intersection between human rights, international corporate governance, and corporate social responsibility and the creation of a new market for virtue in human rights legal services. Her doctoral dissertation looks at the emergence of business and human rights at the United Nations, examining and critiquing the historical trajectories which led to its development from the 1970s to the present day.

Michelle is Co-Founder of ATLAS (Acting Together: Law, Advice, Support) – a women's legal network with over 6,000 members on all five continents, whose vision is to secure equal representation of women lawyers at all stages of their careers in the field of international law and policy across the globe.

Mr. Edmund W. Sim is currently Partner at international law firm, Appleton Luff, and an international trade attorney and regular editorial contributor to the *Singapore Straits Times* and *OpinionAsia* on trade and diplomacy in ASEAN, as well as editing the ASEAN Economic Community blog. He received his AB magna cum laude degree from Dartmouth College with Phi Beta Kappa honors, and a JD cum laude from the University of Michigan Law School. He has participated in over 180 trade remedy (antidumping, countervailing duty, and safeguard) proceedings in the US, EU, Canada, Australia, Korea, China, Turkey, Indonesia, South Africa, India, Russia, the Philippines, Malaysia, Thailand, and Singapore. Mr. Sim has provided assistance to government trade ministries in Asia and has participated in dispute resolution proceedings under the World Trade Organization, the General Agreement on Tariffs and Trade, the North American Free Trade Agreement, and the US–Canada Free Trade Agreement. Mr. Sim has represented companies in dealing with the economic integration of the ASEAN economies under the ASEAN Free Trade Agreement, and teaches a course on this subject at the National University of Singapore Faculty of Law. Mr. Sim was the lead lawyer for the Vietnamese seafood industry in the US antidumping investigation of frozen tra and basa fillets from Vietnam, the Malaysian and Philippine steel industries in the EU antidumping and antisubsidy investigations on stainless steel fasteners from Malaysia and the Philippines, as well as the Malaysian and Thai plastic industries in the US and EU antidumping and antisubsidy investigations on plastic bags from Malaysia and Thailand. He has served as Vice Chairman and Treasurer of the Board of Governors of the American Chamber of Commerce, Singapore; Committee Vice Chair at the American Bar Association, Inter Pacific Bar Association, American Society of International Law, and International Bar Association, and on the panel of FTA advisors maintained by the Singapore government.

Prof. Dr. Kevin Y.L. Tan specializes in constitutional and administrative law, international law and international human rights. He graduated with an LLB (Hons) from the Faculty of Law at the National University of Singapore and holds an LLM and JSD from the Yale Law School. He currently holds Adjunct Professorships at the Faculty of Law, National University of Singapore (NUS) as well as at the S. Rajaratnam School of International Studies, Nanyang Technological University (NTU) where he teaches constitutional law, international law, and international human rights. He has published widely in his areas of specialization and has written and edited over 40 books on the law, history, and politics of Singapore. Among his publications are: *Constitutional Law in Malaysia and Singapore; Managing Political Change in Singapore: The Elected Presidency* (Routledge, 1997); *Lee's Lieutenants: Singapore's Old Guard* (Allen & Unwin, 1999) (both with Lam Peng Er); *The Singapore Legal System* (Singapore University Press, 1999); *Essays in Singapore Legal History* (Marshall-Cavendish Academic, 2004); *Introduction to Singapore's Constitution* (Talisman, 2014); *The Constitution of Singapore: A Contextual Analysis* (Hart, 2015); *The Evolution of a Revolution: 40 Years of the Singapore Constitution* (with Thio Li-ann) (Routledge-Cavendish, 2009); and *50 Constitutional Moments That Defined a Nation* (Marshall-Cavendish, 2015) (with Thio Li-ann). Kevin has been on the Editorial Board of several leading legal journals. From 1998–2000, he was also Chief Editor of the *Singapore Journal of International and Comparative Law* and from 2000–2003 was the journal's Adjunct Editor. He is currently Editor-in-Chief of the *Asian Yearbook of International Law* (since 2010); Executive Editor of the *Asian Journal of Comparative Law* (since 2016); and Editorial Board Member of the *Korean Journal of International and Comparative Law* (since 2013). Kevin also serves on the Board of Governors of the Human Rights Resource Centre (HRRC).

Preface

This volume comes at an opportune time in the trajectory of ASEAN Community development. On the one hand, we are now ten years past the adoption of the ASEAN Charter and thus in a position to assess what has been achieved in implementing its ambitious framework of a "rules-based ASEAN." On the other hand, a realistic of assessment of the current political situation in many, if not most, of the ASEAN Member States indicates deep fractures within the community as to fundamental political values and principles expressed in the Charter as well as in regard to the way in which ASEAN should respond to the pressing issues posed by regional and global challenges. This raises the question of whether ASEAN's institutional structures, or lack thereof, are adequate for dealing with such challenges as opposed to pretending that they do not impinge upon ASEAN's mantra of "one vision, one identity, one community." ASEAN still clings to its tri-partite three-pillar structure and its foundational principles of consensus, non-interference, and reliance upon the ASEAN Summit as the ultimate and sole decision-making body. Whether that foundation is sufficient to meet present challenges or to create the integrated ASEAN Community envisioned by the Charter and the subsequent ASEAN Blueprints 2016–2025 is one of the questions that runs throughout the chapters of this book and is addressed by this group of authors who have all worked extensively with ASEAN institutions for many years. Likewise running through the volume is the question of how an ASEAN defined by the silos of its three pillars can possibly respond adequately on issues that inevitably cut across those pillars.

The tension between the vision of an increasingly integrated ASEAN and the silo mentality embodied in its three-pillar structure and their institutional expression appears clearly in the document adopted by the ASEAN leaders in 2015 and intended to guide ASEAN through the ensuing decade. That document, "ASEAN 2025: Forging Ahead Together," contains a section entitled "ASEAN Community Vision 2025." That section, comprising some six pages, is followed only by the blueprints of the three pillars that the ASEAN Secretariat published separately: the "ASEAN Political Security Blueprint 2025," the "ASEAN Economic Community Blueprint 2025," and the "ASEAN Socio-Cultural Community Blueprint 2025." The document ends there, giving no account of how these three blueprints can be "forged together" as the title "ASEAN 2025: Forging

Ahead Together" suggests they should be. That is hardly surprising, however, as an effective integrated approach to the cross-cutting issues that define the three blueprints would require ASEAN to create permanent professional standing structures for the development, implementation, and evaluation of policies and rules. This, of course, is something ASEAN is fundamentally loathe to do as it would undermine the ability of Member States to continue to do exactly as they please regardless of whether their policies and conduct conflict with the principles and commitments of the Charter and with "ASEAN Law," as explored in several chapters of this volume. The growing body of ASEAN conventions, declarations, and other instruments raises another issue that ASEAN is loath to address. While since the adoption of the Charter the mantra of a "rules-based ASEAN" has been constantly invoked, what it means to have a "rules-based community" in the ASEAN context is far from clear. This issue is also addressed by the authors of the ensuing chapters. Take, for example, the following provision of the "ASEAN Community Vision" in "ASEAN 2025: Forging Ahead Together":

> 4. We resolve to consolidate our Community, building upon and deepening the integration process to realise a rules-based, people-oriented, people-centred ASEAN Community, where our peoples enjoy human rights and fundamental freedoms, higher quality of life and the benefits of community building, reinforcing our sense of togetherness and common identity, guided by the purposes and principles of the ASEAN Charter.

At the moment, ASEAN does not have a coherent set of "rules," nor any mechanism for their authoritative drafting, adoption, interpretation and implementation, let alone for adjudication in the case of violations and associated disputes. And yet ASEAN Law does indeed exist as binding regional law for Southeast Asia, even as ASEAN and its Member States wrestle with institutional, normative, and polemical issues on the implementation, enforcement, and compliance with ASEAN Law. It is, for the present, very much a State-driven endeavor, much to the detriment of ASEAN's vast prospects for the populations of Southeast Asia. While ASEAN resolves to create a rules-based, people-centered community, the peoples of ASEAN have no opportunity to address the obvious failure of multiple Member States to respect the "human rights and fundamental freedoms" mentioned in the passage above and enshrined in the Charter. The ASEAN human rights bodies, such as the AICHR, remain adamant against receiving or investigating individual complaints, let alone dealing with humanitarian crises such as that of the Rohingya or other systematic abuses of state power. The challenge of making a "rules-based ASEAN" into a meaningful reality for the benefit of a truly "people-centered" ASEAN remains elusive and the chapters of this volume assess the areas where the most has been achieved and where the most remains to be done in fulfilling the promise and vision of the Charter and 2025 Blueprints for rule of law as the genuine pathway to lasting development for Southeast Asia.

Much remains to be done in the region in its prospects for rule of law-based development. We remain committed to working with our institutional partners and colleagues throughout ASEAN and Southeast Asian universities, think-tanks, non-profit organizations, counsels' organizations, among others, with whom we have had the privilege of working for many years. We are grateful to our respective institutions – the University of Notre Dame (Keough School of Global Affairs, and its Klau Center for Civil and Human Rights; the Kellogg Institute for International Studies; the Liu Institute for Asia and Asian Studies; and the Notre Dame Initiative for Global Development), and Stanford University (Classics Department and Stanford Global Studies' WSD Handa Center for Human Rights and International Justice) for their continued support of our academic scholarship and policy assistance work in ASEAN. We are grateful to Philippine Ambassador H.E. Elizabeth Buensuceso at the Committee of Permanent Representatives to ASEAN and former Philippine President Fidel V. Ramos for his insights on ASEAN's evolution; Mr. Un Sovannasam (Head, ASEAN Legal Affairs Division) and Mr. Pratap Parameswaran (former Director, APSC); our colleagues at the Human Rights Resource Centre in ASEAN (Jakarta, Indonesia); former Principal Counsel at the Asian Development Bank, Dr. Kala Mulqueeny; Singapore's Ambassador-at-Large and former Secretary-General of ASEAN H.E. Ong Keng Yong; and the host of family, friends, fellow human rights defenders on the ground in the Southeast Asian region imperiled in uncertain times – with whom for years we have been honored and blessed to see Southeast Asia as home.

Professor Diane A. Desierto, Notre Dame, Indiana, USA
Professor David Cohen, Stanford, California, USA

1 Development, governance, and the rule of law in ASEAN

Diane A. Desierto

We, the Peoples of the Member States of the Association of Southeast Asian Nations (ASEAN) …

Adhering to the principles of ***democracy****, the* ***rule of law****, and* ***good governance****,* ***respect for and protection of human rights and fundamental freedoms****;*

Resolved to ensure ***sustainable development*** *for the benefit of present and future generations and to place the* ***well-being, livelihood and welfare of the peoples at the centre of the ASEAN community building process****;*

Convinced of the need to strengthen existing bonds of regional solidarity to realise an ASEAN Community that is politically cohesive, economically integrated and socially responsible in order to effectively respond to current and future challenges and opportunities;

Committed to intensifying community building through enhanced regional cooperation and integration, in particular by establishing an ASEAN Community comprising the ASEAN Security Community, the ASEAN Economic Community and the ASEAN Socio-Cultural Community …

Hereby establish, through this Charter, the legal and institutional framework for ASEAN …[1]

Development and rule of law as cross-pillar objectives for ASEAN

ASEAN's origins have always been rooted in shared aspirations towards regional development and rule of law, no matter how much these terms have proven to be interpretively contested, easily amorphous, or conveniently ambiguous in actual State usages or regional practices in Southeast Asia.[2] Depending on one's

1 Charter of the Association of Southeast Asian Nations (hereafter "ASEAN Charter"), Singapore, 20 November 2007, at https://asean.org/storage/2012/05/The-ASEAN-Charter-26th-Reprint.pdf (last accessed 1 June 2020). Emphasis added.

2 *See among others* Joel Ng, *Rule of Law as a Framework within the ASEAN Community,* 5 Journal of East Asia and International Law 2 (2012), pp. 327–342; Paul Davidson, *The ASEAN Way and the Role of Law in ASEAN Economic Cooperation,* 8 Singapore Yearbook of International Law (2004), pp. 165–176; Antonia Hussey, *Regional Development and Cooperation through ASEAN,* 81 Geographical Review 1 (January 1991), pp. 87–98; Michael Ewing-Chow and Tan Hsien-Li, *The Role of the Rule of Law in ASEAN Integration,* EUI RSCAS Working Paper No. 2013/

analytical and historical lens, one could observe that the aspirations have been achieved somewhat in 2019. In over 50 years thus far of ASEAN's existence, it has witnessed the successful transformation of various Southeast Asian economies as a "region on the rise",[3] "one of the world's fastest growing markets",[4] with "Southeast Asia's roaring economies".[5] However, economic growth alone is not the barometer of regional sustainable development, and neither does it demonstrate how ASEAN Member States have (or have not) adhered to their own commitments to principles of democracy, the rule of law, and good governance, respect for and protection of human rights and fundamental freedoms. There is a wealth of robust scholarship that very usefully focuses on the stunning economic success of Southeast Asia and various policy and legal dimensions of the unique horizontally driven intergovernmental approach of ASEAN integration,[6] but current scholarship also appears somewhat more muted when it comes to openly debating any discontents over ASEAN integration,[7] the development

16, March 2013, at http://cadmus.eui.eu/bitstream/handle/1814/26452/RSCAS_2013_16.pdf?sequence=1&isAllowed=y (last accessed 1 June 2020); IMELDA DEINLA, THE DEVELOPMENT OF THE RULE OF LAW IN ASEAN: THE STATE AND REGIONAL INTEGRATION (Cambridge University Press, 2017), at pp. 1–49.

3 Chang Yong Rhee, *Reaching the Next Level,* 55 Finance and Development 3 (September 2018), at www.imf.org/external/pubs/ft/fandd/2018/09/southeast-asia-progress-and-reform-rhee.htm (last accessed 1 June 2020).

4 Vinayak HV, Fraser Thompson, and Oliver Tonby, "Understanding ASEAN: Seven Things You Need to Know", McKinsey and Company, May 2014, at www.mckinsey.com/industries/public-sector/our-insights/understanding-asean-seven-things-you-need-to-know (last accessed 1 June 2020).

5 Shannon Teoh, Wahyudi Soeriaatmadja, Raul Dancel, and Tan Hui Yee, "Southeast Asia's roaring economies", The Straits Times, 17 November 2017, at www.straitstimes.com/asia/south-east-asias-roaring-economies (last accessed 1 June 2020).

6 *See among others* MICHAEL G. PLUMMER AND CHIA SIOW YUE (EDS.), REALIZING THE ASEAN ECONOMIC COMMUNITY: A COMPREHENSIVE ASSESSMENT (ISEAS-Yusof Ishak Institute, November 2009), at pp. 1–19; SIOW YUE CHIA AND MICHAEL G. PLUMMER, ASEAN ECONOMIC COOPERATION AND INTEGRATION: PROGRESS, CHALLENGES, AND FUTURE DIRECTIONS (Cambridge University Press, 2015), pp. 74–156; SANCHITA BASU DAS, THE ASEAN ECONOMIC COMMUNITY AND BEYOND: MYTHS AND REALITIES (ISEAS, Singapore, 2016), at Parts I and II; KIYOSHI KOBAYASHI, KHAIRUDDIN ABDUL RASHID, MASAHIKO FURUICHI, AND WILLIAM P. ANDERSON (EDS.), ECONOMIC INTEGRATION AND REGIONAL DEVELOPMENT: THE ASEAN ECONOMIC COMMUNITY (Routledge, 2017), at Chapters 1 and 2; Hidetaka Yoshimatsu, *Collective Action Problems and Regional Integration in ASEAN,* 28 Contemporary Southeast Asia 1 (April 2006), at pp. 115–140; Pasha L. Hsieh and Bryan Mercurio, *ASEAN Law in the New Regional Economic Order: An Introductory Roadmap to the ASEAN Economic Community,* pp. 3–21 in PASHA L. HSIEH AND BRYAN MERCURIO (EDS.), ASEAN LAW IN THE NEW REGIONAL ECONOMIC ORDER: GLOBAL TRENDS AND SHIFTING PARADIGMS (Cambridge University Press, 2019); JACQUES PELKMANS, THE ASEAN ECONOMIC COMMUNITY: A CONCEPTUAL APPROACH (Cambridge University Press, 2016), at pp. 75–115.

7 *See among others* UNITED NATIONS CONFERENCE ON TRADE AND DEVELOPMENT (UNCTAD), ASEAN AT 50: ACHIEVEMENTS AND CHALLENGES IN REGIONAL INTEGRATION (United Nations, New York and Geneva, 2017), at https://unctad.org/en/PublicationsLibrary/gdsecidc2017d2_en.pdf (last accessed 1 June 2020), at pp. 7–14; Joshua Kurlantzick, "The Failures of the ASEAN Economic Community", Council of Foreign Relations, 12 September 2014, at www.cfr.org/blog/failures-asean-economic-community (last accessed 1 June 2020); Irina Onyusheva, Lalita Thammashote, and Sebastian Kot, *ASEAN: Problems of Regional Integration,* 39 Revista Espacios (2018), at www.revistaespacios.com/a18v39n36/a18v39n36p02.pdf (last accessed 1 June 2020); Michael

paradigms followed (or not) by ASEAN,[8] and whether the regional integration process itself completely internalizes and embeds the rule of law not just in the commitments perennially articulated by ASEAN Member States, but in actual regional actions (or inactions) of ASEAN as a whole against rule of law challenges in Southeast Asia.[9]

This book thus examines over a decade of ASEAN's integration not just from the lionizing perspective of rapid raw economic growth and ASEAN Member States' individual strategic preferences,[10] but also from the structural, institutional, and polemical undersides of how this "development" is being achieved as a matter of regional law and authoritative operational policy. ASEAN integration has always been envisaged under the ASEAN Charter as a cross-pillar endeavor towards development and regional governance under rule of law – uniquely uniting ASEAN's Political-Security, Economic, and Socio-Cultural Communities in coordinated horizontal action,[11] in a sharp contrast to other deeper forms of integration such as that of the European Union.[12]

Our review of twelve years of integration efforts thus far reveals not just contested development philosophies and conceptions of rule of law, but also: 1) lingering institutional deficits within the ASEAN administrative structure that do not bode well for timely and adequate responses to regional challenges;[13]

Ewing-Chow, *Translating the Design into a Bloc: The Domestic Implementation of the ASEAN Charter*, pp. 66–86 in S. Tiwari (Ed.), ASEAN: Life After the Charter (ISEAS, Singapore, 2010).

8 *Among the few sources critically scrutinizing development trajectories in ASEAN integration, see* Hans C. Blomqvist, *ASEAN as a Model for Third World Regional Economic Co-operation?*, 10 ASEAN Economic Bulletin 1 (July 1993), pp. 52–67; Mely Caballero-Anthony, *Revisioning Human Security in Southeast Asia,* 28 Asian Perspective 3 (2004), pp. 155–189; see among others Katherine McKinnon, *What is development in Southeast Asia and who benefits?, Progress, power, and prosperity,* Chapter 2; Simon Springer, *Neoliberalism in Southeast Asia,* Chapter 3; both in Andrew McGregor, Lisa Law, and Fiona Miller (Eds.), Routledge Handbook of Southeast Asian Development (Routledge, 2017).

9 *See among others* Simon Chesterman, From Community to Compliance? The Evolution of Monitoring Obligations in ASEAN (Cambridge University Press, 2015), at pp. 7–58 (on ASEAN's approach to monitoring).

10 On individual strategic preferences of ASEAN Member States, see Min-hyung Kim, *Theorizing ASEAN Integration,* 35 Asian Perspective 3 (July to September 2011), pp. 407–435.

11 ASEAN Charter, Articles 1(5), 1(6), 1(7), 1(11), 1(13), 5(2), 9(4), 20(1), and 20(2). See also Thomas Parks, Larry Maramis, Apichai Sunchindah, Weranuch Wongwatanakul, ASEAN as the Architect for Regional Development Cooperation: Advancing ASEAN Centrality and Catalyzing Action for Sustainable Development (The Asia Foundation, 2018), at https://asiafoundation.org/wp-content/uploads/2018/09/ASEAN-as-the-Architect-for-Regional-Development-Cooperation.pdf (last accessed 1 June 2020), at pp. VIII-IX.

12 *See among others* Leonard Felix Hutabarat, *European Union Integration Process: A Lesson Learned for ASEAN,* 13 Indonesian Journal of International Law 2 (January 2016), pp. 171–187; Laura Allison, The EU, ASEAN, and Interregionalism: Regionalism Support and Norm Diffusion Between the EU and ASEAN (Palgrave Macmillan, 2015), pp. 76–123.

13 *See among others* Donald E. Weatherbee, ASEAN's Half-Century: A Political History of the Association of Southeast Asian Nations (The Rowman & Littlefield Publishing Group, Inc., 2019), at pp. 227–264 (arguing for a fourth reinvention in ASEAN to better respond as an institution to regional conflicts); Chng Meng Kng, *ASEAN's Institutional Structure and Economic Co-operation,* 6 ASEAN Economic Bulletin 3 (March 1990), pp. 268–282; Kei Koga, *ASEAN's*

2) continuous normative proliferation without counterpart deepening of cross-border legal harmonization;[14] and 3) significant gaps in deliberative decision-making that ought to be premised on people-based "ASEAN Centrality" but remain opaque to local communities, groups, and peoples of Southeast Asia who are the actual constituents of development policies but which are neither fully informed nor conferred specific substantive participation rights in shaping the regional agendas that affect them.[15] To this end, while this book acknowledges the expansion of post-ASEAN Charter-based scholarship elaborating on many dimensions of the ASEAN integration process, our particular focus here is on evaluating how cross-pillar coordination (or lack thereof) responds to ASEAN's continuing aspirations, pre- and post-Charter, for regional development and rule of law-based governance.

Evolving visions of development and the rule of law in ASEAN

A brief survey of key ASEAN instruments confirms a consistent articulated emphasis on the objectives of "development" and "rule of law" as the basis for regional governance, albeit with quite variable understandings and elaborations of these concepts over time. To recall, before ASEAN passed its Charter in 2007, it existed as a loose regional intergovernmental cooperation that was often vulnerable to the postwar fragility of a constellation of newly independent States of Southeast Asia, often making pragmatic choices to achieve the region's rapid economic development and political stability through rule of law.[16] The 1976

Evolving Institutional Strategy: Managing Great Power Politics in South China Sea Disputes, 11 Chinese Journal of International Politics 1 (Spring 2018), pp. 49–80; Amitav Acharya, *ASEAN 2030: Challenges of Building a Mature Political and Security Community,* Asian Development Bank Institute (ADBI) Working Paper Series No. 441, October 2013, at www.adb.org/sites/default/files/publication/156296/adbi-wp441.pdf (last accessed 1 June 2020).

14 Erman Rajagukguk, *Harmonization of Law in ASEAN Countries Towards Economic Integration,* 9 Indonesian Journal of International Law 4 (October 2012), pp. 529–538; Basil C. Bitas, *Legal Convergence, Transnational Rule-Making, and Regional Integration in ASEAN – From Open Regionalism to Open Legal Architecture,* 2014 LawAsia Journal 1 (2014), pp. 1–22; Sohini Chatterjee, "ASEAN's Legal Architecture Critical to Addressing Transboundary Challenges", The Asia Foundation, 17 May 2017, at https://asiafoundation.org/2017/05/17/aseans-legal-architecture-critical-addressing-transboundary-challenges/ (last accessed 1 June 2020).

15 *See among others* Amitav Acharya, *The Myth of ASEAN Centrality?,* 39 Contemporary Southeast Asia 2 (August 2017), pp. 273–279; Anna Meijknecht and Byung Sook de Vries, *Is There a Place for Minorities' and Indigenous Peoples' Rights within ASEAN? Asian Values, ASEAN Values, and the Protection of Southeast Asian Minorities and Indigenous Peoples,* 17 International Journal on Minority and Group Rights (2010), pp. 75–110; Ronald Holzhacker, *Introduction: Sustainable Development Goals in Southeast Asia and ASEAN,* pp. 3–38 in Ronald Holzhacker and Dafri Agussalim (Eds.), Sustainable Development Goals in Southeast Asia and ASEAN (Brill, 2019).

16 *See* Kishore Mahbubani and Jeffery Sng, The ASEAN Miracle: A Catalyst for Peace (NUS Press, 2017), at pp. 48–75; Diane A. Desierto, *ASEAN's Constitutionalization of International Law: Challenges to Evolution under the ASEAN Charter,* 49 Columbia Journal of Transnational Law 2 (2011), pp. 268–320; Vincent K. Pollard, *ASA and ASEAN, 1961–1967: Southeast Asian Regionalism,* 10 Asian Survey 3 (March 1970), pp. 244–255; William P. Bundy, *New Tides in*

Declaration of ASEAN Concord emphasized that the primary concern of the original ASEAN Five Member States (Indonesia, Malaysia, the Philippines, Singapore, and Thailand) was "the elimination of poverty, hunger, disease, and illiteracy ... economic and social development, with particular emphasis on the promotion of social justice and on the improvement of the living standards of their peoples."[17] The 1976 Treaty of Amity and Cooperation (TAC) emphasized rule of law-based principles as fundamental governing principles for ASEAN and any external partners (e.g. mutual respect for independence, sovereignty, equality, territorial integrity and national identity of all nations; the right of every State to lead its national existence free from external interference, subversion or coercion; non-interference in the internal affairs of one another; settlement of differences or disputes by peaceful means; renunciation of the threat or use of force; and effective cooperation[18]), similar to the Ten Bandung Principles[19] established by the postwar Non-Aligned Movement that prescribed respect for human rights, international law, the UN Charter, and sovereignty for all nations, especially in the postcolonial and postwar international system.

The 1987 Manila Declaration issued by the 3rd ASEAN Heads of Government Summit emphasized "promoting the principle of sustainable development and systematically integrating it into all aspects of development".[20] The 1992 Singapore Declaration issued by the 4th ASEAN Heads of Government Summit heavily anchored political and security cooperation in ASEAN on international law, regional instruments such as the TAC, the Declaration of ASEAN Concord, as well as the UN Charter.[21] This reference to international law, the UN Charter, and regional instruments as the basis for regional cooperation and development would thereafter be reiterated frequently by ASEAN in subsequent Heads of Government Summits up to the 35th Summit held in 2019.[22] During the 1998

Southeast Asia, 49 Foreign Affairs 2 (January 1971), pp. 187–200; J.L.S. Girling, *Regional Security in Southeast Asia,* 2 Journal of Southeast Asian Studies 1 (March 1971), pp. 56–65.

17 The Declaration of ASEAN Concord, Bali, Indonesia, 24 February 1976, Clause 3, at https://asean.org/?static_post=declaration-of-asean-concord-indonesia-24-february-1976 (last accessed 1 June 2020).

18 Treaty of Amity and Cooperation in Southeast Asia, Indonesia, 24 February 1976, Article 2(a) to 2(f), at https://asean.org/treaty-amity-cooperation-southeast-asia-indonesia-24-february-1976/ (last accessed 1 June 2020).

19 *See* Luis Eslava, Michael Fakhri, and Vasuki Nesiah, *The Spirit of Bandung,* pp. 3–32 in Luis Eslava, Michael Fakhri, and Vasuki Nesiah (Eds.), Bandung, Global History, and International Law: Critical Pasts and Pending Futures (Cambridge University Press, 2017).

20 Manila Declaration, Philippines, 15 December 1987, at Clause 20, at https://asean.org/?static_post=manila-declaration-philippines-15-december-1987 (last accessed 1 June 2020).

21 Singapore Declaration, 28 January 1992, Clauses 3 and 4, at https://asean.org/?static_post=singapore-declaration-of-1992-singapore-28-january-1992 (last accessed 1 June 2020).

22 *See among others* Bangkok Summit Declaration, Thailand, 14–15 December 1995, Clauses 7 to 9, at https://asean.org/?static_post=bangkok-summit-declaration-of-1995-bangkok14-15-december-1995 (last accessed 1 June 2020); Hanoi Summit Declaration, Viet Nam, 16 December 1998, Clauses 28 to 32, at https://asean.org/?static_post=ha-noi-declaration-of-1998-16-december-1998 (last accessed 1 June 2020); Hanoi Plan of Action, Clauses 7.1 to 7.17, at https://asean.org/?static_post=hanoi-plan-of-action (last accessed 1 June 2020).

summit held in Hanoi and against the backdrop of the 1998 Asian financial crisis, ASEAN emphatically declared that its objectives of regional development transcended purely economic metrics into one of actual ***human development***:

> We recognize that the ultimate objective of economic development is to raise standards of living and to promote human development in all its dimensions, so as to enable the people of ASEAN to have the fullest potential to realize their potential.[23]

ASEAN Member States further refined this understanding of human development in the 2003 Declaration of ASEAN Concord II (Bali Concord II) along lines of sustainability and equality, where they recognized "that ***sustainable economic development*** requires a secure political environment based on a strong foundation of mutual interests generated by economic cooperation and political solidarity",[24] as well as "the importance of rules-based multilateral trading system that is *equitable* and that contributes towards the pursuit of development".[25]

By the time ASEAN held its 10th Summit in Laos in 2004, with membership already beyond the original ASEAN Five (Indonesia, Malaysia, the Philippines, Singapore, Thailand) to a roster of ten Member States, including the CMLV (Cambodia, Myanmar, Laos, Vietnam) countries plus the Sultanate of Brunei Darussalam, ASEAN itself was prioritizing the glaring development gap within Southeast Asia itself, even as ASEAN was cautiously moving towards gradual regional economic integration: "bridging the development gap is extremely important for regional economic integration and is a crucial part of confidence-building efforts to assist members to cope with challenges".[26] The Vientiane Action Programme issued by the same 10th ASEAN Summit called for ASEAN Member States to develop "a strategy for rule of law, judiciary systems and legal infrastructure, effective and efficient civil services, and good governance in public and private sectors".[27] At this juncture in ASEAN's existence with the ASEAN Member States anticipating regional economic integration, it is highly significant that ASEAN regarded sustainable development as human development in all dimensions, for which the rule of law in all Member States was critically decisive. At the 11th ASEAN Summit in Kuala Lumpur, Malaysia, in 2005 (and while the

23 Hanoi Summit Declaration, Viet Nam, 16 December 1998, Clause 21, at https://asean.org/?static_post=ha-noi-declaration-of-1998-16-december-1998 (last accessed 1 June 2020).

24 Declaration of ASEAN Concord II (Bali Concord II), 7 October 2003, Preamble, ninth paragraph, at https://asean.org/?static_post=declaration-of-asean-concord-ii-bali-concord-ii (last accessed 1 June 2020). Italics added.

25 Ibid., at footnote 24, at Preamble, eleventh paragraph. Italics added.

26 Chairman's Statement of the 10th ASEAN Summit, Vientiane, 29 November 2004, Clause 10, at https://asean.org/?static_post=chairman-s-statement-of-the-10th-asean-summit-vientiane-29-november-2004 (last accessed 1 June 2020).

27 Vientiane Programme of Action, 2004, at p. 6, Clause 1.1(iv), at www.asean.org/wp-content/uploads/images/archive/VAP-10th%20ASEAN%20Summit.pdf (last accessed 1 June 2020).

ASEAN Charter was already in the drafting process), ASEAN Member States acknowledged that

> the region is being confronted with challenges such as the threat of terrorism, the outbreak of avian influenza, and the rise of oil prices which have a direct negative impact on regional economic development and public health … [they] agreed that ASEAN should step up efforts to address these challenges at the bilateral, regional, and multilateral levels ***in accordance with [their] obligations under international law*** and with respect for national sovereignty, territorial integrity, and the principle of non-interference in the internal affairs of other countries.[28]

The 12th ASEAN Summit in Cebu, the Philippines in 2007 would yield the Cebu Declaration on the Blueprint of the ASEAN Charter, focusing on key challenges of regional economic integration from the socio-cultural community perspective, particularly challenges for migrant workers, transboundary environmental challenges and sustainability, and narrowing the development gaps remaining within Southeast Asia.[29]

The signing of the ASEAN Charter on 20 November 2007 entrenched the regional understanding of "development" as ***human development*** in all its dimensions (including sustainable development), and the intrinsic importance of governance based on the rule of law, democracy, human rights and fundamental freedoms to achieve Southeast Asia's desired human development. The ASEAN Charter articulates organizational Purposes centered on a premise of human development achieved through a "thick"[30] conception of rule of law (one that specifically includes democracy, human rights and fundamental freedoms):

> 4. To ensure that the peoples and Member States of ASEAN live in peace with the world at large in a just, ***democratic,*** and harmonious environment;
>
> 5. To create a single market and production base which is stable, prosperous, highly competitive and economically integrated with effective facilitation for trade and investment in which there is free flow of goods, services, and investment; facilitated movement of business persons, professionals, talents and labour; and freer flow of capital;

28 Chairman's Statement of the 11th ASEAN Summit, Kuala Lumpur, 12 December 2005, Clause 43, at https://asean.org/?static_post=chairman-s-statement-of-the-11th-asean-summit-one-vision-one-identity-one-community (last accessed 1 June 2020).

29 Chairperson's Statement of the 12th ASEAN Summit, H.E. the President Gloria Macapagal-Arroyo, 13 January 2007, at https://asean.org/?static_post=chairperson-s-statement-of-the-12th-asean-summit-he-the-president-gloria-macapagal-arroyo-one-caring-and-sharing-community (last accessed 1 June 2020); Cebu Declaration on the Blueprint of the ASEAN Charter, 13 January 2007, at https://asean.org/?static_post=cebu-declaration-on-the-blueprint-of-the-asean-charter-cebu-philippines-13-january-2007 (last accessed 1 June 2020).

30 *See* Jørgen Møller and Svend Erik-Skaaning, *Systematizing Thin and Thick Conceptions of Rule of Law,* 33 The Justice System Journal 2 (2012), pp. 136–153, at p. 138.

> 6. To *alleviate poverty and narrow the development gap* within ASEAN through mutual assistance and cooperation;
>
> 7. To *strengthen democracy, enhance good governance, and the rule of law, and to promote and protect human rights and fundamental freedoms*, with due regard for the rights and responsibilities of the Member States of ASEAN;
>
> ...
>
> 9. To promote *sustainable development* so as to ensure the protection of the region's environment, the sustainability of its natural resources, the preservation of its cultural heritage, and the high quality of life of its peoples;
>
> ...
>
> 11. To enhance the well-being and livelihood of the peoples of ASEAN by providing them with *equitable access to opportunities for human development*, social welfare, and justice;
>
> ...
>
> 13. To promote a *people-centered ASEAN in which all sectors of society are encouraged to participate in, and benefit from, the process of ASEAN integration and community building*.[31]
>
> (Italics added)

The participatory, equitable, sustainable, and inclusive nature of human development contemplated in a "people-centered ASEAN" democratically governed by rule of law, human rights, and fundamental freedoms appears consistent with the expansive definition of the right to development in the 1986 Declaration on the Right to Development, which recognizes that "the human person is the central subject of the development process and that development policy should therefore make the human being the main participant and beneficiary of development".[32] Article 1(1) of the Declaration on the Right to Development stresses that the right to development

> is an inalienable human right by virtue of which every human person and all peoples are entitled to participate in, contribute to, and enjoy economic, social, cultural and political development, in which all human rights and fundamental freedoms can be fully realized.[33]

The subsequent Community Blueprints issued at the 15th ASEAN Summit in Cha-am, Thailand, in 2009 all likewise reflect the deep intertwining of rule of law

31 ASEAN Charter, Article 1(4) to 1(7), 1(9), 1(11), and 1(13).

32 United Nations General Assembly, *Declaration on the Right to Development*, A/RES/41/128, 4 December 1986, at thirteenth paragraph, at www.un.org/documents/ga/res/41/a41r128.htm (last accessed 1 June 2020).

33 Ibid. at footnote 32, at Article 1(1).

with human development drawing from moorings in the ASEAN Charter. The ASEAN Political-Security Community (APSC) Blueprint committed to

> promote political development in adherence to the principles of democracy, the rule of law and good governance, respect for and promotion and protection of human rights and fundamental freedoms as inscribed in the ASEAN Charter … [the Blueprint shall be] a means by which ASEAN Member States can pursue closer interaction and cooperation to forge shared norms and create common mechanisms to achieve ASEAN's goals and objectives in the political and security fields … it promotes a people-oriented ASEAN in which all sectors of society, regardless of gender, race, religion, language, or social and cultural background, are encouraged to participate in, and benefit from, the process of ASEAN integration and community building."[34]

The ASEAN Socio-Cultural Community (ASCC) Blueprint (2009–2015) emphasizes the ASCC's "culture of regional resilience, adherence to agreed principles, spirit of cooperation, collective responsibility … to promote human and social development, respect for fundamental freedoms, gender equality, the promotion and protection of human rights and the promotion of social justice".[35] The ASEAN Economic Community (AEC) Blueprint set the goal of transforming ASEAN into a "single market and production base, a highly competitive region, a region of equitable economic development, and a region fully integrated into the global economy",[36] where ASEAN "shall act in accordance to principles of an open, outward-looking, inclusive, and market-driven economy consistent with multilateral rules as well as adherence to rules-based systems for effective compliance and implementation of economic commitments".[37]

Much as these initial Community Blueprints were expansive and encompassing in their vision of human development achieved through rule of law, it was equally significant that none of the Community Blueprints elaborated on cross-pillar collaboration to achieve all dimensions of human development under a premise of rule of law, human rights, and fundamental freedoms. Quite problematically, the initial Community Blueprints indicate a segmented approach to cross-cutting regional issues involving human development and rule of law. For example, much as the ASEAN Political-Security Community acknowledged

34 ASEAN Political-Security Community Blueprint, at para. 7, at www.asean.org/wp-content/uploads/images/archive/22337.pdf (last accessed 1 June 2020).

35 Blueprint for the ASEAN Socio-Cultural Community (2009–2015), at para. 6, at www.asean.org/wp-content/uploads/images/archive/22336.pdf (last accessed 1 June 2020).

36 ASEAN Economic Community Blueprint, *Declaration on the ASEAN Economic Community Blueprint*, para. 1, at https://asean.org/wp-content/uploads/archive/5187-10.pdf (last accessed 1 June 2020).

37 ASEAN Economic Community Blueprint, para. 5, at https://asean.org/wp-content/uploads/archive/5187-10.pdf (last accessed 1 June 2020).

"interwoven relationships of political, economic, socio-cultural, and environmental dimensions of development",[38] the APSC Blueprint did not contain any provision or facility for formalized cross-pillar collaboration with the ASEAN Socio-Cultural Community or the ASEAN Economic Community. The ASEAN Economic Community's Blueprint merely acknowledged that "all three pillars are expected to work in tandem in establishing the ASEAN Community in 2020",[39] without spelling out clear pathways for operational cooperation and coordination with the ASEAN Political-Security Community and the ASEAN Socio-Cultural Community. Likewise, even as the ASEAN Socio-Cultural Community Blueprint focused on "human development" through education, human resource and skills development, promotion of decent work, science and technology, entrepreneurship, civil service capabilities, as well as "social welfare and social protection" through poverty alleviation, social safety nets, food security, healthcare, ensuring a drug-free ASEAN, disaster resilience, disability rights, migrant worker rights, environmental sustainability, among others – this ASCC Blueprint for 2009–2015 is completely silent on cross-pillar collaboration with the ASEAN Political-Security Community and the ASEAN Economic Community. These issue silos militate against the laudably expansive ambitions of the ASEAN Charter towards human development based on rule of law, human rights, and fundamental freedoms.

Even the ASEAN Master Plan on Connectivity,[40] which was devised by the ASEAN Member States to provide strategic direction and a plan of action for physical infrastructural connectivity, institutional connectivity, and people-to-people connectivity throughout Southeast Asia, fails to cultivate and systematize cross-pillar collaboration between the ASEAN Political-Security Community, the ASEAN Economic Community, and the ASEAN Socio-Cultural Community. Regional physical infrastructure projects – which are expected to involve dimensions of economic integration, political-security considerations, as well as generate socio-cultural impacts – are encouraged in the ASEAN Master Plan on Connectivity but there is no provision for cross-pillar collaboration on such projects. Institutional connectivity issues focusing on impediments to the cross-border movements of persons, goods, services, labor, and vehicles in Southeast Asia implicate all three pillar communities, but there is again nothing in the ASEAN Master Plan on Connectivity that strategically concretizes cross-pillar collaboration for ASEAN's broad vision of human development premised on rule of law, human rights, and fundamental freedoms.

The ASEAN Community Vision 2025 is equally silent about cross-pillar collaboration between the ASEAN Political-Security Community, the ASEAN Economic Community, and the ASEAN Socio-Cultural Community, even as the

38 Id. at footnote 34, at para. 9 therein.

39 Id. at footnote 37, at para. 2 therein.

40 Master Plan on ASEAN Connectivity, ASEAN Secretariat, 2009, at para. 5, at www.asean.org/storage/images/ASEAN_RTK_2014/4_Master_Plan_on_ASEAN_Connectivity.pdf (last accessed 1 June 2020).

ASEAN Member States appear to espouse greater ambitions towards achieving human development through rule of law, human rights, and fundamental freedoms in Southeast Asia, stating in particular that:

> We resolve to consolidate our Community, building upon and deepening the integration process to realise a rules-based, people-oriented, people-centred ASEAN Community, where our peoples enjoy human rights and fundamental freedoms, higher quality of life and the benefits of community building, reinforcing our sense of togetherness and common identity, guided by the purposes and principles of the ASEAN Charter.[41]

Thus, the ASEAN Political-Security Community by 2025 is expected to be

> a rules-based community that fully adheres to ASEAN fundamental principles, shared values and norms as well as principles of international law governing the peaceful conduct of relations among states; an inclusive and responsive community that ensures our peoples enjoy human rights and fundamental freedoms as well as thrive in a just, democratic, harmonious, and gender-sensitive environment in accordance with the principles of democracy, good governance, and the rule of law.[42]

In parallel, the ASEAN Economic Community by 2025 is expected not just to be a highly integrated regional economy in trade, investment, and capital as Southeast Asia's single market, but also as a resilient, inclusive, people-oriented, and people-centred community that engenders equitable development and inclusive growth.[43] Finally, the ASEAN Socio-Cultural Community by 2025 is envisioned to be a

> committed, participative, socially-responsible community through an accountable and inclusive mechanism for the benefit of [Southeast Asian] peoples, upheld by the principles of good governance … a sustainable community that promotes social development and environmental protection through effective mechanisms to meet the current and future needs of [Southeast Asian] peoples.[44]

Notwithstanding the broadest scope of human development and rule of law in ASEAN Community Vision 2025, the updated Community Blueprints still do not reflect any specific provision that designs cross-pillar collaboration and coordination between the three pillar communities, which, at best, adopts hortatory

41 ASEAN Community Vision 2025, at para. 4, at www.asean.org/wp-content/uploads/images/2015/November/aec-page/ASEAN-Community-Vision-2025.pdf (last accessed 1 June 2020).

42 Id. at footnote 41, at paras. 8.1 and 8.2.

43 Id. at footnote 41, at para. 10.4.

44 Id. at footnote 41, at paras. 12.2 and 12.3.

language that merely encourages (rather than obligates) such cross-pillar collaboration and coordination.[45] This significant law and policy vacuum within ASEAN integration (and one that seriously undermines achieving the broad goals of human development under rule of law), has spurred recent proposals in ASEAN to create a fourth oversight pillar that would be dedicated to ensuring cross-pillar collaboration and coordination.[46]

Governance constraints in realizing ASEAN's vision of human development under rule of law

ASEAN's unique structure and institutional history often attract its own share of naysayers regarding the intergovernmental organization's actual operational ability to produce a regional governance paradigm that delivers on its pre- and post-Charter ambitious normative commitments.[47] Beyond the usual observations made about the under-resourced nature of the ASEAN Secretariat or the regional bureaucracy serving ASEAN's pillar communities,[48] the more significant governance constraints, in my view, are twofold: 1) any regional decisions taken at the ASEAN level variably depend on ASEAN Member States' respective abilities, resource capacities, and political will to meet their overarching obligation under Article 5(2) of the ASEAN Charter to "take all necessary measures, including the enactment of appropriate legislation, to effectively implement the provisions of this Charter and to comply with all the obligations of membership";[49] and

45 *See* ASEAN Political-Security Community Blueprint 2025, at paras. 14.A.iii (on strengthening cross-pillar coordination); para. A.2.5.vii (on human rights mainstreaming across all pillars) www.asean.org/wp-content/uploads/2012/05/ASEAN-APSC-Blueprint-2025.pdf (last accessed 1 June 2020); ASEAN Economic Community Blueprint 2025, at www.asean.org/storage/2016/03/AECBP_2025r_FINAL.pdf (last accessed 1 June 2020) (which does not contain any provision on cross-pillar coordination); ASEAN Socio-Cultural Community Blueprint 2025, paras. 18, 23 and 24 (identifying possible cross-pillar and cross-sectoral coordination points without making cross-pillar collaboration mandatory or institutionalizing such collaboration formally with the AEC and the APSC), at www.asean.org/wp-content/uploads/2016/04/8.-March-2016-ASCC-Blueprint-2025.pdf (last accessed 1 June 2020).

46 *See* Joycee Teodoro, "An ASEAN Fourth Pillar: Is It Necessary?", 1 CIRSS Commentaries 8, September 2014, at www.fsi.gov.ph/wp-content/uploads/2014/09/2014-09-30-Vol-1-No-8-An-ASEAN-Fourth-Pillar-Is-It-Necessary-Teodoro.pdf (last accessed 1 June 2020).

47 *See among others* Roda Mushkat, *"Loose" Regionalism and Global Governance: The Association of Southeast Asian Nations (ASEAN) Factor*, 17 Melbourne Journal of International Law 1 (June 2016), pp. 238–256; Donald K. Emmerson, *Challenging ASEAN: A "Topological" View*, 29 Contemporary Southeast Asia 3 (December 2007), pp. 424–446; Paruedee Nguitgarool and Jürgen Rüland, ASEAN as an Actor in International Fora: Reality, Potential, and Constraints (Cambridge University Press, 2015), at pp. 249–272.

48 *See* Deepak Nair, "A Strong Secretariat, a Strong ASEAN? A Re-Evaluation", 8 ISEAS Perspective (19 February 2016), at www.iseas.edu.sg/images/pdf/ISEAS_Perspective_2016_8.pdf (last accessed 1 June 2020); Termsak Chalermpalanupap, *The ASEAN Secretariat and Legal Issues Arising from the ASEAN Charter*, 6 Indonesian Journal of International Law 2 (January 2009), at pp. 178–186.

49 ASEAN Charter, Article 5(2).

2) there remains lacking any hard legal mechanism or transparent monitoring, verification, and/or accountability system under the Charter-based ASEAN, to regionally respond to any ASEAN Member State's failure to meet ASEAN obligations, in a manner that ensures the ASEAN Member State will ultimately be brought to full compliance with ASEAN decisions.[50] For any serious breach of the ASEAN Charter or any non-compliance by any ASEAN Member State with ASEAN decisions will be referred to the ASEAN Summit (the highest governing body of ASEAN comprising all Heads of State of ASEAN Member States) for decision, still under its consensus decision-making rule.[51] One therefore has to take the explosion and proliferation of ASEAN legal instruments – which contain all of ASEAN Member States' legal commitments regionally as well as to their respective external partners – with a fair degree of pragmatism concerning ASEAN's lingering governance constraints.

Achieving human development under rule of law – the most challenging of ASEAN's objectives – will be a glacial and opaque process if the levers of compliance with ASEAN regional decisions are left up to relative silence, inaction, or paralysis that ensues from the strict demands of consensus decision-making among the ASEAN Member States.[52] As one scholar observes:

> Can ASEAN remain relevant if it continues to be hampered by consensus decision-making? The choice of holding fast to the consensus model to keep the peace and maintain unity instead of exploring other modalities of decision-making is a false one. An ASEAN that is united and held together by the thread of deafening silence would only push the regional organization closer to irrelevance … ASEAN has been organized around the premise of consensus, which in itself is a highly idealistic aspiration, but it does not have effective mechanisms to deal with instances where ideals are not translated into reality. ASEAN works best when there is consensus but fares poorly in managing differences.[53]

50 *On soft compliance monitoring mechanisms through the role of the ASEAN Secretariat and coordinating mechanisms or treaty-based bodies in ASEAN instruments, see* Robert Beckman, Leonardo Bernard, Hao Duy Phan, Hsien-Li Tan, and Ranyta Yusran, Promoting Compliance: The Role of Dispute Settlement and Monitoring Mechanisms in ASEAN Instruments (Cambridge University Press, 2016), pp. 101–159; Hao Duy Phan, *Promoting Compliance: An Assessment of ASEAN Instruments since the ASEAN Charter,* 41 Syracuse Journal of International Law and Commerce 2 (Spring 2014), pp. 379–412.

51 ASEAN Charter, Article 20(4).

52 Kim Hyung Jong and Lee Poh Ping, *The Changing Role of Dialogue in the International Relations of Southeast Asia,* 51 Asian Survey 5 (September/October 2011), pp. 953–970, at p. 954 ("… the ASEAN dialogue is increasingly shifting from an approach where consensus is assumed, to one where decision by consensus is getting less effective and more rational … increasing asymmetry in ASEAN in terms of identity, interests, and motives … makes for difficulty in achieving consensus.").

53 Tang Siew Mun, *Is ASEAN Due for a Makeover?,* 39 Contemporary Southeast Asia 2 (August 2017), pp. 239–244, at p. 241.

Even beyond the strict demands of consensus decision-making (with no recorded practice thus far of ASEAN Member States availing of the ASEAN Charter Article 20(2) mechanism allowing the ASEAN Summit to "decide how a specific decision can be made"[54] if consensus cannot be reached), concerns have been raised about the lack of professionalization in ASEAN such as that more like a regional "civil service" bureaucracy responsible for institutional governance,[55] instead of perennially confronting the entrenched politicization of appointments at the ASEAN Secretariat that largely depend on which ASEAN Member State holds the chairmanship in any given year:

> The ASEAN Secretary-General (S-G) has always been a political appointee. Each ASEAN Member State takes turns to nominate the S-G. How they choose is left to them ... The Charter provided the opportunity to professionalize the [ASEAN Secretariat] by making the [Deputy Secretaries-General or DSGs] non-political. Open recruitment would have allowed [ASEAN Secretariat] to develop a stronger core of long-term professionals ... Theoretically, the S-G and DSGs are not supposed to promote the interests of their home countries. But when the incumbent is a member of a country's diplomatic service and has to return home after a three or five year stint, how independent can he/she really be?[56]

Somewhat unusually for any development bank, the Asian Development Bank also did not mince words in 2014, when it pressed for serious institutional reforms in ASEAN and its governance structure to achieve ASEAN's short- and long-term development goals:

> ASEAN's institutional framework and basic governing principles were designed mainly to cover political and security matters. But economic and social issues have become the group's main focus, requiring more flexibility, timely decision making, and efficiency. Therefore, ASEAN needs to structurally reform its basic governing principles. Areas for improvement include the group's basic approach to decision making, financial contributions, and the delegation of powers from national to regional agencies. Innovation is needed to upgrade the current system, which does not provide for proper treatment of sanctions, feedback, and compensating mechanisms for groups and countries where the costs of integration exceed its benefits ... A general lack of resources also limits the effectiveness of national agencies in charge of

54 ASEAN Charter, Article 20(2).

55 *See* Cheong Kee Cheok and Yong Chen, *Assessing ASEAN's Relevance: Have the Right Questions Been Asked?*, 36 Journal of Southeast Asian Economies 1 (Special Issue: ASEAN Towards Economic Convergence, April 2019), pp. 11–24, at p. 14 ("ASEAN was, and has remained, very much a top-down project driven by member country leadership and in which civil society has minimal involvement and hence little knowledge.").

56 Walter Woon, *The ASEAN Charter Ten Years On*, 39 Contemporary Southeast Asia 2 (August 2017), pp. 245–271, at pp. 247–248.

> ASEAN affairs, as well as other subregional and regional agencies involved with the ASEAN process.[57]

What complicates ASEAN's incremental approach to regional rules-based institutional governance under these conditions is the lack of fundamental clarity about the long-term execution of a shared *regional* understanding of human development through rule of law, and what that entails for each ASEAN Member State. Because ASEAN chairmanships rotate before every ASEAN Summit, agendas for operationally implementing the vast commitments in all three Community Blueprints are thus largely defined by whichever ASEAN Member State holds the chairmanship for that given year.[58]

Most importantly, all three Community Blueprints suggest different – albeit related – perspectives on development, but do not contain any formal coordination mechanism with the other pillar communities, let alone shared oversight for monitoring and realizing regional human development through rule of law. To this end, examining what precisely ASEAN sets out to realize by way of human development is critical – each pillar community's approach is distinct but also functionally related to the other two pillar communities' mandates for development. The ASEAN Political-Security Community Blueprint 2025 seeks to establish: 1) a

> rules-based, people-oriented, people-centred community bound by fundamental principles, shared values and norms, in which our peoples enjoy human rights, fundamental freedoms and social justice, embrace the values of tolerance and moderation, and share a strong sense of togetherness, common identity, and destiny.[59]

2) "a resilient community in a peaceful, secure and stable region, with enhanced capacity to respond effectively and in a timely manner to challenges for the common good of ASEAN, in accordance with the principle of comprehensive security";[60] 3) "an outward-looking community that deepens cooperation with our external parties, upholds and strengthens ASEAN Centrality in the evolving regional architecture, and plays a responsible and constructive role globally based on an ASEAN common platform on international issues";[61] and 4)

> a community with strengthened institutional capacity through improved ASEAN work processes and coordination, increased effectiveness and

57 Asian Development Bank Institute, ASEAN 2030: Toward a Borderless Economic Community (2014, ADB Institute, Japan), at pp. xxix and xxx.

58 On controversies regarding Myanmar's chairmanship in 2006, for example, see Mikio Oishi and Nina Ghani, *Developing a Way to Influence the Conduct of Government in Intrastate Conflict: The Case of Myanmar*, pp. 89–110, at pp. 101–102, in Mikio Oishi (Ed.), Contemporary Conflicts in Southeast Asia: Towards a New ASEAN Way of Conflict Management (Springer, 2016).

59 ASEAN Political-Security Community Blueprint 2025, at Part. II.5.1, at www.asean.org/wp-content/uploads/2012/05/ASEAN-APSC-Blueprint-2025.pdf (last accessed 1 June 2020).

60 Id. at Part II.5.2.

61 Id. at Part II.5.3.

efficiency in the work of ASEAN Organs and Bodies, including a strengthened ASEAN Secretariat, as well as with increased ASEAN institutional presence at the national, regional, and international levels.[62]

The ASEAN Economic Community 2025 Blueprint, on the other hand, seeks to realize the following:

i. Create a deeply integrated and highly cohesive ASEAN economy that would support sustained high economic growth and resilience even in the face of global economic shocks and volatilities;

ii. Engender a more equitable and inclusive economic growth in ASEAN that narrows the development gap, eliminates if not reduces poverty significantly, sustains high growth rates of per capita income, and maintains a rising middle class;

iii. Foster robust productivity growth through innovation, technology and human resource development, and intensified regional research and development that is designed for commercial application increase ASEAN's competitive edge in moving the region up the global value chains (GVCs) into higher technology and knowledge-intensive manufacturing and services industries;

iv. Promote the principles of good governance, transparency, and responsive regulatory regimes through active engagement with the private sector, community-based organisations, and other stakeholders of ASEAN;

v. Widen ASEAN people-to-people, institutional, and infrastructure connectivity through ASEAN and sub-regional cooperation projects that facilitate movement of capital as well as skilled labour and talents;

vi. Create a more dynamic and resilient ASEAN, capable of responding and adjusting to emerging challenges through robust national and regional mechanisms that address food and energy security issues, natural disasters, economic shocks, and other emerging trade-related issues as well as global mega trends;

vii. Incorporate a sustainable growth agenda that promotes a science-based use of, and support for, green technology and energy;

viii. Promote the use of the ASEAN Protocol on Enhanced Dispute Settlement Mechanism (EDSM) and develop other approaches to speed up economic dispute resolution;

ix. Reinforce ASEAN centrality in the emerging regional economic architecture by maintaining ASEAN's role as the centre and facilitator of economic integration in the East Asian region; and

x. Work towards a common position and enhance ASEAN's role and voice in global economic fora.[63]

62 Id. at Part II.5.4.

63 ASEAN Economic Community Blueprint 2025, at Part I.6(i) to (x), at www.asean.org/storage/2016/03/AECBP_2025r_FINAL.pdf (last accessed 1 June 2020).

Out of the three pillar communities, it is the ASEAN Socio-Cultural Community that has the most expansive Blueprint 2025 for realizing human development through rule of law in Southeast Asia. It prescribes that the ASEAN Community "shall be characterized as one that engages and benefits its peoples, upheld by the principles of good governance",[64] focusing on multi-sectoral and multi-stakeholder engagements such as ASEAN's Dialogue and Development Partners, sub-regional organizations, academia, local governments, communities, labor organizations, social enterprises, and civil society organizations, among others.[65] The ASEAN Socio-Cultural Community Blueprint 2025 also emphasizes that ASEAN

> is envisioned to move towards a more inclusive community. This would entail the promotion of equitable access to opportunities for ASEAN peoples, and the promotion and protection of human rights of women, children, youths, the elderly/older persons, persons with disabilities, migrant workers, ethnic minority groups, and vulnerable and marginalized groups, throughout their life cycle, guided by a life cycle approach and adhering to rights-based principles in the promotion of ASEAN policies and programmes ... Complementing the inclusive growth agenda of the ASEAN Economic Community (AEC), this Characteristic focuses on addressing the concerns of all peoples of ASEAN on matters related to welfare, social protection, women empowerment, gender equality, promotion and protection of human rights, equitable access to opportunities, poverty eradication, health, decent work, education and information.[66]

Apart from these ambitious objectives, ASEAN is also enjoined to "promote and ensure balanced social development and sustainable environment that meet the needs of the peoples at all times ... for an ASEAN Community with equitable access to sustainable environment that can support its social development and its capacity to work towards sustainable development".[67] For a heavily maritime and land-based region often subject to the hazards of natural disasters, ASEAN also emphasizes the objective of creating resilient communities, where

> resilience is an essential aspect of human security and sustainable environment ... [with] an enhanced capacity to collectively respond and adapt to current challenges and emerging threats. This recognizes that socio-cultural resilience has cross-pillar linkages within the ASEAN Community as an effective force for moderation for the common good, and one that

64 ASEAN Socio-Cultural Community Blueprint 2025, at Part II.A.6, at www.asean.org/wp-content/uploads/2016/04/8.-March-2016-ASCC-Blueprint-2025.pdf (last accessed 1 June 2020).

65 Id. at Part II.A.7.

66 Id. at Part II.B.10 and 7.

67 Id. at Part II.C.15.

> is prepared for natural and human-induced disasters, and socio-economic crises, while fully embracing the principles of comprehensive security.[68]

As of this writing, ASEAN's latest annual report (2017–2018) indicates variable challenges for all three pillar communities in realizing their respective visions of human development through rule of law.[69] With respect to the ASEAN Political-Security Community, ASEAN

> anticipates growing uncertainties in the global strategic environment and increasingly complex non-traditional and transnational security challenges ... It is crucial for ASEAN to play a key role in developing the evolving geopolitical strategic architecture. This means that ASEAN-led mechanisms, such as the [East Asia Summit or EAS], the [ASEAN Regional Forum or ARF], and the [ASEAN Defence Ministers Meeting Plus or ADMM-Plus] have to be inclusive, transparent, and most importantly proactive in promoting cooperation and addressing emerging challenges in a timely manner.[70]

The ASEAN Economic Community pointed out numerous milestones (including the elimination of 98.7 per cent of intra-ASEAN tariffs) in trade and non-trade matters, investment, financial integration, competition law harmonization, micro small and medium enterprises (MSME) development, connectivity, energy security and infrastructure, and innovation, but was markedly silent about the nature of ASEAN Member States' development paradigms or the extent to which human development was being realized (or not) through rule of law.[71] The Initiative for ASEAN Integration (IAI) within the ASEAN Economic Community, which specifically covers development projects on food and agriculture, trade facilitation, MSMEs, education, and health, for Cambodia, Myanmar, Laos, and Viet Nam (the CMLV countries within ASEAN), remains thinly resourced under a slow implementation pace,[72] in contrast with the ASEAN Economic Community milestones. Significantly, the ASEAN Socio-Cultural Community reported more normative regional approaches it has led thus far on various aspects of human development in Southeast Asia (e.g. regional instruments such as the ASEAN Consensus on the Protection and Promotion of the Rights of Migrant Workers;[73] the ASEAN Declaration on Culture of Prevention for a Peaceful, Inclusive,

68 Id. at Part II.D.17 and 18.

69 The ASEAN Secretariat, A Resilient and Innovative ASEAN Community: Annual Report 2017–2018 (Jakarta, July 2018), at https://asean.org/wp-content/uploads/2018/08/ASEAN-Annual-Report-2017–2018.pdf (last accessed 1 June 2020).

70 Id. at p. 11.

71 Id. at pp. 15–20.

72 Id. at pp. 21–22.

73 *See* ASEAN Consensus on the Protection and Promotion of the Rights of Migrant Workers, March 2018, at https://asean.org/storage/2019/01/3.-March-2018-ASEAN-Consensus-on-the-Protection-and-Promotion-of-the-Rights-of-Migrant-Workers.pdf (last accessed 1 April 2019).

Resilient, Healthy, and Harmonious Society;[74] among others), but without elaborating on actual operational outcomes for all the broad sectors covered in its mandate.

Beyond the proliferation of many regional decisions, pronouncements, communiques, among others, ASEAN has not yet created a centralized monitoring and compliance mechanism for assessing each pillar community's progress against their respective Blueprint objectives. The ASEAN Coordinating Council (composed of the Foreign Ministers of all ASEAN Member States) is not a standing institutional body in ASEAN, and yet it is tasked under Article 8 of the ASEAN Charter with the pivotal functions of coordinating implementation of all agreements and decisions of the ASEAN Summit and coordinating with all three ASEAN Communities "to enhance policy coherence, efficiency, and cooperation among them".[75] As of this writing, the latest Community Scorecards indicate more rapid progress AEC than in the APSC or the ASCC. As of 2012, the AEC reported reaching around 73.6 per cent of ASEAN's collective targets (e.g. indicators for single market and production base, competitive economic region, equitable economic development, integration with the global economy),[76] but under selected data points or data indicators previously agreed upon by ASEAN Member States. (Whether or not measuring "equitable economic development" was adequately or accurately captured by data indicators such as MSME development, or increased assistance to the CLMV countries through the Initiative for ASEAN Integration, is, of course, another polemical and methodological matter.[77])

The ASEAN Political-Security Community does not have a Scorecard evaluating its progress in realizing its Blueprint 2025, consistent with ASEAN's non-confrontational tendencies in its political and security relations.[78] The ASEAN Socio-Cultural Community Scorecard, on the other hand, admitted to many serious methodological problems in trying to monitor the ambitious scope of its Blueprint for human development through rule of law in Southeast Asia:[79]

74 *See* ASEAN Declaration on Culture of Prevention for a Peaceful, Inclusive, Resilient, Healthy, and Harmonious Society, November 2017, at https://asean.org/wp-content/uploads/2017/11/9.-ADOPTION_12-NOV-ASCC-Endorsed-Culture-of-Prevention-Declaration_CLEAN.pdf (last accessed 1 June 2020).

75 ASEAN Charter, Article 8.

76 ASEAN Economic Community Scorecard 2012, p. 12, at www.asean.org/wp-content/uploads/images/archive/publications/AEC%20Scorecard.pdf (last accessed 1 June 2020).

77 *See* Sanchita Basu Das, *Assessing the Progress and Impediments Towards an ASEAN Economic Community*, pp. 1–19, at pp. 12–15, in Sanchita Basu Das (Ed.), ASEAN Economic Community Scorecard: Performance and Perception (Institute of Southeast Asian Studies, 2013).

78 *See* Termsak Chalermpalanupap, *ASEAN: Managing External Political and Security Relations*, Southeast Asian Affairs (2014), pp. 53–75; Alan Collins, Building a People-Oriented Security Community the ASEAN Way (Routledge, 2013), at pp. 6–7.

79 ASEAN Socio-Cultural Community Scorecard, 2016, at pp. 5–6, at www.asean.org/wp-content/uploads/2016/04/9.-March-2016-2015-ASCC-Scorecard-1.pdf (last accessed 1 June 2020).

- Lack of agreed indicators by ASCC sectoral bodies for some of the strategic objectives of the ASCC Blueprint, thus leading to a more qualitative assessment and descriptive analysis of the status of ASCC with regard to these objectives.
- Lack of complete set of data for all [ASEAN Member States or AMS], and data corresponding to different years for each indicator makes it difficult to make sensible assessment of the region's collective performance.
- Insufficient data due to lack of updating and verification of data by AMS (as required by the ASEAN Secretariat), even though updated data is publicly available from UN and other reputable databases.
- Trend analysis could not be made as comparable data is not available for the reference years 2009 (baseline) and 2015 (year of reporting).
- Lack of most recent data (majority of data sets are only up to 2012), thus the Scorecard assessment may not be representative of the actual state of affairs as of 2015. Ideally a lag of one year from the reference year 2015 would be appropriate.
- Inconsistencies in data format reported and verified by AMS, thus assessing progress from 2009 to 2015 is similarly not feasible, unless amended by the researchers to conform to the agreed reporting format to allow for comparison.
- Lack of details and clarification on some indicators in terms of its definition, methodology, or the rationale for adopting the indicator.

The above problems are not just problems of data gathering or methodology at the ASEAN Socio-Cultural Community, but reveal an overall lack of coordination with the other two pillar communities to investigate and verify the state of affairs of human development through rule of law in ASEAN as a whole. As discussed throughout the rest of this book, ASEAN's progress on the establishment of a single market is narrowly focused according to specific sectors of trade, investment, and finance, among others, and remains methodologically incremental in the strategies that it can adopt. This is precisely because ASEAN is drawing from its pre-Charter practices as a loose intergovernmental cooperation while stalemated by governance constraints under the present Charter and a strict reliance on mainly the individual implementation of ASEAN Law by ASEAN Member States. So long as these situations endure, achieving ASEAN's rule of law-based vision of human development will prove difficult in the long run.[80]

The structure for this book: asking the development and rule of law questions for an ASEAN Law-based single market

There is a wealth of international legal scholarship on ASEAN integration, particularly other series that helpfully delve in authoritative detail on mapping and

80 *See* Ravichandran Moorthy and Guido Benny, *Is an "ASEAN Community" Achievable?*, 52 Asian Survey 6 (November/December 2012), pp. 1043–1066.

examining the normative regimes now appearing from Charter-based ASEAN integration.[81] We have benefited from these collaborative exchanges with ASEAN and European Union scholars fostered by the National University of Singapore (NUS) Center for International Law and Centre for Asian Legal Studies, and greatly appreciate the pioneering efforts taken by NUS to explore emerging ASEAN Law in fine-grained detail.

Our own work in this book is a product of considerable collaboration in the past six years. It has been informed by two previous symposia that my co-editor David Cohen and I organized while we were Co-Directors of the ASEAN Law & Integration Center (ALIC) and co-faculty members at the University of Hawaii Richardson School of Law, and a third conference hosted by David Cohen at Stanford University The first was an Authors' Workshop conducted in September 2014 in Jakarta, Indonesia, organized by the East-West Center (where I served as Adjunct Fellow and where David Cohen led its Asian International Justice Initiative for the East-West Center), where we identified several preliminary issues with the ASEAN integration process. This was followed by the April 2016 ALIC-Asia Pacific Law & Policy Journal International Symposium on Governance, Development, and Civil Society, where we raised broader concerns about the interrelated development concerns suffusing all three pillar communities in ASEAN. In October 2016, David Cohen hosted the seminar "The Rise of ASEAN and the Future of the US-ASEAN Strategic Partnership", where we focused on interrelated AEC, development, and maritime security issues in Southeast Asia. At the University of Notre Dame Keough School of Global Affairs, I have been fortunate to keep finding avenues for my academic and policy work on ASEAN, this time in conjunction with my role as Expert for the United Nations' Intergovernmental Working Group on the Right to Development, where I assist in the drafting of the new legally binding instrument (treaty) on the right to development for the United Nations. My co-editor David Cohen continues his Expert assistance for the ASEAN Intergovernmental Commission on Human Rights, and in January 2018, we both had the opportunity to again elaborate our positions on rule of law-based development in ASEAN as Resource Experts/Speakers for the Human Rights Resource Centre for ASEAN's Summer Institute on Trade, Investment, and the Rule of Law in Bali, Indonesia.

This book, therefore, is not intended to be a treatise or textbook on ASEAN Law which has already been laudably done by so many others. We aim to introduce scholars to various fundamental topics of ASEAN Law as it relates to its emerging single market – trade in goods, trade in services, foreign investment, ASEAN's economic regulators – but to contextualize our inquiry against

81 *See among others* the Integration through law: The Role of Law and the Rule of Law in ASEAN Integration monograph series at Cambridge University Press (series editors Joseph H.H. Weiler and Hsien-Li Tan), at www.cambridge.org/core/series/integration-through-lawthe-role-of-law-and-the-rule-of-law-in-asean-integration/87C637DF557C415ED79612CF8C121F56 (last accessed 1 June 2020); Pasha L. Hsieh and Bryan Mercurio (Eds.), ASEAN Law in the New Regional Economic Order: Global Trends and Shifting Paradigms (Oxford University Press, 2019).

the broader prism of ASEAN's rule of law-based development objectives. In Chapter 2 (Pre-Charter and post-Charter-based ASEAN: cross-pillar decision-making in the master plan for ASEAN Connectivity 2025), I draw from earlier work published with the *Columbia Journal of Transnational Law* in 2011, as well as a recorded lecture at the United Nations Audio-Visual Library of International Law in January 2017, to summarize the key structural innovations of a post-Charter ASEAN, juxtaposing these innovations with unexplored deficits in cross-pillar development decision-making as seen in the nascent implementation of the Master Plan for ASEAN Connectivity 2025. National University of Singapore Constitutional Law, Administrative Law, and International Law Professor Kevin Y.L. Tan then demonstrates in Chapter 3 (ASEAN Law: content, applicability, and challenges) how emerging regional law in Southeast Asia – ASEAN Law – is internalized throughout the different constitutional law systems among the ASEAN Member States.

Economist, lawyer, and Chief of Party for USAID and the US State Department's ASEAN Connectivity through Trade and Investment (ACTI) Project Dr. Timothy Buehrer then focuses in Chapter 4 (ASEAN's regional economic regulators) on the complex layering of regional governance, particularly from the ASEAN Economic Community Context, and the proliferation of regional economic coordination and cooperative bodies to realize the AEC Blueprint 2025. International trade lawyer Edmund W. Sim then analyzes the Southeast Asian regional trade in goods regime in Chapter 5 (ASEAN trade in goods), finding that the

> continuing influence of national borders in the [ASEAN Economic Community or AEC] also affects the creation of a single market in ASEAN. Trade in services, investment flows, and movement of natural persons are also affected by national policies. ASEAN's relative lack of a unified policy on competition, government procurement, subsidies, taxation, labor mobility, and other issues accordingly present challenges to the formation of a single market in ASEAN.

Singapore Management University Law Professor Pasha L. Hsieh examines the counterpart Southeast Asian regional trade in services regime in Chapter 6 (ASEAN trade in services), observing that the regional legal framework governing services negotiations and commitments, while promoting the movement of natural persons and labour within Southeast Asia, nevertheless requires continued regulatory reform to ensure intensification of services integration in a manner most consistent with the development prospects of ASEAN as a single market. In Chapter 7 (Horizontal embeddedness, business, and human rights: fostering the corporate responsibility to respect human rights within the ASEAN Community), SOAS University of London Lecturer in International Law Dr. Michelle Staggs Kelsall then zeroes in on the asymmetries of protection in business and human rights controversies within the ASEAN Economic Community – a lingering deficit notwithstanding the development and rule of law objectives of the ASEAN

Charter. I then proceed to sketch out in Chapter 8 (ASEAN's foreign investment regime) regulatory freedom and public policy issues from ASEAN's regional investment treaties vis-à-vis ASEAN Member States' remaining individual bilateral investment treaty programs, drawing from previous analysis conducted for the ASEAN Coordinating Committee on Investment at their June 2015 intergovernmental session in Da Nang, Viet Nam. Finally, in Chapter 9 (The rule of law and human rights in ASEAN: towards a "rules-based" community?), David Cohen exposes the development paradox that the rule of law

> cuts across all three pillars of ASEAN … the greater the impingement of the rule of law through corruption, political interference, lack of judicial independence, influence peddling, and many other factors, the greater will be the drag that impedes and holds back the implementation of the goals of the AEC.

It has been well over a decade since the start of ASEAN integration and ASEAN's shift to a fully rules-based intergovernmental organization purposely seeking regional development through rule of law. We do not expect the topics in this book to have exhausted all development and rule of law issues that continue to suffuse individual ASEAN Member States – particularly with the rise of authoritarian regimes in Southeast Asia,[82] or the proliferation of different development paradigms among ASEAN Member States and the rise of corresponding impacts from rapid infrastructure, "smart cities", "fintech", automation, and other burgeoning technologies altering the land and marine environment, climate change adaptation and mitigation measures, as well as changing human rights situations in Southeast Asia.[83] But the cross-pillar discussion on both the architecture and details of how to achieve ASEAN's regional development through rule of law has to begin even among academics and policy experts, even if it is not formally taking place for now throughout ASEAN's three pillar communities. Well beyond our immediate fascination with the continuing exponential economic performance of Southeast Asia under its single market and production base, should lie our enduring core inquiries on what our understanding of regional development is, and for whom and to what ends we strive for rule of law in ASEAN.

82 *See* Rainer Einzenberger and Wolfram Schaffar, *The Political Economy of New Authoritarianism in Southeast Asia,* 11 Austrian Journal of Southeast Asian Studies 1 (2018), pp. 1–12; Thitinan Pongsudhirak, "Authoritarianism is accelerating in Southeast Asia", Nikkei Asian Review, 1 January 2018, at https://asia.nikkei.com/Editor-s-Picks/Looking-ahead-2018/Authoritarianism-is-accelerating-in-Southeast-Asia (last accessed 1 June 2020).

83 *See among others* Hal Hill (Ed.), The Economic Development of Southeast Asia (Edward Elgar Publishing, 2002), Volumes 1–4; Michael T. Rock, *The Last Fifty Years: Development Strategy and Development Performance in Southeast Asia,* 35 Journal of Southeast Asian Economies 1 (April 2018, ISEAS-Yushof Ishak Institute), pp. 39–49; Thomas Parks, "ASEAN: Shaping the Future of Regional Development in Southeast Asia", The Asia Foundation, 24 October 2018, at https://asiafoundation.org/2018/10/24/asean-shaping-the-future-of-regional-development-in-southeast-asia/ (last accessed 1 June 2020).

2 Pre-Charter and post-Charter ASEAN

Cross-pillar decision-making in the Master Plan for ASEAN Connectivity 2025

Diane A. Desierto[1]

Structural comparisons: ASEAN before and after the 2008 Charter system

There are five key structural differences in ASEAN that should be emphasized before and after the passage of the ASEAN Charter in 2008. *First, there is a qualitative legal difference now to the array of international instruments ASEAN Member States regionally conclude under the Charter-based system.* Article 5(2) of the ASEAN Charter expressly obligates ASEAN Member States to "take all necessary measures, including the enactment of appropriate domestic legislation, to effectively implement the provisions of this Charter and to comply with all obligations of membership".[2] In the pre-Charter system practices of ASEAN Member States for over 40 years, ASEAN Member States issued numerous communiques, declarations, and commitments – some in explicit treaty form such as the Treaty of Amity and Cooperation – and others in more cooperative "softer" international instruments. Differentiating the binding legal effects and scope of those pre-Charter instruments was an opaque and archaeologically difficult exercise, as ASEAN itself did not provide explicit guidance on how to treat such pre-Charter instruments, much less where to find authoritative sources for such instruments outside of the ASEAN Secretariat headquarters archives in Jakarta, Indonesia. (Although in 2012, ASEAN Member States concluded the Rules of Procedure for the Interpretation of the ASEAN Charter, which permits the ASEAN Secretariat to issue good faith, non-binding, and non-authoritative interpretations of the ASEAN Charter upon the request of any ASEAN Member

1 This chapter draws from a recorded lecture on ASEAN Law and Regional Integration that I delivered at the United Nations Audiovisual Library in January 2017, at http://legal.un.org/avl/ls/Desierto_RO_video_1.html (last accessed June 1, 2020), and from a previously published article, Diane A. Desierto, *ASEAN's Constitutionalization of International Law: Challenges to Evolution under the New ASEAN Charter*, 49 Columbia Journal of Transnational Law 2 (2011), pp. 268–320.

2 ASEAN Charter, Article 5(2).

State or any ASEAN organ.[3]) Significantly, the ASEAN Charter itself removes the ambiguity by specifically providing for the legal effect of pre-Charter instruments – whatever the nature or tenor of the instrument – according to the following terms in Article 52:

> *Article 52*
>
> LEGAL CONTINUITY
>
> 1. All treaties, conventions, agreements, concords, declarations, protocols and other ASEAN instruments which have been in effect before the entry into force of this Charter *shall continue to be valid*.
> 2. In case of inconsistency between the rights and obligations of ASEAN Member States under such instruments and this Charter, the Charter shall prevail.[4]
>
> (Italics added)

The deliberate use of the term "valid" in Article 52(1) is significant. Denotatively, "valid" means "having legal efficacy or force".[5] Article 52(1) of the ASEAN Charter did not distinguish between the legal effects of different pre-Charter ASEAN instruments, when it could have done so easily differentiating between the "hard law" effects of treaties and conventions, with the softer legal quality of regional cooperation instruments such as concords, declarations, protocols, and other ASEAN instruments. This makes it reasonable to infer today that each pre-Charter ASEAN instrument has been conferred legal force and effect, even if the language in which the instrument is couched is stated in terms that are more cooperative, voluntarist, or suggestive of "best-efforts" endeavors of ASEAN Member States.[6] While pre-Charter ASEAN was often derided for the more marginal influence of hard law,[7] one also has to appreciate that ASEAN's in its pre-Charter years was also steadily marching toward deepened legalization in the regional framework for economic cooperation and what ASEAN Member States expected of each other in their regional relations.[8]

3 Rules of Procedure for the Interpretation of the ASEAN Charter, 2012, at www.asean.org/uploads/2012/05/ROP%20for%20Interpretation%20of%20ASEAN%20Charter.pdf (last accessed June 1, 2020).
4 ASEAN Charter, Article 52.
5 Merriam-Webster Legal Dictionary, at www.merriam-webster.com/dictionary/valid#legalDictionary (last accessed June 1, 2020).
6 On the reasons why states use soft law (e.g. resolving a coordination game, loss avoidance theory, delegation theory, or an evolving "international common law"), see Andrew T. Guzman and Timothy L. Meyer, *International Soft Law*, 2 Journal of Legal Analysis 1 (Spring 2010), pp. 171–225.
7 Purificacion Valera-Quisumbing, *Can ASEAN Forge a Viable Legal Regime for Regional Cooperation?*, 56 Philippine Law Journal 2 (June 1981), pp. 209–224.
8 *See* Paul J. Davidson, *The ASEAN Way and the Role of Law in ASEAN Economic Cooperation*, 8 Singapore Yearbook of International Law (2004), pp. 165–176, at p. 177.

The second key structural difference in pre-Charter and post-Charter ASEAN is in the clarified and more predictable regional legislative process under more identifiable Charter-based regional institutions and a more permanent ASEAN regional bureaucracy than the loose configuration that existed in pre-Charter ASEAN. Pre-Charter ASEAN depended on decisions and instruments issued by what was then the ASEAN Heads of Government meetings, expediently complemented by a variable constellation of ad hoc committees and councils:

> The main constitutive documents of the pre-Charter ASEAN are the 1976 Treaty of Amity and Cooperation (TAC) and the 1967 ASEAN Bangkok Declaration. Both instruments clearly defined the terms of Southeast Asian regional economic, political, and socio-cultural cooperation under an intergovernmental framework operating through Member States' consensus vote (otherwise known as the "ASEAN Way"). The 1967 ASEAN Bangkok Declaration provided for narrow institutional machinery, governed by Southeast Asian governments through their respective foreign ministers at Annual Meetings and Special Meetings. Pending these Annual and/or Special Meetings, ASEAN would undertake implementation of the region's cooperation agenda through a semi-permanent administrative cohort of Standing Committees, ad hoc Committees and Permanent Committees of Specialists, working alongside counterpart National Secretariats in ASEAN Member States.[9]

In contrast, ASEAN under its Charter-based system establishes a clear hierarchy of decision-making, with the ASEAN Summit (composed of the Heads of State of all ASEAN Member States) at the top of the hierarchy. The ASEAN Summit uniquely possesses executive, legislative, and judicial functions under the ASEAN Charter. The ASEAN Summit is the "supreme policy-making body of ASEAN",[10] which "deliberate(s), provide(s) policy guidance and take(s) decisions on key issues pertaining to the realization of the objectives of ASEAN, important matters of interest to Member States and all issues referred to it by the ASEAN Coordinating Council, the ASEAN Community Councils and ASEAN Sectoral Ministerial Bodies".[11] The ASEAN Summit meets twice annually,[12] and as convened for special or ad hoc meetings.[13] The ASEAN Summit has broad and sweeping emergency powers spanning unspecified innumerable situations affecting the Southeast Asian region, including the power to instruct

9 Diane A. Desierto, *ASEAN's Constitutionalization of International Law: Challenges to Evolution under the New ASEAN Charter,* 49 Columbia Journal of Transnational Law 2 (2011), pp. 268–320, at pp. 282–283.
10 ASEAN Charter, Article 7(2)(a).
11 ASEAN Charter, Article 7(2)(b).
12 ASEAN Charter, Article 7(3(a).
13 ASEAN Charter, Article 7(3)(b).

relevant ministers in each of the ASEAN Community Councils (for Political-Security, Economic, and Socio-Cultural pillar communities) to "hold ad hoc inter-Ministerial meetings, and address important issues concerning ASEAN that cut across Community Councils",[14] as well as the overarching power to "address emergency situations affecting ASEAN by taking appropriate actions".[15]

The ASEAN Summit also decides on any serious breaches of the Charter or non-compliance by any ASEAN Member State with ASEAN Law,[16] as well as any unresolved disputes remaining even after the application of the dispute settlement provisions in Chapter VIII of the ASEAN Charter.[17] Finally, the ASEAN Summit has residual powers to establish and dissolve ASEAN Sectoral Ministerial Bodies and other ASEAN institutions, as well as to appoint the Secretary-General of ASEAN.[18] As of this writing, however, there are so far no reported unresolved regional disputes, serious Charter breaches, or non-compliance issues that have been referred directly to the ASEAN Summit – although it could very well do so with respect to a full range of regional emergency situations such as the South China Sea maritime security issues,[19] regional marine environmental crises from China's island-building and land reclamation activities in the South China Sea,[20] or even the cross-border human security and human rights situation facing the exodus of Rohingya minority from Myanmar into Southeast Asian neighboring territories.[21] Neither has the ASEAN Summit created the standing dispute settlement system (analogous to that of the World Trade Organization's Appellate Body and Panels) to which ASEAN Member States committed under the Vientiane

14 ASEAN Charter, Article 7(c).
15 ASEAN Charter, Article 7(d).
16 ASEAN Charter, Article 20(4) in relation to Article 7(e.)
17 ASEAN Charter, Article 26 in relation to Article 7(e).
18 ASEAN Charter, Articles 7(f) and (g).
19 *See* Lynn Kuok, "South China Sea Dispute Undermines Maritime Security in Southeast Asia", The Asia Foundation, August 23, 2017, at https://asiafoundation.org/2017/08/23/south-china-sea-dispute-undermines-maritime-security-southeast-asia/ (last accessed June 1, 2020); Clive Schofield, *Dangerous ground: a geopolitical overview of the South China Sea*, pp. 7–25 in Sam Bateman and Ralf Emmers (Eds.), Security and International Politics in the South China Sea: Towards a Cooperative Management Regime (Routledge, 2009).
20 *See* Chloe Houdre, "Environmental Ramifications of the South China Sea Conflict: Vying for Regional Dominance at the Environment's Expense", Georgetown Environmental Law Review, July 12, 2018, at www.law.georgetown.edu/environmental-law-review/blog/environmental-ramifications-of-the-south-china-sea-conflict-vying-for-regional-dominance-at-the-environments-expense/ (last accessed June 1, 2020); Matthew Southerland, *China's Island Building in the South China Sea: Damage to the Marine Environment, Implications, and International Law*, US China Economic and Security Review Commission, 2016, at https://seasresearch.files.wordpress.com/2016/04/chinas-island-building-in-the-south-china-sea_0.pdf (last accessed June 1, 2020).
21 *See* Human Rights Watch, "ASEAN: Don't Whitewash Atrocities Against Rohingya, Repatriation Report Ignores Dire Situation in Myanmar", June 19, 2019, at www.hrw.org/news/2019/06/19/asean-dont-whitewash-atrocities-against-rohingya (last accessed June 1, 2020).

2004 ASEAN Protocol on Enhanced Dispute Settlement Mechanism.[22] There is no regional ASEAN court, but rather a diffuse system for various tiers of dispute settlement, as described in the 2004 ASEAN Protocol which contains an Annex enumerating all "covered agreements" therein – specifically pertaining to economic treaties and agreements of ASEAN concluded as of the Protocol as well as "future ASEAN economic agreements".[23]

Notwithstanding the absence of a centralized regional court, the diffusion of compliance monitoring mechanisms in the ASEAN Charter and in post-Charter agreements of ASEAN demonstrates various strategies at work to determine compliance with ASEAN Law. As carefully discussed by Hao Duy Phan,[24] these strategies include: 1) the use of monitoring bodies; 2) reports on implementation progress by the ASEAN Secretariat or ASEAN Sectoral Bodies; 3) self-reporting by ASEAN Member States; 4) review, evaluation, and recommendations submitted by monitoring and evaluation bodies; 5) capacity building and technical assistance with ASEAN Dialogue Partners; and 6) consultations.

The third key structural difference between pre-Charter and post-Charter ASEAN is the formalized role and delimited scope of responsibilities of the ASEAN Chair. In pre-Charter ASEAN practices, whichever ASEAN Member State was chairing the Heads of Government (and other sectoral) meeting had the significant opportunity to define and shape the agenda (including marshaling the corresponding ASEAN resources) for the majority of (if not all) ASEAN meetings for the given year – a largely "undemocratic" process that arose from customary ASEAN practices and is not strictly codified anywhere.[25] The influential role of the ASEAN Chair is such that even in 2006, Myanmar's chairmanship of ASEAN was internally questioned by ASEAN heads of State given all of Myanmar's democratization challenges.[26] By contrast, Article 32 of the ASEAN Charter clearly subordinates the ASEAN chairmanship to the authority of the ASEAN Summit, even as it defines the specific parameters of the Chair's responsibilities:

22 *See* ASEAN Protocol on Enhanced Dispute Settlement Mechanism, 2004, at https://asean.org/?static_post=asean-protocol-on-enhanced-dispute-settlement-mechanism (last accessed June 1, 2020).

23 Id. at Article 1(1) ("The rules and procedures of this Protocol shall apply to disputes brought pursuant to the consultation and dispute settlement provisions of the Agreement as well as agreements listed in Appendix 1 and future ASEAN economic agreements. [the 'covered agreements']").

24 Hao Duy Phan, *Promoting Compliance: An Assessment of ASEAN Instruments Since the ASEAN Charter,* 41 Syracuse Journal of International Law and Commerce 2 (Spring 2014), pp. 379–412, at pp. 388–407.

25 *See among others* Donald K. Emmerson, *Challenging ASEAN: A "Topological" View,* 29 Contemporary Southeast Asia 3, pp. 424–446; Anowar Zahid and Anisah Che Ngah, *Completion of ASEAN Chairmanship,* 9 Journal of East Asia and International Law 2 (Autumn 2016), pp. 540–542; Daniel Seah, *The ASEAN Charter,* 58 The International and Comparative Law Quarterly 1 (January 2009), pp. 197–212.

26 Mikio Oishi and Nina Ghani, *Developing a Way to Influence the Conduct of the Government in Intrastate Conflict,* pp. 89–110, at p. 101, in Mikio Oishi (Ed.), Contemporary Conflicts in Southeast Asia: Towards a New ASEAN Way of Conflict Management (Springer, 2016).

Article 32

ROLE OF THE CHAIRMAN OF ASEAN

The Member State holding the Chairmanship of ASEAN shall:

(a) Actively promote and enhance the interests and well-being of ASEAN, including efforts to build an ASEAN Community through policy initiatives, coordination, consensus and cooperation;
(b) Ensure the centrality of ASEAN;
(c) Ensure an effective and timely response to urgent issues or crisis situations affecting ASEAN, including providing its good offices and such other arrangements to immediately address these concerns;
(d) Represent ASEAN in strengthening and promoting closer relations with external partners; and
(e) Carry out such other tasks and functions as may be mandated.[27]

For the given calendar year, the ASEAN Chair will assume the chairmanship of the ASEAN Summit and related summits; the ASEAN Coordinating Council; the three ASEAN Community Councils; as appropriate, relevant ASEAN Sectoral Ministerial Bodies and Senior Officials meetings; and the Committee of Permanent Representatives.[28] This provides clarity not just in presiding over the actual ASEAN meetings, but also predictability as to the scope of ASEAN bodies and organs covered by an ASEAN chairmanship.

The fourth key structural difference in pre-Charter and post-Charter ASEAN lies with the mandated implementation of ASEAN Law – using all and any means necessary – for all ASEAN Member States. Prescinding from the Charter's recognition of ASEAN Member States' equal rights and obligations,[29] all ASEAN Member States are required to "take all necessary measures, including the enactment of appropriate domestic legislation, to effectively implement the provisions of this Charter and to comply with all obligations of membership".[30] The scope of measures that ASEAN Member States are expected to take are broad and sweeping – what is necessary to "effectively implement" the Charter as well as all that is necessary to achieve compliance with membership obligations. This language is particularly significant, because membership obligations are left unenumerated in the ASEAN Charter, even as the admission of any Member State to ASEAN includes the criterion of "ability and willingness to carry out the obligations of Membership".[31] At the minimum, obligations of membership should include all Charter obligations – including ASEAN and ASEAN Member States' overarching commitment to "act in accordance with" the key Principles enumerated in Article 2(a) to 2(n) of the Charter, as well as to execute all ASEAN

27 ASEAN Charter, Article 32.
28 ASEAN Charter, Article 31(2).
29 ASEAN Charter, Article 5(1).
30 ASEAN Charter, Article 5(1).
31 ASEAN Charter, Article 6(d).

Summit decisions in light of the Article 7(2)(a) Charter provision making the ASEAN Summit the "supreme policy-making body of ASEAN".

Much has been written about Article 3 (Legal Personality of ASEAN) of the ASEAN Charter having supposedly "conferred legal personality" on ASEAN as an intergovernmental organization.[32] This is a moot point. Article 3 did not "create" nor constitute ASEAN, but it does contain ASEAN Member States' express Charter commitment to declare and recognize ASEAN's existing international legal personality as a regional organization. The International Law Commission's 2011 Draft Articles on the Responsibility of International Organizations defines "international organization" as "an organization established by a treaty or other instrument governed by international law and possessing its own international legal personality".[33] The establishment of ASEAN under the 1976 Treaty of Amity and Cooperation (TAC)[34] satisfies this precise definition.

The fifth key structural difference between pre-Charter and post-Charter ASEAN is the prominent Charter status given to the norm of "ASEAN Centrality"[35] in Articles 1(15) and 2(2)(m) of the ASEAN Charter. Article 1(15) of the ASEAN Charter states that one of ASEAN's Purposes is to "maintain the centrality and proactive role of ASEAN as the *primary* driving force in its relations and cooperation with its external partners in a regional architecture that is open, transparent, and inclusive".[36] In turn, ASEAN and its Member States commit in Article 2(2)(m) to "act in accordance with ... the centrality of ASEAN in external political, economic, social and cultural relations while remaining actively engaged, outward-looking, inclusive, and non-discriminatory".[37] The Charter status of ASEAN Centrality is a marked departure from pre-Charter ASEAN, when ASEAN Member States readily concluded agreements with fellow ASEAN Member States with or without ASEAN's facilitation. The Charter's emphasis on ASEAN Centrality – heightening the primary role of ASEAN in the Southeast Asian region's external partnerships and cooperative relationships with ASEAN's numerous Dialogue Partners – at the same time evolves the meaning and content

32 *See among others* Hao Duy Phan, *The Association of Southeast Asian Nations: International Legal Personality and its Treaty-Making Power,* 13 International Organizations Law Review 2 (2016), pp. 273–307; Simon Chesterman, *Does ASEAN Exist: The Association of Southeast Asian Nations as an International Legal Person,* 12 Singapore Yearbook of International Law (2008), pp. 199–212.

33 International Law Commission, *Draft Articles on Responsibility of International Organizations,* 2011, Article 2(a), at https://legal.un.org/ilc/texts/instruments/english/draft_articles/9_11_2011.pdf (last accessed August 27, 2020).

34 Treaty of Amity and Cooperation in Southeast Asia, Indonesia, February 24, 1976, at https://asean.org/treaty-amity-cooperation-southeast-asia-indonesia-24-february-1976/ (last accessed June 1, 2020).

35 *See* Amitav Acharya, *The Myth of ASEAN Centrality?,* 39 Contemporary Southeast Asia 2 (August 2017), pp. 273–279, at p. 273 ("it is related to a number of concepts: ASEAN as the 'leader', the 'driver', the 'architect', the 'institutional hub', the 'vanguard', the 'nucleus', and the 'fulcrum' of regional processes and institutional designs in the Asia-Pacific region").

36 ASEAN Charter, Article 1(15).

37 ASEAN Charter, Article 2(2)(m).

of ASEAN neutrality, which is an equally fundamental norm in Article 2(2), paragraphs (a) to (f), and (k), of the ASEAN Charter:

> 2. ASEAN and its Member States shall act in accordance with the following Principles:
>
> (a) Respect for the independence, sovereignty, equality, territorial integrity and national identity of all ASEAN Member States;
> (b) Shared commitment and collective responsibility in enhancing regional peace, security and prosperity;
> (c) Renunciation of aggression and of the threat or use of force or other actions in any manner inconsistent with international law;
> (d) Reliance on peaceful settlement of disputes;
> (e) Non-interference in the internal affairs of ASEAN Member States;
> (f) Respect for the right of every Member State to lead its national existence free from external interference, subversion and coercion;
>
> ...
>
> (k) Abstention from participation in any policy or activity, including the use of its territory, pursued by any ASEAN Member State or non-ASEAN State or any non-State actor, which threatens the sovereignty, territorial integrity or political and economic stability of ASEAN Member States.[38]

The primacy of ASEAN in driving Southeast Asia's external political and economic relationships under ASEAN Centrality does not in any way mean abandoning its Charter norms on the region's neutrality. This is understandable given the evolution of ASEAN neutrality as practiced in the Southeast Asian region, which Ralf Emmers argues is a transition from the pre-Charter framing of ASEAN neutrality as autonomy and non-external interference, into a post-Charter concept of ASEAN neutrality as impartiality within a broader Asia-Pacific architecture:

> In the last two decades, ASEAN has attempted to build an institutional architecture that includes all the major and middle powers in the Asia Pacific. The architecture consists of overlapping multilateral bodies – such as the East Asia Summit (EAS), ASEAN Plus Three, the ASEAN Regional Forum (ARF) and the ASEAN Defence Ministers' Meeting Plus (ADMM-Plus) – that provide venues for participants to exchange strategic perspectives and work towards mutual understanding on security issues. Based on the notion of inclusiveness, these platforms have focused on dialogue and confidence building measures to improve the climate of relations. Significantly, the ASEAN-led architecture suggests a change in the meaning and applicability of ASEAN neutrality. It constitutes a shift in strategy from keeping the major powers at bay to a new imperative centred at locking them in. ASEAN has

38 ASEAN Charter, Articles 2(2)(a) to (f), and (k).

therefore evolved from being dedicated to keeping Southeast Asia free from Great Power conflict to accepting the involvement of external powers.[39]

ASEAN Centrality in post-Charter ASEAN is thus a key structural difference which should be noted alongside the paradigmatic shift in ASEAN's evolved conception of neutrality into regional impartiality. As seen in the next section, these structural differences are significant for understanding how ASEAN navigates development and rule of law decision-making in the post-Charter ASEAN pillar communities.

Post-Charter development and rule of law cross-pillar decision-making: possibilities for the Master Plan on ASEAN Connectivity 2025

The five key structural differences discussed in the previous section between pre-Charter and post-Charter ASEAN all bear significantly upon ASEAN's ability to undertake cross-pillar decision-making on its development and rule of law objectives under the ASEAN Charter. Giving legal effect and validity to ASEAN instruments, whether pre-Charter or post-Charter, does not only allow for predictability and reliability of ASEAN development policies, but concretely expresses ASEAN decision-making as the rule of law in Southeast Asia. Having a predictable regional legislative process and an identifiable permanent ASEAN bureaucracy is also valuable not just to ensure compliance with ASEAN Law and institutional or official accountability for such compliance, but also to help promote operational and sectoral implementation in a manner that could avoid functional replication and resource inefficiencies among ASEAN bodies and organs. The clearer delineation of the role of the ASEAN Chair assists in avoiding any leadership vacuum for the full range of ASEAN meetings each year, likewise preventing the hosting State from ever overreaching against ASEAN Summit decisions. The required mandatory implementation of ASEAN Law by all the Member States within their respective national jurisdictions provides mutual and external assurances that ASEAN decisions will be localized through all necessary measures by the Member States. Finally, with the Charter status of ASEAN Centrality in tandem with an evolved notion of ASEAN neutrality as impartiality, ASEAN's development and rule of law decision-making conveys global inclusiveness with, and responsiveness to, ASEAN's myriad of Dialogue Partners and other non-State Development Partners.

The prospects for cross-pillar decision-making in a post-Charter ASEAN are particularly visible in the Master Plan on ASEAN Connectivity 2025.[40] The

39 Ralf Emmers, *Unpacking ASEAN Neutrality: The Quest for Autonomy and Impartiality in Southeast Asia*, 40 Contemporary Southeast Asia 3 (December 2018), pp. 349–370, at pp. 355, and 362–363.

40 See The ASEAN Secretariat, *Master Plan on ASEAN Connectivity 2025*, Jakarta, 2016, at https://asean.org/storage/2016/09/Master-Plan-on-ASEAN-Connectivity-20251.pdf (last accessed June 1, 2020).

Master Plan on ASEAN Connectivity 2025 (MPAC 2025) seeks "improved physical, institutional, and people-to-people linkages, by promoting greater competitiveness, prosperity, inclusiveness, and sense of [ASEAN] Community",[41] which is seen as the foremost cross-pillar rule of law-based development plan for ASEAN.[42] According to the Master Plan, connectivity in ASEAN

> encompasses the physical (e.g. transport, [information and communications technology or ICT], and energy), institutional (e.g. trade, investment, and services liberalization), and people-to-people linkages (e.g. education, culture, and tourism) that are the foundational supportive means to achieving the economic, political-security, and socio-cultural pillars of an integrated ASEAN Community.[43]

The Master Plan focuses on five key development areas for the heavily maritime and land-based Southeast Asian region with over 620 million in population: 1) Sustainable Infrastructure; 2) Digital Innovation; 3) Seamless Logistics; 4) Regulatory Excellence; and 5) People Mobility.[44]

ASEAN identified various barriers and common challenges to the ASEAN Connectivity projects, such as: 1) *financing barriers* (e.g. the lack of sufficiently attractive return on investment to encourage private sector investment, "even if there were large potential societal benefits";[45] the different fiscal capacities of ASEAN Member States involving budgetary choices between long-term infrastructure investment and immediate priorities in health, education, and social services; as well as capital availability from other sources such as multilateral funds, bond markets, other governments, the private sector); 2) *decision-making barriers* (e.g. how ASEAN decision-makers prioritize infrastructure projects as national priorities versus other national priorities; inter-agency coordination and delegation to ensure sustained readiness to realize long-term infrastructure projects, especially if they are cross-border such as the ASEAN Highway Network – a 132-kilometer road from Ban Lao to Nam Phao; information asymmetries in regard to the costs and benefits of ASEAN Connectivity projects, due diligence, and the assessment of project viability); and 3) *implementation barriers* (e.g. gaps in the supply chain preventing access to critical components of ASEAN

41 Vientiane Declaration on the Adoption of the Master Plan on ASEAN Connectivity 2025, at Preamble, fourth paragraph, at https://asean.org/storage/2016/09/Master-Plan-on-ASEAN-Connectivity-20251.pdf (last accessed June 1, 2020).

42 Id. at fifth paragraph ("Emphasizing the importance of the Master Plan on ASEAN Connectivity 2025 in building the ASEAN Community as well as in supporting the implementation of the ASEAN Political-Security Community Blueprint 2025, the ASEAN Economic Community Blueprint 2025, the ASEAN Socio-Cultural Community Blueprint 2025, ASEAN sectoral workplans, and the Initiative for ASEAN Integration (IAI) Work Plan III, as well as in enhancing synergies with other sub-regional and inter-regional frameworks").

43 Id. at footnote 42, at Executive Summary, paragraph 1, at page 8.

44 Id. at footnote 42, at p. 9, paragraph 5.

45 Id. at footnote 42, at p. 23, at para. 15(i).

Connectivity projects; lack of coordination with other initiatives where the ASEAN Connectivity project may have interdependencies; a lack of regulatory structures to support implementation of ASEAN Connectivity projects).[46] The same Master Plan identified six core areas as ASEAN's implementation strategy for ASEAN Connectivity projects going forward: 1) *strong focus and targets* (e.g. focus on a small set of programmes that are prioritized for potential return and speed of implementation); 2) *clear governance and ownership* (e.g. clearly identify the lead implementing sector and design process to ensure adequate oversight); 3) *clear and aligned plans* (e.g. improve on the consistency and clarity of the narrative on ASEAN Connectivity at different levels of government); 4) *presence of core skills, incentives, finance* (e.g. harness ASEAN Member States' National Focal Points and relevant implementing agencies in their respective jurisdictions); 5) *proactive stakeholder engagement* (e.g. cultivating relationships with the private sector as well as a two-way dialogue with external stakeholders); and 6) *robust performance management* (e.g. data-driven, fact-based mechanisms for performance tracking, with regular cycles for updates on project accomplishment).[47]

The Master Plan was particularly silent on how it would ensure cross-pillar collaboration between the relevant bodies and organs in the ASEAN Political-Security Community, the ASEAN Socio-Cultural Community, and the ASEAN Economic Community. This is a significant omission, considering that long-term infrastructure development projects (particularly the range of five core areas that ASEAN seeks to develop in its Master Plan 2025) heavily involve political-security interests of ASEAN Member States individually as well as regionally, and generates inter-generational socio-cultural, environmental, and other welfare impacts on Southeast Asian populations. For a vision of ambitious scope as the Master Plan on ASEAN Connectivity 2025, it was a missed opportunity to leverage the key structural innovations presented by the ASEAN Charter. The Master Plan did not discuss how to use the legal validity of ASEAN decisions to best effect when it comes to planning for either regulatory excellence or regulatory harmonization with best practices for short-term and long-term development projects. While it identified key sectors in the ASEAN bureaucracy that would serve as lead implementation sectors for ASEAN Connectivity projects, the Master Plan omitted to establish a systematic chain of command that situates each Connectivity project within the broader ASEAN leadership structure and bureaucracy. The Master Plan also did not emphasize the highly influential role of the ASEAN Chair in agenda-setting, and in galvanizing the ASEAN Member States throughout project implementation, monitoring, and oversight of ASEAN Connectivity projects. The Master Plan did not elaborate on how to ensure ASEAN Member States enforce ASEAN decisions with respect to the ASEAN Connectivity projects – which ought to have had, at the very least, the status of ASEAN Law that was to be implemented by "all means necessary" as envisioned

46 Id. at footnote 42, at pp. 23–26.

47 Id. at footnote 42, at pp. 69–74.

in Article 5(2) of the ASEAN Charter. With respect to seeking external capital sources, skills, and incentives for long-term ASEAN Connectivity projects, it was equally surprising that the Master Plan 2025 did not build on ASEAN Centrality under the Charter to push ASEAN's ministerial levels to formally and routinely engage its numerous Dialogue Partners to collaborate on ASEAN Connectivity projects. (As of this writing, ASEAN has ten Dialogue Partners, namely, Australia, Canada, China, European Union, India, Japan, Republic of Korea, New Zealand, Russia, and the United States.)

The compartmentalized approaches taken to implement the Master Plan on ASEAN Connectivity 2025 thus far sub-optimally uses the structural innovations in the ASEAN Charter. The Master Plan on ASEAN Connectivity 2025 is a ripe opportunity for post-Charter ASEAN to institutionalize cross-pillar collaboration between the ASEAN Economic Community (which looks to the economic dimensions of the ASEAN Connectivity projects), with that of the ASEAN Political-Security Community (whose mandate includes ensuring the implementation of the ASEAN Charter and all ASEAN agreements,[48] such as the Master Plan on ASEAN Connectivity) and the ASEAN Socio-Cultural Community (whose mandate includes engaging stakeholders on all ASEAN processes involving policy-making, policy development, implementation, and monitoring,[49] such as that of local community consultations, due diligence review, and environmental-social impacts assessment for ASEAN Connectivity projects). Somewhat inexplicably, much as ASEAN insists that the Master Plan on ASEAN Connectivity is intended to support all Community Blueprints, it does not contain any specific mechanism for coordination across all pillars.

Notably, in June 2019, ASEAN publicized its Initial Rolling Priority Pipeline of Potential ASEAN Infrastructure Projects under the Master Plan on ASEAN Connectivity 2025. The process for identifying 19 regional infrastructure projects was described in the following terms:

> Despite being one of the world's fastest-growing regions, ASEAN still faces budget constraints and competing demands for resources to address infrastructure investment needs. The Initial Pipeline is a list of ASEAN infrastructure projects that have satisfied a set of screening criteria and are expected – if certain pre-conditions are met – to attract robust investments. The list covers transport, energy, and information and communication technology sectors which will potentially contribute to improving the movement of people, services, goods and innovations among the ASEAN Member States.

48 ASEAN Political-Security Community Blueprint 2025, at Parts A.1.1 and A.1.2, at p. 3, at www.asean.org/wp-content/uploads/2012/05/ASEAN-APSC-Blueprint-2025.pdf (last accessed June 1, 2020).

49 ASEAN Socio-Cultural Community Blueprint, at Part II.A.1., pp. 4–5, in www.asean.org/wp-content/uploads/2016/04/8.-March-2016-ASCC-Blueprint-2025.pdf (last accessed June 1, 2020).

> ASEAN, with the technical support from the World Bank and funding support from the ASEAN-Australia Development Cooperation Program Phase II, developed the Initial Pipeline through a process to identify and prioritise infrastructure projects at the regional level. ASEAN Member States submitted projects based on their respective national priorities. Through an assessment process of the projects' strategic relevance, impact on regional connectivity, environmental and social (E&S) impact, project feasibility, and contracting agencies' implementation capacity, 19 projects have been selected for inclusion in the Initial Pipeline (as appears in the list below). An analysis will be undertaken to determine the appropriate funding/financing options for each of the 19 projects. Pre-feasibility studies, which will include an initial E&S and economic impact assessment, will be carried out for projects that require more detailed supporting studies. Many of the 19 projects are in the early stages of development, and further studies may be needed to determine or verify their underlying economic robustness and identify the risks before a decision is taken to implement these projects.
>
> As a "rolling" Pipeline, projects can be rolled in or rolled out of the Pipeline. New projects can be submitted for future iterations to roll into the Pipeline, and existing projects with limited progress or changes in circumstances can be rolled out of the Pipeline.[50]

The 34th ASEAN Summit emphasized the ASEAN Member States' growing concerns about cross-pillar collaboration among its three pillar communities, as a means of "advancing partnership for sustainability to achieve a people-centered, people-oriented, and forward-looking ASEAN Community".[51]

The ASEAN Political-Security Community has identified ASEAN Connectivity as one of the items in its List of Cross-Pillar and Cross-Cutting Issues, which includes a full range of issues such as maritime security, peacekeeping, human rights, humanitarian assistance, international economic crimes, border management, climate change, food safety, social protection, sustainable development, among many other issues.[52] During the 34th ASEAN Summit hosted in Thailand in June 2019, the ASEAN Summit declared that the ASEAN Defence Ministers Meeting (ADMM) will purposely focus on sustainable security; strengthening defence cooperation; and supporting cross-pillar and cross-sectoral activities.[53]

50 ASEAN Secretariat, "ASEAN identifies potential infrastructure projects", June 10, 2019, at https://asean.org/asean-identifies-potential-infrastructure-projects/ (last accessed June 1, 2020).

51 Chairman's Statement of the 34th ASEAN Summit, Bangkok, June 23, 2019 (Advancing Partnership for Sustainability), para. 1, at www.asean2019.go.th/en/news/chairmans-statement-of-the-34th-asean-summit-bangkok-23-june-2019-advancing-partnership-for-sustainability/ (last accessed June 1, 2020).

52 *See* ASEAN Annual Report, 2018–2019, at p. 14, at https://asean.org/storage/2019/08/ASEAN-Annual-Report-2018-2019-web.pdf (last accessed June 1, 2020).

53 Id. at footnote 54, at para. 9.

The ASEAN Summit also declared that with respect to the Master Plan on ASEAN Connectivity 2025:

> We welcomed the significant progress in implementing the Master Plan on ASEAN Connectivity (MPAC) 2025 towards a seamless and competitive ASEAN Community. To address the sustainable infrastructure needs of the region and unlock opportunities, we are pleased to note that the development of the Initial Rolling Priority Pipeline of Potential ASEAN Infrastructure Projects has progressed well and look forward to the launch of the ASEAN Infrastructure Projects at the sidelines of the 35th ASEAN Summit and Related Summits. Complementing the efforts to advance sustainable infrastructure, we also welcomed the commencement of work on the development of an ASEAN database on trade routes and framework for enhancing supply chain efficiency. We emphasised the importance of promoting links and interface between ASEAN and sub-regional arrangements as well as between ASEAN MPAC 2025 and the connectivity strategies of other countries and regions, using the "Connecting the Connectivities" approach, which could broaden and deepen our partnerships on connectivity. We commended the ASEAN Connectivity Coordinating Committee (ACCC), the Lead Implementing Bodies (LIBs) and relevant ASEAN Sectoral Bodies for their strong support to the implementation of MPAC 2025, and appreciated the continuous contributions of our Dialogue Partners and external parties.[54]

The growing recognition of the need for cross-pillar coordination and collaboration the development decisions, policies, and operational plans to implement the Master Plan on ASEAN Connectivity 2025 is an encouraging step toward fuller use of the structural innovations in a post-Charter ASEAN. How cross-pillar coordination will be systematized and operationalized in the long-term implementation of the Master Plan on ASEAN Connectivity remains a matter undisclosed to ASEAN's many stakeholders. Currently, it appears that ASEAN's Connectivity Coordinating Committee is readily engaging ASEAN's Dialogue, Sectoral, and Development Partners to attract interest, capital financing, partnership, technical expertise, and operational commitments to ASEAN's desired connectivity projects. The Initial Rolling Priority Pipeline of Potential ASEAN Infrastructure Projects under the Master Plan on ASEAN Connectivity 2025 generates the first public list of pre-screened and identified projects, but little is said for now about how and in what form the ASEAN Socio-Cultural Community and ASEAN Political-Security Community have been engaged as active stakeholders, rather than as passive monitors, given the foreseeable and unforeseeable development and rule of law consequences behind an ASEAN Economic Community consolidated list of flagship long-term infrastructure

54 Id. at footnote 54, at para. 23.

projects in Southeast Asia. For now, the focus appears to be on connectivity project promotion, and less on institutionalizing a broader architecture for rule of law-based development governance over the present and future of ASEAN Connectivity projects in Southeast Asia. This is a significantly missed opportunity to embed best practices, for example, such as UNCITRAL's corpus of key recommendations for implementing privately-financed infrastructure projects, which includes, among others, to "ensure transparency, fairness, and the long-term sustainability of projects",[55] as well as to entrust regulatory competences over infrastructure projects to "functionally independent bodies with a level of autonomy sufficient to ensure that their decisions are taken without political interference or inappropriate pressures from infrastructure operators and public service providers". It remains to be seen whether the Master Plan on ASEAN Connectivity 2025 will be implemented as a post-Charter ASEAN cross-pillar endeavor, rather than another example of pre-Charter siloed, ad hoc, and incremental ASEAN practices.

Conclusion

Comparing practices under the pre-Charter ASEAN with the post-Charter ASEAN, one could readily hypothesize that there are no material differences insofar as ASEAN's development decision-making processes are concerned. That would erroneously substitute nascent practice under the post-Charter ASEAN with actual ASEAN Law as set out in the ASEAN Charter, ASEAN Summit decisions, ASEAN treaties and agreements, among others. Much can still be maximized in the structural innovations of the post-Charter ASEAN to enable ASEAN's development decision-making fully according to the vision of a "people-oriented, people-centered" ASEAN. Internalizing the advantages from the five key structural innovations under the ASEAN Charter (e.g. legal effect of ASEAN decisions, a more predictable legislative process from an identifiable regional bureaucracy, delineation of the responsibilities of the ASEAN Chair, mandated implementation of ASEAN Law in national jurisdictions, and ASEAN Centrality) will be a critical threshold for development decision-making in ASEAN in the years to come.

55 UNCITRAL Legislative Guide on Privately Financed Infrastructure Projects (United Nations, 2001), at pp. xi and xii, at www.uncitral.org/pdf/english/texts/procurem/pfip/guide/pfip-e.pdf (last accessed June 1, 2020).

3 ASEAN Law

Content, applicability, and challenges

Kevin Y.L. Tan

Introduction

Since its inception in 1967, the states that comprise the Association of Southeast Asian Nations (ASEAN) have collectively entered into a large number of treaties and regional instruments that are now commonly referred to as 'ASEAN Law'. However, ASEAN Law is not easily defined, unlike 'EU Law' or 'Union Law' in the case of the European Union (EU).[1] In the EU, 'Union Law' is distinct from national law and independent from it.[2] This means that 'rights can be conferred and obligations imposed both on the Member States and on natural and legal persons directly by Union provisions, ie without interference from or intervention by national authorities'.[3] The difference stems from the organic manner in which ASEAN emerged as a regional grouping, and the fact that till 2008, when the ASEAN Charter came into force, ASEAN did not technically have a legal personality. As a result, the nature of these legal instruments and the extent to which they affect or impact the Member States of ASEAN vary greatly. This chapter explores the nature of these legal instruments and considers how they are internalised and implemented within the ASEAN states.

The founding of ASEAN

A key difficulty in determining the subject and content of ASEAN Law writ large stems from the manner ASEAN was formed. Unlike the European Union, which was established as a supranational regional body,[4] ASEAN emerged as a loose

1 See for example, Lorna Woods, *Steiner & Woods EU Law*, 12 ed (New York: Oxford University Press, 2014); PP Craig, *EU Law: Text, Cases and Materials*, 6 ed (Oxford: Oxford University Press, 2015); and Chris Turner, *EU Law* (Abingdon, Oxford: Routledge, 2014).

2 See PSFR Mathijsen & P Dyrberg, *Mathijsen's Guide to European Union Law*, 11 ed (London: Sweet & Maxwell, 2013) at para 4.05.

3 Ibid.

4 See for example, Wolfram Kaiser, Bridgitte Leucht & Morten Rasmussen (eds), *The History of the European Union: Origins of a Trans- and Supranational Polity, 1950–72* (New York & London: Routledge, 2009); Alec Stone Sweet & Wayne Sandholtz, 'European Integration and Supranational Governance' (1997) 4(3) *Journal of European Public Policy* 297–317; and Heather

regional grouping that eschewed supranationalism.[5] ASEAN was born in the aftermath of the tense and destabilising *Konfrontasi* (Confrontation) of 1963–1966 which President Sukarno of Indonesia had launched against the Federation of Malaysia to protest its formation.[6] Thanat Khoman – Foreign Minister of Thailand from 1959 to 1971 – was attempting to broker a reconciliation between Indonesia, the Philippines and Malaysia that he broached the idea of forming a new organisation for regional cooperation to Indonesian Foreign Minister Adam Malik, and on 8 August 1967, the five foreign ministers of Indonesia, Malaysia, the Philippines, Singapore and Thailand came together in the main hall of the Thai Foreign Affairs Department to sign what is now known as the ASEAN Declaration or Bangkok Declaration.

It was a short and plainly-worded document of just five articles declaring the formation of 'an Association for Regional cooperation among the countries of South-East Asia to be known as the Association of South-East Asian Nations (ASEAN)' that is open to all states in the South-East Asian Region. The ASEAN Declaration, with seven objects,[7] and a commitment to establish an Annual Meeting of Foreign Ministers,[8] a Standing Committee 'to carry on the work of the Association' between the meetings of the foreign ministers; Ad-Hoc and Permanent Committees 'of specialists and officials on specific subjects'; and a 'National Secretariat in each member country to carry out the work of the Association on behalf of that country and to service the Annual or Special

AD Mbaye, 'Why National States Comply with Supranational Law: Explaining Implementation Infringements in the European Union, 1972–1993' (2001) 2(3) *European Union Politics* 259–281.

5 On the establishment of ASEAN, see Thanat Khoman, 'ASEAN Conception and Evolution', available at: www.asean.org/?static_post=asean-conception-and-evolution-by-thanat-khoman; and 'The Founding of ASEAN', available at: www.asean.org/?static_post=the-founding-of-asean (last accessed 1 June 2020).

6 See among others on Konfrontasi, David Easter, *Britain and the Confrontation with Indonesia, 1960–1966* (London: IB Tauris, 2004); JAC Mackie, *Konfrontasi: The Indonesian-Malaysia Dispute 1963–1966* (Kuala Lumpur: Oxford University Press, 1974); and M Jones, *Conflict and Confrontation in South East Asia, 1961–1965: Britain, the United States and the Creation of Malaysia* (Cambridge: Cambridge University Press, 2002).

7 The seven aims and purposes of ASEAN are to: (1) Accelerate the economic growth, social progress and cultural development in the region through joint endeavours in the spirit of equality and partnership in order to strengthen the foundation for a prosperous and peaceful community of South-East Asian Nations; (2) Promote regional peace and stability through abiding respect for justice and the rule of law in the relationship among countries of the region and adherence to the principles of the United Nations Charter; (3) Promote active collaboration and mutual assistance on matters of common interest in the economic, social, cultural, technical, scientific and administrative fields; (4) Provide assistance to each other in the form of training and research facilities in the educational, professional, technical and administrative spheres; (5) Collaborate more effectively for the greater utilization of their agriculture and industries, the expansion of their trade, including the study of the problems of international commodity trade, the improvement of their transportation and communications facilities and the raising of the living standards of their peoples; (6) Promote South-East Asian studies; and (7) Maintain close and beneficial cooperation with existing international and regional organizations with similar aims and purposes, and explore all avenues for even closer cooperation among themselves.

8 Known also as the 'ASEAN Ministerial Meeting' or AMM.

Meetings of Foreign Ministers, Standing Committee and such other committees' to be established.

Quite clearly, while the founders of ASEAN saw the organisation as an effort by the nations of Southeast Asia to 'bind themselves together in friendship and cooperation and, through joint efforts and sacrifices, secure for their peoples and for posterity the blessings of peace, freedom and prosperity', they did not envisage the organisation becoming a supranational organisation with its own legal system and institutions capable of enforcing legal norms against and for its Member States and citizens. In the words of the European Court of Justice in the landmark decision in *NW Algemene Transporten Expeditie Onderneming van Gend en Loos v Nederlandse Admniistratie der Belastingen*:

> The Community constitutes a new legal order of international law for the benefit of which the states have limited their sovereign rights, albeit within limited fields, and the subjects of which comprise not only member states but also their nationals. Independently of the legislation of member states, community law therefore not only imposes obligations on individuals but is also intended to confer upon them rights which become part of their legal heritage. These rights arise not only where they are expressly granted by the treaty, but also by reason of obligations which the treaty imposes in a clearly defined way upon individuals as well as upon the member states and upon the institutions of the community.[9]

Notwithstanding ASEAN's avowedly non-legal character and lack of an overt legal personality, the regional body did enter into a number of agreements soon after its formation. The first of these were signed in December 1969, and we shall consider their character and legality in the next section.

What is ASEAN Law?

In this chapter, I use the term 'ASEAN Law' as a collective reference to the treaties and regional instruments entered into by ASEAN since 1967. While this broad definition seems simple enough, it is not possible to say with great certainty exactly what these agreements are. The problem of identifying ASEAN legal instruments is compounded by the fact that the ASEAN Secretariat does not maintain an authoritative list of these documents. The most comprehensive collection of ASEAN documents – in the electronic repository of the Centre for International Law at the National University of Singapore – lists over a thousand documents that potentially form part of this corpus. In February 2015, the Legal Services and Agreements Division (LSAD) of ASEAN Secretariat compiled a list of 81 'ASEAN Legal Instruments' which are defined as 'legal instruments concluded among and between ASEAN Member States' with a focus on

9 [1963] *European Court Reports* 1, at 12.

> legal instruments by which the consent to be bound is expressed through either signature of the authorized representatives of Members States or where the signature is subject to ratification and/or acceptance in accordance with the internal procedures of member states.[10]

The list of 81 key instruments includes legal documents known variously as 'Charters', 'Agreements' and 'Protocols', 'Conventions', 'Treaties' and 'Memoranda of Understanding'. Of these, the oldest is of course the ASEAN Declaration or Bangkok Declaration of 8 August 1967 which established the regional body. Many of these instruments pre-date the ASEAN Charter of 2008 that, among other things, made ASEAN a legal entity. This list was clearly put together after considerable thought and assessment but is not exhaustive. For example, the list does not contain any agreements made between Member States of ASEAN among themselves. Assuming that an exhaustive and authoritative list of ASEAN 'laws' is compiled, the question remains: What is their effect on the Member States of ASEAN and on third parties? To answer this question, it is necessary to look more closely on the kinds of agreements the ASEAN states have individually and collectively entered into.

Types of ASEAN agreements

'Agreements' legal and political

As mentioned earlier, two of the earliest ASEAN Agreements were signed in 1969. These were the Agreement for the Establishment for a Fund for ASEAN, and the Agreement for the Promotion of Cooperation in Mass Media and Cultural Activities, both signed in Malaysia in December 1969. These two agreements offer excellent comparisons of the two very different types of 'Agreements' ASEAN member States enter into and show that not all instruments that are labelled 'Agreements' are binding treaties.

The Agreement for the Establishment of a Fund for ASEAN is the more legalistic of the two, with clear provisions spelling out specific obligations of the parties. For example, Article II(2)(a) of this Agreement provided that each 'member country shall initially contribute to the Fund an amount equivalent to UDS$1 million to be paid in not more than three annual instalments'. In addition, the Fund 'shall be replenished by each member country to the required level as decided by the Foreign Ministers ... taking into account any outstanding claim for reimbursement by member countries'.[11] Amendments to this Agreement may be proposed by any member country but such amendment 'shall only come into force after it has been accepted by all the other member countries'.[12] In addition,

10 See the ASEAN website at: http://agreement.asean.org/explanatory/show.html (last accessed 1 June 2020).

11 Article II(2)(b).

12 Article IV.

the Agreement provides that any contracting party 'may at any time give formal notice of its intention to withdraw' from the Agreement and that 'such withdrawal shall take effect one year from the date of the notification of the Ministry of Foreign Affairs, Malaysia, which shall as soon as possible notify all the other member countries'.[13] The Funds may only be utilised according to the rules set out in the Annex to the Agreement, a fairly lengthy document running into eight pages. This Agreement has all the characteristics of a valid multilateral treaty that binds the states parties. However, unlike most treaties of this sort, this Agreement has no dispute resolution mechanism or provision and there are no provisions dealing with non-performance and breach of the treaty terms. That said, the Agreement is still enforceable against a delinquent state by the other parties. This Agreement has been superceded by three later agreements of the same name, the last of which was done in Vientiane on 26 July 2005, and which is considered by the ASEAN Secretariat to be currently in force.

The Agreement for the Promotion of Cooperation in Mass Media and Cultural Activities is another beast altogether. Comprising just two pages and eight articles, the Agreement obliges the contracting parties to promote 'mass media activities' and 'cultural cooperation' through a series of modalities, such as broadcasting programmes on radio or television or organising film festivals or cultural festivals. It also requires states parties to 'examine the possibility' of exchanging experts, organising seminars in mass media and cultural activities,[14] and establishing ASEAN cultural institutions in member countries.[15] This Agreement looks much less like a treaty than what is commonly called a Memorandum of Understanding. The obligations of parties under the Agreement are broadly worded and vaguely couched and there are very few 'hard' rules which may be breached by any of the parties.

Let us now consider the nature and effect of other kinds of agreements which are part of the corpus of ASEAN Laws.

Agreements between Member States of ASEAN inter se

Bilateral treaties or even multilateral treaties between ASEAN Member States are common and have been entered into from the time these states became independent. For example, the Philippines and the Republic of Indonesia concluded their first Air Transport Agreement on 7 December 1944. Other than air service agreements, other typical bilateral agreements which ASEAN Member States enter into with each other include double-tax avoidance treaties and extradition treaties. For example, Singapore and the Philippines concluded an Avoidance of Double Taxation and the Prevention of Fiscal Evasion with Respect to Taxes on Income Treaty in August 1977; and Malaysia and Indonesia entered into an Extradition Treaty in June 1974. One of the first ASEAN Agreements signed

13 Article VI.
14 Article 3.
15 Article 4.

between all the ASEAN states was the Multilateral Agreement on Commercial Rights on Non-Scheduled Services Among the Association of Southeast Asian Nations signed in Manila on 13 March 1971. Such treaties are not unique and bind states parties in the same manner as all bilateral treaties.

Agreements between ASEAN and others[16]

A difficulty arises in cases where ASEAN Member States act collectively as ASEAN, either in making rules for its members or entering into a treaty with another entity. As we noted above, it was not till the coming into force of the ASEAN Charter in 2008 that ASEAN declared itself to be a legal being. Article 3 of the Charter states: 'ASEAN, as an inter-governmental organisation, is hereby conferred legal personality.' Article 41(7) of ASEAN Charter further provides:

> 47. ASEAN may conclude agreements with countries or sub-regional, regional and international organisations and institutions. The procedures for concluding such agreements shall be prescribed by the ASEAN Coordinating Council in consultation with the ASEAN Community Councils.

Does the Charter's bare pronouncement of ASEAN's legal status properly cloak ASEAN with international legal personality? The answer is rather complicated, for as Professor Simon Chesterman notes:

> Does this mean that ASEAN before that moment had no international legal personality? And that after the entry into force of the Charter such personality miraculously popped into existence? The answer to both questions is a qualified 'no': the lack of such a provision did not mean that ASEAN lacked international legal personality; the presence of one does not mean that it possesses personality in a meaningful sense.[17]

Chesterman suggests several theories that may be used to answer this question. The first, is the 'will theory' which accords with the holding of the International Court of Justice in the *Reparations Case*[18] where the Court held that the United Nations had legal personality because 'its Members, by entrusting certain functions to it, with the attendant duties and responsibilities, have clothed it with the competence required to enable those functions to be effectively discharged'.[19]

16 For a comprehensive survey of this subject, see Marise Cremona, David Leimann, Joris Larik, Rena Lee and Pascal Vennesson, *ASEAN's External Agreements: Law, Practice and the Quest for Collective Action* (Cambridge: Cambridge University Press, 2015) [hereinafter 'Cremona et al.'].

17 Simon Chesterman, 'Does ASEAN Exist? The Association of Southeast Asian Nations as an International Legal Person' (2008) 12 *Singapore Yearbook of International Law* 199–211, at 200 [hereinafter 'Chesterman'].

18 *Reparation for Injuries Suffered in the service of the United Nations*, Advisory Opinion (1949) ICJ Reports 174.

19 Ibid., at 179.

Under the 'will theory', founders of international organisations endow their creations with personality which 'is what it will receive'.[20] Alternatively, one can have recourse to the 'objective theory' of international legal personality to determine ASEAN's status by looking at the attributes it possesses.[21] Objective criteria should thus be applied to ASEAN's case to determine if other states and international organisations *ought* to recognise it as having legal personality. Chesterman proposes using the test advanced by Professor Ian Brownlie[22] – Does the organisation possess the following attributes:

1. a permanent association of states, with lawful objects, equipped with organs;
2. a distinction, in terms of legal powers and purposes, between the organisation and its Member States; and
3. the existence of legal powers exercisable on the international plane and not solely within the national systems of one or more states?

While the first criterion is easily satisfied, Chesterman argues that second and the third criteria prove more problematic. Does ASEAN have legal personality separate and distinct from its Member States? The Charter itself is silent, but Article 20 makes it abundantly clear that all decisions will continue to be made in accordance with the 'ASEAN Way':

Article 20

1. As a basic principle, decision-making in ASEAN shall be based on consultation and consensus.
2. Where consensus cannot be achieved, the ASEAN Summit may decide how a specific decision can be made.
3. Nothing in paragraphs 1 and 2 of this Article shall affect the modes of decision-making as contained in the relevant ASEAN legal instruments.
4. In the case of a serious breach of the Charter or non-compliance, the matter shall be referred to the ASEAN Summit for decision.

According to Professor Walter Woon, one of the architects of the ASEAN Charter, the phrase 'as an inter-governmental organisation' was inserted in Article 3 of the Charter by the High Level Task Force

> in order to make clear that there is no supranational element to ASEAN. It was clear from the very beginning of the Charter-drafting process that member states were not ready to share sovereignty in any way. This reluctance on the part of the member states to pool sovereignty makes them

20 Chesterman, n 16 above, at 202.
21 Ibid., at 203.
22 Ian Brownlie, *Principles of Public International Law*, 5 ed (Oxford: Clarendon Press, 1998) at 679–680.

> ambivalent about creating independent institutions in ASEAN ... Thus one finds that the Secretary-General is still kept on a very tight leash, despite the fact that he has ministerial rank and is supposed to speak for ASEAN as an organisation. Similarly, the member states are reluctant to concede the ASEAN Secretariat any independent role. ASEAN member states have yet to fully come to terms with the fact that they are supposed to have created an independent entity called ASEAN, which is meant to be more than the sum of its constituent members. For the ASEAN member states the legal personality of ASEAN does not imply that the organisation has any independent right of action. All decisions, even mundane ones like human resource management, are subject to the oversight of the member states.[23]

However, if one considers Brownlie's third criterion – whether ASEAN has powers exercisable on the international plane independent of the Member States – it would appear that ASEAN can in limited circumstances, exist separately from its members. Can ASEAN enter into binding treaties with other states or international entities? Can the ASEAN Secretary-General negotiate and enter into agreements on behalf of ASEAN? After all, Article 3(1)(5)(a) of the 1992 Protocol on the Agreement on the Establishment of the ASEAN Secretary designates the Secretary-General as 'spokesman and representative of ASEAN on all matters'. Back in 1979, Datuk Ali bin Abdullah, then ASEAN Secretary-General, signed the Agreement Between Indonesia and ASEAN Relating to the Privileges and Immunities of the ASEAN Secretariat,[24] on behalf of ASEAN. Signing on behalf of Indonesia was its Foreign Minister, Prof Dr Mochtar Kusumaatmadja. This appears to be an aberration, for as Chesterman observed, this Agreement only related to its status within Indonesia, and all ASEAN officials 'travel as nationals of their respective member states' outside of Indonesia.

As noted, Article 41(7) of the ASEAN Charter stipulates that ASEAN 'may conclude agreements with countries or sub-regional and international organisations and institutions'. However, there is a caveat, since this power is subject to procedures to be 'prescribed by the ASEAN Coordinating Council (comprising the ASEAN Foreign Minister)[25] in consultation with the ASEAN Community Councils'.[26] As Walter Woon noted, this caveat militates against appointing the Secretary-General as ASEAN's representative for negotiations though he 'may be appointed to sign agreements on behalf of ASEAN, often a purely symbolic act'.[27] Examples of such designations were when the

23 Walter Woon, *The ASEAN Charter: A Commentary* (Singapore: NUS Press, 2016), at 77–78 [hereinafter 'Woon'].

24 Agreement Between the Government of the Republic of Indonesia and the ASEAN Relating to the Privileges and Immunities of the ASEAN Secretariat, done on 20 January 1979.

25 Article 8(1) ASEAN Charter.

26 Article 41(7) ASEAN Charter. On the ASEAN Community Councils, see Article 9 ASEAN Charter.

27 Woon, n 22 above, at 226. Under the 2011 Rules of Procedure for the Conclusion of International Agreements by ASEAN (done on 17 November 2011), Rule 8(5) empowers the ASEAN Foreign

Secretary-General executed the 2012 Agreement on Hosting and Granting Privileges and Immunities Between ASEAN and Indonesia, and the 2012 Memorandum of Understanding between ASEAN and the Asian Development Bank, both done in Phnom Penh, Cambodia in April 2012.[28] Quite clearly, the power to negotiate, enter into and ratify treaties on behalf of ASEAN lie in the hands of the ASEAN Foreign Ministers Meeting. This is made explicit in the 2011 Rules of Procedure for the Conclusion of International Agreements by ASEAN.[29]

For all other important treaties and agreements, the ASEAN Member States sign and ratify in their individual capacities. One pre-Charter example is the Agreement Between the Government of Member Countries of ASEAN and the Government of Canada on Economic Cooperation, signed on 25 September 1981. The Agreement was signed by:

> The Governments of the Republic of Indonesia, Malaysia, the Republic of the Philippines, the Republic of Singapore and the Kingdom of Thailand, member countries of the Association of Southeast Asian Nations (hereinafter referred to as the member countries of ASEAN) of the one part and the Government of Canada (hereinafter referred to as Canada) of the other part.

In the post-Charter period, key and important agreements have been signed by ASEAN Member States in their individual capacities while agreements of lesser import are signed by ASEAN as an international organisation. One of the first and most important of these was the 2008 Agreement on Comprehensive Economic Partnership Among Japan and ASEAN[30] which was entered into by:

> The Governments of Japan, and Brunei Darussalam, the Kingdom of Cambodia, the Republic of Indonesia, the Lao People's Republic, Malaysia, the Union of Myanmar, the Republic of the Philippines, the Republic of Singapore, the Kingdom of Thailand and the Socialist Republic of Viet Nam.

Similar wording can be found in the 2009 Agreement Establishing the ASEAN-Australia-New Zealand Free Trade Area, the 2009 ASEAN Multilateral Agreement on Air Services, and 2009 Agreement on Trade in Goods Under the Framework

Ministers Meeting 'on its own or through the Committee of Permanent Representatives to ASEAN, may appoint the Secretary-General of ASEAN or any other person to sign the international agreement on behalf of ASEAN'.

28 See Woon, ibid.

29 See Rule 3 (Authorisation of the Commencement of Negotiation and Appointment of Representative(s)); Rule 5 (Obligation of Information and Consultation); Rule 6 (Initialling the Draft Text of the International Agreement); Rule 7 (Endorsement of the Draft Text of the International Agreement); Rule 8 (Signature and Act of Formal Confirmation); and Rule 9 (Full Powers).

30 Agreement on Comprehensive Economic Partnership Among Japan and Member States of Association of Southeast Asian Nations, 2008.

Agreement on Comprehensive Economic Cooperation Between ASEAN and the Republic of India, among several others. However, the Memorandum of Understanding Between ASEAN and China on Cooperation in the Field of Non-Traditional Security Issues of November 2009[31] was signed by ASEAN Secretary-General Surin Pitsuwan on behalf of the 'Association of Southeast Asian Nations (ASEAN)' and Zhang Xinfeng, Vice Minister of Public Security for 'the Government of the People's Republic of China'.

ASEAN's unique evolution as an international organisation has resulted in its distinct and peculiar treaty-making practice. As some scholars have observed:

> The treaty-making practice of ASEAN shows that there exists a mode of ASEAN external relations – and the most often used – whereby the member states appear as the actors by whom or on whose behalf ASEAN external instruments are concluded or issued. At times, this authority is delegated to one of the members or to the Secretariat, but the individual member countries remain nonetheless the bearers of the rights and responsibilities resulting from these instruments. A hallmark of this mode is the rather consistent use of the ASEAN label. This does not alter the fact that the member states are the parties, but they still insist on being identified as 'ASEAN member states' or 'collectively' representing ASEAN. However, in certain cases this labelling is done in such a way that it become unclear which entity is the actual party and which would incur responsibility in case of violations of international law.[32]

Determining exactly who the parties to the various treaties are is crucial in the event a dispute arises. It raises 'questions as to which parties to these agreements have what rights and obligations in relation to other parties, which they can claim in the framework of the agree dispute settlement procedures'.[33]

Treaty monitoring

Assuming that it is possible to exhaustively map out the entire corpus of ASEAN Laws, it then becomes necessary to put in place some form of monitoring mechanism to ensure compliance, implementation and interpretation.[34] However, the

31 Memorandum of Understanding Between the Association of Southeast Asian Nations (ASEAN) and the Government of the People's Republic of China on Cooperation in the Field of Non-Traditional Security Issues, done on 18 November 2009 in Siem Reap, Cambodia.

32 Cremona et al., n 16 above, at 130.

33 See Pieter Jan Kuijper, James H Mathis and Natalie Y Morris-Sharma, *From Treaty-Making to Treaty-Breaking: Models for ASEAN External Trade Agreements* (Cambridge: Cambridge University Press, 2015) at 189.

34 Chesterman offers five reasons for a monitoring mechanism: (a) compliance *sensu stricto*; (b) implementation; (c) interpretation; (d) facilitation; and (e) symbolism. See Simon Chesterman, *From Community to Compliance: The Evolution of Monitoring Obligations in ASEAN* (Cambridge: Cambridge University Press, 2015), chapter 2.

ASEAN Charter offers no monitoring facility for ASEAN agreements. It is thus necessary to look to each ASEAN agreement to see if and what kind of reporting of monitoring mechanisms exist and, if so, what obligations are imposed on the states parties. One of the biggest problems in ensuring compliance is that 'many ASEAN agreements are intentionally vague in their objectives, often framed in the language of promotion and cooperation rather than the achievement of clear goals'.[35]

The same may be said of implementation provisions. Even the 2002 ASEAN Agreement on Transboundary Haze Pollution only required states to take 'appropriate measures to monitor' (a) all fire prone areas; (b) all land and/or forest fires; (c) the environmental conditions conducive to such land and/or forest fires; and (d) haze pollution arising from such land and/or forest fires.[36] Under this Agreement, parties are also obliged to develop and implement 'legislative and other regulatory measures … to promote zero burning policy to deal with land and/or forest fires resulting in transboundary haze pollution'. However, there is no monitoring body to ensure compliance, and disputes 'as to the interpretation or application or, or compliance with, this Agreement or any protocol thereto, shall be settled amicably by consultation or negotiation'.[37]

ASEAN's general reluctance to put in place an effective monitoring mechanism is symptomatic of its overall aversion to supranationalism and Member States' jealous preservation of their sovereignty. That said, Chesterman concludes, in his study of trends in monitoring in ASEAN, that since the coming into force of the ASEAN Charter, 'monitoring of all types is becoming more common … even if the powers and resources of that mechanism are weak'.[38] There is also a greater willingness to 'accept stronger monitoring regimes in economic rather than political-security and socio-cultural contexts'.[39]

Dispute settlement mechanism[40]

One other aspect of ensuring rule-compliance is to establish some kind of dispute settlement mechanism. This is necessary to resolve questions on rule interpretation and disputes over the meaning, extent and compliance with Member States' treaty obligations. No provisions were made for dispute settlement in the Bangkok Declaration of 1967. Indeed, it was only in 1971 that there was any discussion about dispute resolution. The Zone of Peace, Freedom and Neutrality (ZOPFAN) Declaration stated it its Preamble that the 'peaceful settlement of

35 Ibid., at 60.
36 Article 7(1).
37 Article 27.
38 See Simon Chesterman, *From Community to Compliance: The Evolution of Monitoring Obligations in ASEAN* (Cambridge: Cambridge University Press, 2015) at 77.
39 Ibid.
40 See Jean-Claude Piris and Walter Woon, *Towards A Rules-Based Community: An ASEAN Legal Service* (Cambridge: Cambridge University Press, 2015) at 71–106.

international disputes' was mentioned. Yet, no infrastructure or mechanism was established to manifest this intention.

In 1976, the Treaty of Amity and Cooperation in Southeast Asia (TAC) – signed by the heads of government of the five ASEAN Member States – provided for the pacific settlement of disputes. Article 13 of the TAC requires the parties to 'have determination and good faith to prevent disputes from arising' but in the event that disputes arise, such disputes shall be settled 'among themselves through friendly negotiations'. A High Council – comprising ministerial representatives from the Member States – is constituted to 'take cognizance of the dispute … and shall recommend to the parties in the dispute appropriate means of settlement such as good offices, mediation, inquiry or conciliation'.[41] In addition, the High Council may 'offer its good offices' or 'constitute itself into a committee of mediation, inquiry or conciliation', and where deemed necessary, 'recommend appropriate measures for the prevention of a deterioration of the dispute, or the situation'. The TAC does not, however, require states parties to utilise this dispute resolution mechanism. Article 16 provides that the mechanism 'shall not apply to a dispute unless all the parties to the dispute agree to their application to that dispute', and Article 17 does not 'preclude recourse to the modes of peaceful settlement contained in Article 33(1) of the Charter of the United Nations' although the parties are 'encouraged to take initiatives to solve it by friendly negotiations before resorting to other procedures' under the UN Charter. The content of Article 17 of the TAC has in essence been preserved and repeated in Article 28 of the ASEAN Charter.[42]

Woon points to three major weaknesses in the scheme for dispute settlement under the TAC.[43] First, parties to the dispute *must* agree before the dispute is brought to the High Council. Any of the parties can easily block the use of the dispute settlement mechanism. For example, former ASEAN Secretary-General Rudolfo Severino stated that Indonesia had tried to bring the Ligitan-Sipadan territorial dispute to the High Council under the Treaty of Amity and Cooperation but Malaysia refused, fearing that the other ASEAN members would be partial to Indonesia.[44] Second, the TAC procedure allows countries other than ASEAN Member States to get involved in the dispute settlement process especially since the 1987 amendment to the TAC allowed for the accession of states outside Southeast Asia and Rule 14 of the Rules of Procedure allowed non-ASEAN Member States to be represented as observers at High Council meetings. The presence of non-ASEAN members on the High Council militates against the use

41 Article 15, TAC.

42 Article 28 of the ASEAN Charter provides:

> Unless otherwise provided for in this Charter, Member States have the right of recourse to the modes of peaceful settlement contained in Article 33(1) of the Charter of the United Nations or any other international legal instruments to which the disputing Member States are party.

43 Woon, n 23 above, at 172–174.

44 R Severino, *Southeast Asia in Search of an ASEAN Community* (Singapore: Institute of Southeast Asian Studies, 2006) at 12–13.

of the Council for the resolution of intra-ASEAN disputes. Third, 'there is no explicit provision for arbitration or adjudication by a court or tribunal'[45] and this only offers the use of 'good offices', mediation, inquiry and conciliation as supplementary modalities to what remains essentially a political process. This will not facilitate neutral, rules-based solutions to disputes.

The problems endemic under the TAC's dispute settlement process have been carried into the ASEAN Charter. Under the Charter, all disputes 'relating to specific ASEAN instruments shall be settled through the mechanisms and procedures provided for in such instruments'[46] while all disputes 'which do not concern the interpretation or application of any ASEAN instrument shall be resolved peacefully in accordance with' the TAC and its rules of procedure.[47] Disputes concerning 'the interpretation or application of ASEAN economic agreements shall be settled in accordance with the ASEAN Protocol on Enhanced Dispute Settlement Mechanism'.[48] Under Article 25 of the Charter, where 'not otherwise specifically provided, appropriate dispute settlement mechanisms, including arbitration, shall be established for disputes which concern the interpretation or application of this Charter and other ASEAN instruments'. In the event that a dispute remains unresolved following the application of the Charter's dispute settlement procedures, the dispute 'shall be referred to the ASEAN Summit, for its decision'.[49] The ASEAN Secretary-General is charged with monitoring 'the compliance with the findings, recommendations or decisions resulting from an ASEAN dispute settlement mechanism, and submit a report to the ASEAN Summit'[50] and any Member State who is 'affected by non-compliance with the findings, recommendations or decisions resulting from an ASEAN dispute settlement mechanism, may refer the matter to the ASEAN Summit for decision'.[51]

Things are only slightly better in cases where there is an economic dispute. The Protocol on Enhanced Dispute Settlement Mechanism (EDSM), which was signed in 2004 at the 10th ASEAN Summit in Vientiane (hence 'the Vientiane Protocol'), provides for a mandatory procedure for dispute settlement. This Protocol is administered by the Senior Economic Officials Meeting (SEOM) to whom any dispute arising from any of the covered agreements may be submitted. This is known as a 'request for consultation' and the other party has ten days to reply and 30 days to enter into consultations.[52] The SEOM is then required to establish a panel to hear the dispute unless it decides – by consensus – not to do so. This decision must be taken within 45 days. The panel is then required to consider the dispute and competing claims and make a recommendation to

45 Woon, n 23 above, at 173.
46 Article 24(1), ASEAN Charter.
47 Article 24(2), ASEAN Charter.
48 Article 24(3), ASEAN Charter.
49 Article 26, ASEAN Charter.
50 Article 27(1), ASEAN Charter.
51 Article 27(1), ASEAN Charter.
52 Article 5(1), Vientiane Protocol.

the SEOM within 60 days.[53] The SEOM is required to adopt the report within 30 days unless it 'decides by consensus not to adopt the report'.[54] The disputants are then required to accept the panel's report unconditionally and comply within 60 days.[55] Article 12 of the Protocol further provides for reports to be appealed to an Appellate Body to be established by the ASEAN Economic Ministers (AEM). Comprising seven persons and of whom three shall serve on any case, the Appellate Body is given up to 60 days to determine the appeal although it may request an extension of up to 90 days.[56] Such appeals are 'limited to issues of law covered in the panel report and legal interpretations developed by the panel'.[57] This mechanism has never been invoked even though there was at least one dispute that could have been resolved under the Vientiane Protocol. This arose out of a World Trade Organisation (WTO) dispute between Thailand and the Philippines, which was resolved under the WTO dispute settlement mechanism instead.[58] Woon, citing one senior ASEAN official, opines that the main problems facing the EDSM 'are lack of resources, the unenthusiastic attitude of the member states (who prefer consultation and mediation) and the fact that the timelines are not workable'.[59]

All this points to a non-rules-based neutral solution to problems within ASEAN. As two scholars observed:

> The ASEAN Charter thus reflects ambivalence about ASEAN's own operating rules and procedures. ASEAN wished to introduce a rules-based system through the creation of the ASEAN Charter yet did not create obligations to use the ASEAN institutions to resolve disputes and other issues related to those rules. This ambivalence reflects some discomfort within ASEAN with both the effectiveness of its legal institutions and the nature of a confrontational approach to dispute resolution. Due to both considerations, no ASEAN dispute has ever reached the arbitration process established by the EDSM and its predecessor. Nor has the High Council anticipated by the TAC ever been called in to resolve a dispute.[60]

Is ASEAN Law part of the domestic law of Member States?

Notwithstanding the difficulties in determining exactly what constitutes the corpus of ASEAN Law, it is clear that many agreements entered into by the ASEAN Member States, acting collectively or as ASEAN, do in fact create

53 Article 8(2), Vientiane Protocol.
54 Article 9(1), Vientiane Protocol.
55 Article 15(1), Vientiane Protocol.
56 Article 12(5), Vientiane Protocol.
57 Article 12(6), Vientiane Protocol.
58 See Woon, n 23 above, at 179.
59 Ibid.
60 Stafano Idama and Edward Sim, *The Foundation of the ASEAN Economic Community: An Institutional and Legal Profile* (Cambridge: Cambridge University Press, 2015) at 45–46.

obligations on the part of states parties. How are these obligations manifested in the domestic laws of ASEAN Member States? Are treaty obligations directly incorporated into domestic law?The ASEAN Charter does not deal specifically with this matter although Article 5(2) of the Charter requires all member States to 'take all necessary measures, including the enactment of appropriate domestic legislation, to effectively implement the provisions of the Charter and to comply with all obligations of membership'. State practice among the ASEAN states suggests that with the exception of the Philippines, transformation is necessary to turn international legal obligations into domestic ones.[61]

The Brunei Constitution is silent on the status of international law in a domestic setting, but it appears from recent state practice that transformation is necessary. For example, it was announced in August 2011 that Brunei was proceeding to ratify the Convention on Domestic Workers but that most of the standards under the Convention were already part of Brunei law by virtue of the Employment Order 2009. Provisions in the Constitution of Cambodia also suggest a dualist, rather than a monist approach to international law. Article 31 of the Constitution provides that the state 'shall recognize and respect human rights as stipulated in the United Nations Charter, the Universal Declaration of Human Rights, the covenants and conventions related to human rights, women's and children's rights', suggesting the automatic application of international human rights law in the state. However, Article 55 states that any 'treaty and agreement incompatible with the independence, sovereignty, territorial integrity, neutrality and national unity of the Kingdom of Cambodia shall be abrogated'.

The communist states of Vietnam and Laos have also adopted a clearly dualist approach to international law. Article 6(3) of the Vietnamese Law on the Conclusion, Accession to and Implementation of Treaties, 2001 provides:

> On the basis of the requirements, contents and nature of a treaty, the National Assembly, the State President or the Government, when deciding to consent to be bound by the treaty, shall also decide on the direct application of the whole or part of the treaty to agencies, organizations and/or individuals in case the provisions of the treaty are explicit and specific enough for implementation; or decide or propose to amend, supplement, cancel or promulgate legal documents for the implementation of the treaty.

This means that an international treaty may – if determined by the National Assembly, President or Government – apply directly to the domestic system either in whole or in part. This may also be supplemented by additional laws to be enacted to implement the treaty. A similar provision is found in the Laotian Presidential Ordinance on the Conclusion, Accession, and Implementation of International Treaties, 2009.

61 See Diane Desierto, 'ASEAN's Constitutionalization of International Law: Challenges to Evolution Under the New ASEAN Charter' (2010–2011) 49 *Columbia Journal of Transnational Law* 268, at 299–305.

Malaysia and Singapore also adopt a dualist approach to the implementation of international treaties. In Malaysia, Article 74(1) of the Constitution empowers Parliament to make laws with respect to matters in Federal List which includes in Ninth Schedule: 'Treaties, agreements and conventions with other countries and all other matters which bring the Federation into relations with other countries.' And in a recent Court of Appeal decision, it was held that for 'a treaty to be operative in Malaysia, Parliament must legislate'.[62] Similarly, in Singapore, Article 38 vests all legislative power in Parliament, and local courts have interpreted this to mean that no international obligation is self-executing and has the force of law until and unless it has been transformed.[63]

Article 23 of the Thai Constitution of 2014 which provides that 'A treaty which … requires an enactment of an Act for its implementation … shall be approved by the National Legislative Assembly' suggests that, to date, Thailand has not changed its dualist view on the implementation of international law in a domestic setting. Indeed, at the Special Event on the Convention on the Rights of Persons with Disabilities at the 4th Session of the Human Rights Council in Geneva on 26 March 2007, the Thai delegate stated:

> as a country with a dualist legal system, obligations under an international treaty which Thailand becomes party to are not automatically enforceable within the Kingdom. The treaty provisions have to be transformed into Thai laws for it to be enforceable and a domestic process needs to be undertaken before becoming party to an international treaty, in order to determine whether new domestic laws need to be enacted and parliamentary approval needs to be sought.[64]

In the case of Myanmar, Article 456 of the 2008 Constitution mandates the state to 'honour all legitimate obligations arising out of treaties or agreements which before the commencement of this Constitution have been in operation between the Government of the Union of Myanmar and the Government of other State'. It does not, however, have any provision for the direct implementation of international treaties in the domestic legal system. In 2004, Myanmar enacted the Mutual Assistance in Criminal Matters Law in conformity with its obligations under the Convention Against Transnational Organised Crime which it acceded to in March that year. The situation in Indonesia is rather complex

62 See *Air Asia Berhad v. Rafizah Shima Binti Mohamed Aris* and *Pathmanathan Krishnan v Indira Gandhi Mutho & Other Appeals* [2016] 1 CLJ 911, at para 68.

63 See *Yong Vui Kong v Public Prosecutor* [2015] 2 Singapore Law Reports 1129.

64 Statement by the Thai Delegation during the Special Event on the Convention of the Rights of Persons with Disabilities at the 4th Session of the Human Rights Council (HRC), 26 March 2007, Geneva, available at: www.un.org/esa/socdev/enable/documents/hrcdocs/soThailand.pdf (last accessed 1 June 2020). See also, Kriangsak Kittichaisaree, 'Effectuation of International Law in the Municipal Legal Order of Thailand' (1995) 4 *Asian Yearbook of International Law* 171–184.

given that state practice on the implementation of treaties has been inconsistent.[65] Recent practice has, however, suggested that Indonesia, like most of other ASEAN states, adopt a dualist, rather than a monist conception of international law. For example, Indonesia ratified the Convention on the Rights of Persons with Disabilities in November 2011[66] and then proceeded to pass a new Law on Persons with Disabilities in April 2016.[67]

The Philippines is the only ASEAN country which adopts a monist approach to international treaties. Article II, Section 2 of its Constitution provides that 'The Philippines … adopts the generally accepted principles of international law as part of the law of the land …' while Article VII, Section 21 provides that 'No treaty or international agreement shall be valid *and effective* unless concurred in by at least two-thirds of all the Members of the Senate.' A plain reading of these two provisions suggests a monist legal order and this is buttressed by the fact the Philippines Supreme Court has declared the Universal Declaration of Human Rights to have full and binding effect in the Philippines.[68]

Quite clearly, ASEAN state practice – save perhaps for the Philippines – militates strongly against the application of ASEAN international agreements and obligations in the domestic legal systems of its Member States. And while Article 5(2) of the ASEAN Charter requires Member States to 'take all necessary measures, including the enacting of appropriate domestic legislation' to implement provisions of the Charter 'and to comply with all obligations of membership', there is nothing to compel them to do so or to prevent them from citing 'their respective inter-internal or constitutional laws in order to justify suspending, delaying or declining to comply with ASEAN Summit decisions, ASEAN Law and international law norms subsumed in the ASEAN Charter'.[69]

Conclusion

For ASEAN to become a 'rules-based' organisation, it is imperative that its legal framework be strengthened. Despite the best efforts of the Eminent Persons Group and the High Level Task Force, the ASEAN Charter and its attendant framework is still very much a political rather legal in character. And even where

65 See Sari Azia and Ranyta Yusran, 'Indonesia's Country Report' CIL Research Project on International Maritime Crimes (Singapore: Centre for International Law, National University of Singapore, 2011) at 13.

66 Law No. 19 of 2011.

67 Law No. 8 of 2016.

68 See *Government of Hongkong Special Administrative Region v Hon Felixberto T Olalia Jr*, GR No. 153675 (2007); *Republic of the Philippines v Sandiganbayan*, GR No. 104768 (2003); *Boris Mejoff v The Director of Prisons*, GR No. L-2855 (1949); and *Victor Borovsky v The Commissioner of Immigration et al.*, GR No. L-2852 (1949).

69 Diane Desierto, 'ASEAN's Constitutionalization of International Law: Challenges to Evolution Under the New ASEAN Charter' (2010–2011) 49 *Columbia Journal of Transnational Law* 268, at 305.

ASEAN, acting collectively, intends to create legally binding instruments, provisions are crafted in ways that are so deferential to state sovereignty as to make these 'legal obligations' little more than motherhood statements. Take for example the recent ASEAN Convention on the Trafficking in Persons. Article 4(1) requires that states parties 'carry out their obligations ... in a manner consistent with the principles of sovereign equality and territorial integrity of States and that of non-intervention in the domestic affairs of other States'. Article 4(2) further states that nothing in the Convention 'entitles a Party to undertake in the territory of another Party, the exercise of jurisdiction and performance of functions that are reserved exclusively for the authorities of that other Party by its domestic laws'. Almost identical wording is to be found in the ASEAN Convention on Counter Terrorism, 2007.[70]

Despite these reservations and prevarications, ASEAN continues to move steadily towards a community based on its three pillars, especially with the establishment of the ASEAN Economic Community in 2015. Sooner or later, the time will come for ASEAN as a community to focus more closely on its commitment towards forging a rules-based order that will make more certain what laws apply to the community as a whole and what needs to be done to implement individual state obligations; what to do when disputes arise and how differences are resolved.

70 See Articles III and IV.

4 ASEAN's regional economic regulators

Timothy Buehrer

While ASEAN began as a meeting of foreign ministers with a strong focus on international relations, it has evolved dramatically over its nearly 50 years of existence. It was not until 1976 that the first meeting of the heads of state of ASEAN was held. This was an auspicious event as it launched what has become known as the Bali Concord I that contained the concept of the ASEAN Community and institutionalized a broader mandate for ASEAN that covered political, economic, social, culture and information, and security matters.[1] In the area of economics, it called for Cooperation on Basic Commodities, particularly Food and Energy; Industrial Cooperation; Cooperation in Trade; and Joint Approach (sic) to International Commodity Problems and Other World Economic Problems. This laid the structure for much of the cooperation that has followed in the next 40 years.

The Bali Concord I also called for the establishment of ministerial meetings

> on economic matters shall be held regularly or as deemed necessary in order to: i) formulate recommendations for the consideration of Governments of member states for the strengthening of ASEAN economic cooperation; ii) review the coordination and implementation of agreed ASEAN programmes and projects on economic cooperation; iii) exchange views and consult on national development plans and policies as a step towards harmonizing regional development; and iv) perform such other relevant functions as agreed upon by the member Governments.

Shortly thereafter the ASEAN Economic Ministers held their first meeting and by February of 1977 the first key economic agreement, the Agreement on the ASEAN Preferential Trading Arrangements, was signed. This was the first of 59 official high level ASEAN economic agreements signed through the end of 2015, more than twice the number of agreements signed in other areas.

1 Declaration of the ASEAN Concord, www.asean.org/?static_post=declaration-of-asean-concord-indonesia-24-february-1976 (last accessed 1 June 2020).

To enable this kind of regional decision making ASEAN has established a wide range of committees in what is now the ASEAN Economic Community, though the committee structure pre-dates the ASEAN Community or its blueprints. This chapter examines how the current ASEAN decision-making system operates, identifying its strengths and weaknesses. This will include select case studies of key policy issues of the past and for the future.

Earlier chapters have discussed how ASEAN, through the ASEAN Charter, has sought to transform itself into a rules-based institution. This chapter will examine what this means for the ASEAN Economic Community and its committee structure. Finally, we will make recommendations on how ASEAN could further reform itself to better address the challenges, particularly the cross-sectoral challenges, that it faces today.

ASEAN economic committee structure

From the modest call of the first ASEAN heads of state meeting for ASEAN Economic Ministers to meet to implement the Bali Concord I's plan for deeper economic integration, ASEAN has developed a wide-ranging set of economic ministerial meetings. This structure has served ASEAN well for many years supporting the development of key agreements like the ASEAN Trade in Goods Agreement,[2] the ASEAN Framework Agreement on Services,[3] and the ASEAN Comprehensive Investment Agreement,[4] among others. The structure that is discussed below has been further formalized in the ASEAN Charter which will be discussed briefly later in this chapter. A complete description of all of the 11 ministerial meetings and their subsidiary bodies is not attempted here. Instead, we focus on the core groups engaged in ASEAN decision making in the economic sphere.

ASEAN Economic Ministers Meeting

The ASEAN Economic Ministers Meeting (AEM) has responsibility for the trade-related agenda of ASEAN. In fact, most of the participants are the trade ministers of the ASEAN member States. The trade ministers also sit as the ASEAN Free Trade Agreement Council and the ASEAN Investment Council. The ASEAN Economic Ministers and the Councils along with their subsidiary bodies are responsible for the development of the critical ASEAN economic agreements on trade and investment.

The AEM is supported by the Senior Economic Officials Meeting which generally consists of the Director Generals for ASEAN in the trade ministries. Supporting these two bodies are an array of additional committees that cover

2 *See* www.asean.org/storage/images/archive/22223.pdf (last accessed 1 June 2020).
3 www.asean.org/?staticpost=asean-framework-agreement-on-services (last accessed 1 June 2020).
4 www.asean.org/storage/images/2013/economic/aia/ACIAFinalText26%20Feb%202009.pdf (last accessed 1 June 2020).

specific topics. The list below highlights the breadth and scope of the AEC and the expressed ambition of the organization on trade issues. The challenge for ASEAN is ensuring that all of these activities move forward quickly.

Coordinating Committee on the Implementation of the ATIGA

The Coordinating Committee on the Implementation of the ATIGA (CCA) is responsible for the implementation of the ASEAN Trade in Goods Agreement (ATIGA). It has two sub-groups under it: The Sub-committee on ATIGA Rules of Origin (SC-AROO) and the Meeting of the Legal Experts on the ATIGA. SC-AROO is responsible for managing the process by which goods qualify for preferential tariff rates under ATIGA. These are the rules by which it is determined whether a traded good should be treated as having been made in the sending country.

ATIGA and its predecessor agreement, the Agreement on a Common Preferential Tariff for the ASEAN Free Trade Area, represent a signature success of ASEAN in economic integration. Tariffs on intra-ASEAN trade among the ASEAN-6[5] have fallen to zero on nearly all goods. Average tariffs in CLMV[6] countries have fallen to an average of slightly more than 1 per cent by 2013.[7] Under ASEAN's preferential trade agreements, intra-ASEAN trade has grown from US$82 billion in 1993 to US$608 billion in 2014.[8] The significantly lower tariff rates that are applied to international trade creates a need for a strong set of rules to ensure that only goods from the region receive the preference. ASEAN's rules of origin as established under ATIGA and managed through the CCA play that role for ASEAN. A key current effort of the CCA is to design and implement a new system of self-certification of origin by exporters for ASEAN that would facilitate qualification for preferential tariff treatment.

But CCA is also responsible for managing ASEAN's effort to limit non-tariff barriers. This is a complicated area as countries have legitimate health and safety reasons for setting standards and other rules for products, thus not all rules are barriers to trade. To address this, the CCA has worked to create a non-tariff barrier database and, more recently, to implement the ASEAN Trade Repository that is designed to list on the internet all border regulations in the region. The idea being that transparency in trade regulations promotes trade facilitation and provides information to Member States should they wish to challenge specific trade regulations as being inconsistent with commitments to reduce non-tariff measures.

5 Brunei Darussalam, Indonesia, Malaysia, the Philippines, Singapore, and Thailand.

6 Cambodia, Laos PDR, Myanmar, and Vietnam.

7 ASEAN Community in Figures, Special Addition 2014, p. 7.

8 Ibid., p. 8 and ASEAN Statistics Table 18, www.asean.org/storage/2016/01/statistic/table18_asof21Dec2015.pdf (last accessed 1 June 2020). Intra-ASEAN trade grew faster than external trade over that period but the share of intra-ASEAN trade in total trade is virtually unchanged. While some observers interpret this as showing the limits of ASEAN integration, the rise of China as the factory to the world during this period makes holding one's share constant while the share of China grows rapidly a significant accomplishment.

Coordinating Committee on Investment

The Coordinating Committee on Investment (CCI) is responsible for the implementation of ASEAN's investment agreements, in particular now the ASEAN Comprehensive Investment Agreement (ACIA), including managing the ACIA's built in agenda on issues like performance requirements and for considering how best to continue ASEAN's effort to facilitate intra-ASEAN investment. The committee consists of representatives of the investment boards of ASEAN member States.

Intra-ASEAN investment is significant and is rising. Foreign direct investment (FDI) within the region from all sources grew by more than a factor of five from 2000 to 2013, the last year for which data is available. Intra-ASEAN FDI grew by a factor of over 17, reaching over $21 billion.[9] Ensuring that the ASEAN Comprehensive Investment Agreement is fully implemented and that investment liberalization in the region is expanded will be critical to the continued growth of regional FDI.

Coordinating Committee on Services

The Coordinating Committee on Services (CCS) is in charge of the implementation of the ASEAN Framework Agreement on Services (AFAS) and in particular the negotiation of the series of services trade liberalization packages agreed to be finalized pursuant to AFAS. CCS is also responsible for the negotiation of any changes in AFAS, including now the negotiation of a new ASEAN Trade in Services Agreement. CCS has four active working groups covering business services, healthcare services, logistics and transport services, and telecommunication and IT services. The business and healthcare services sectoral working groups have subcommittees on the mutual recognition agreements covering engineering, architecture, accountancy, surveying, nursing, medical practitioners, and dental practitioners. The committee is generally comprised of representatives from ministries of trade but some Member States send officials from planning and other ministries.

The main work program of the CCS has been the negotiation of the ten packages of services trade liberalization commitments under AFAS.[10] To date, nine packages have been adopted and the 10th and final package is under discussion.

ASEAN Coordinating Committee on Standards and Quality

The ASEAN Coordinating Committee on Standards and Quality (ACCSQ) manages ASEAN's technical regulations and standards regimes.[11] This involves

9 Ibid., p. 86.

10 The packages cover all services sectors except those in finance which are negotiated under the supervision of the ASEAN Finance Ministers' Meeting.

11 The ASEAN web site states "ASEAN through the ASEAN Consultative Committee on Standards and Quality (ACCSQ) has endeavored to harmonize national standards with international standards and implement mutual recognition arrangements on conformity assessment to achieve its

a wide range of issues relating to quality standards for goods produced and consumed in ASEAN. The committee is comprised of representatives of the heads of ASEAN Member State standards organizations.

The ACCSQ has created 11 different sub-groups to address various aspects of standards. Three of the working groups are more general and cover standards and mutual recognition agreements, conformity assessment, and legal metrology. The other eight working groups and committees are sectoral in nature covering medical devices, traditional medicines and health supplements, rubber-based products, electrical and electronic equipment, cosmetics, automotive products, prepared foodstuffs, and pharmaceuticals. These sectors were selected based on their importance to the region. The sub-groups have task forces that address specific issues under the purview of the sub-group.

ASEAN's focus on cooperation in standards helps to minimize the possibility that non-tariff barriers will be expanded in the region to counter the liberalization of trade created by tariff reductions. By commonly adopting international standards or at least adopting similar regulatory schemes, trade can be promoted within the region and beyond. ASEAN has successfully reached agreements in the areas of cosmetics,[12] electrical and electronic equipment,[13] and medical devices.[14] Agreements have also been reached on guidelines for accreditation of laboratories, good regulatory practices, and on policy guidelines on good regulatory practices among other matters.

Case Study: Medical devices – sector-specific regulation

In 2005, the ACCSQ established the Medical Devices Product Working Group (MDPWG) to develop a regional approach to the licensing of medical devices. Sitting on the MDPWG were the head medical device regulators from the ASEAN Member States.

In developing an ASEAN approach to medical device regulation, the MDPWG had the advantage of being able to leverage ongoing international efforts on medical device regulation. Conceived in 1992, the Global Harmonization Task Force (GHTF) brought together medical device

end-goal of 'One Standard, One Test, Accepted Everywhere'." www.asean.org/asean-economic-community/sectoral-bodies-under-the-purview-of-aem/standards-and-conformance/overview/ (accessed February 2016).

12 Agreement on the ASEAN Harmonized Cosmetics Regulatory Regime, www.asean.org/storage/2012/10/20707.pdf (last accessed 1 June 2020).

13 ASEAN Sectoral Mutual Recognition Arrangement for Electrical and Electronic Equipment, www.asean.org/?static_post=asean-sectoral-mutual-recognition-arrangement-for-electrical-and-electronic-equipment-preamble and Agreement on the ASEAN Harmonized Electrical and Electronic Equipment (EEE) Regulatory Regime, www.asean.org/?static_post=agreement-on-the-asean-harmonized-electrical-and-electronic-equipment-eee-regulatory-regime-kuala-lumpur-9-december-2005-2 (last accessed 1 June 2020).

14 ASEAN Agreement on Medical Devices Directive, www.asean.org/storage/images/pdf/2014_upload/AMDD%20Signed%20November%202014.pdf (last accessed 1 June 2020).

regulators and experts from the medical devices industry to harmonize the process of registering medical devices around the world. By 2012 when the GHTF was brought to a close and replaced by the International Medical Devices Regulators Forum, the GHTF had developed the GHTF Regulatory Model and a range of other guidance documents for medical device regulation that were being adopted around the world. The MDPWG Group was able to use these documents to help frame its own directive.

From 2005 to 2014, the MDPWG deliberated with the help of technical assistance from the United States government and the medical device industry on how best to adapt international best practices as set out by the GHTF for use in ASEAN. This effort ultimately resulted in the adoption of the ASEAN Medical Devices Directive at the end of 2014.[15]

This effort, like similar standards development efforts in the other Product Working Groups, benefitted from the fact that the MDPWG was composed leaders of the key regulatory bodies in the region and they did not need input from other organizations to complete their work. The ASEAN process may still take years as countries at varying stages of development work to reach consensus on policy, but the process is relatively straight forward. Moving on to implementation is still a challenge. The ASEAN Medical Devices Directive has only been adopted by two ASEAN governments, though the rest are working to incorporate its provisions into their laws. This highlights one of the other challenges facing ASEAN: national implementation of regional agreements.

ASEAN Directors-General of Customs Meeting

The ASEAN Directors-General of Customs Meeting is unusual in that it reports to both the Economic Ministers and the Finance Ministers. It supervises all work on customs operational matters under the AEC. This includes the ASEAN Single Window Steering Committee. It also supervises the Coordinating Committee on Customs with its working groups on Customs Procedure and Trade Facilitation (including the committee on the ASEAN Custom Transit system and the ASEAN Harmonized Tariff Nomenclature Task Force), Customs Enforcement and Compliance and Customs Capacity Building.

Many core trade facilitation issues must be addressed by customs authorities. The adoption of a common set of tariff nomenclature in the region simplifies trade processing for governments and the private sector. As does sharing of best practices in customs processing. The Customs DG meeting was responsible for the negotiation and implementation of the ASEAN Agreement on Customs

15 The ASEAN Medical Device Agreement can be found at http://agreement.asean.org/media/download/20141204115621.pdf (last accessed 1 June 2020).

that sets out basic standards for the operation of customs authorities in the region.[16]

ASEAN Single Window Steering Committee

The ASEAN Single Window Steering Committee was created as a dedicated body to supervise the establishment of the ASEAN Single Window, which is discussed at length in Appendix 1. It supervises the Working Group on Technical Matters for the ASW and the Working Group on Legal and Regulatory Matters. The Steering Committee reports to both SEOM and the Customs Deputies, though it takes primary direction from SEOM. This reflects the fact that the ASW brings together a range of government agencies and thus has a broader impact than most sectoral focused entities. The ASW is an inherently cross-sectoral effort that is challenging in the ASEAN environment.

Case study: promoting trade facilitation through automation and information sharing

If the ASEAN Economic Community is to succeed, trade among ASEAN Member States must become as seamless as possible. Beginning in 2003, ASEAN recognized that filing and processing paperwork for cross-border trade imposed significant costs on imports and exports. To address this problem, the ASEAN leaders agreed to establish the ASEAN Single Window to facilitate trade both nationally and regionally through the consolidation of permit and other processing through a single electronic window in each country and the exchange of information among countries to facilitate pre-arrival clearance of goods.

The challenge that ASEAN faced was that while customs authorities were the broad gate-keeper for cross-border trade, a wide range of other government agencies were involved in the export and import process. Ministries of trade or commerce are often involved in determining whether goods should be granted preferential tariff terms. Ministries of agriculture or quarantine agencies must grant permits for the importation and sometimes exportation of plant products. Ministries of health must issue permits for the importation of drugs and medical devices. And the list goes on. Clearly no single sectoral body can address this issue.

ASEAN's solution was to create the ASEAN Single Window Steering Committee to supervise the design and implementation of the ASW. This committee consists of representatives of customs authorities and ministries of trade. The Steering Committee and its working groups also collaborate with other sector bodies as required to implement the ASW.

16 www.asean.org/wp-content/uploads/images/archive/DG%2021%2014%20Annex%2003%20AAC%20True%20Certified%20Copy.pdf (last accessed 1 June 2020).

Despite this cross-sectoral design, the implementation of the ASW has been a challenge. As of March 2016, National Single Windows have been established in six Member States and only two countries are exchanging information, though four more countries should be joining by md-2016.

ASEAN SME Working Group

Beginning with Indonesia's Chairmanship of ASEAN in 2012, ASEAN significantly expanded its focus on SME development for the region. But even before that date, the ASEAN SME Working Group was tasked with developing and implementing ASEAN's support for SMEs in the region. The working group consists of the heads of national SME offices around the region. It has an extensive work program focused on helping to prepare SMEs to be competitive in the ASEAN Economic Community through sharing of best practices in training, finance, and market access. Given the nature of SMEs, much of the focus of the SME Working Group is on improving the operation of national programs to promote SME development. But these efforts are critical to ensuring that SMEs can continue to compete as ASEAN integration leads to an ever-more competitive ASEAN Economic Community.

Other sectoral bodies reporting to the AEM

There are also a range of other groups reporting to the AEM. The development of competition policy in the region has been a focus of ASEAN for some time. Leading that effort under the ambit of the SEOM is the *ASEAN Experts Group on Competition*. It has promoted the adoption of competition laws and the formation of competition authorities throughout the region. Under the new Blueprint this group will be tasked with developing an agreement on regional cooperation on competition policy. Another important issue for ASEAN in promoting a fair and equitable society is consumer protection. The *ASEAN Committee on Consumer Protection (ACCP)* was created to manage ASEAN's efforts in this area. It consists of representatives from government consumer protection agencies and offices from around the region. ASEAN's agenda in these town areas are designed to ensure that the AEC does not just benefit large companies but benefits all of ASEAN.

The *ASEAN Working Group on Intellectual Property Cooperation (AWGIPC)* supports the development of the patent, trade mark, and other intellectual property rights systems among ASEAN Member States and promotes coordination within the region. It has sought to promote regional registration of intellectual property rights. The *Sanitary and Phytosanitary Committee* supports cooperation on food standards and quarantine. The *ASEAN Heads of Statistical Offices Meeting* coordinates the collection of data on ASEAN Member States and its dissemination through the Secretariat.

ASEAN Finance Ministers Meeting

While the ASEAN Economic Ministers supervise the trade agenda for ASEAN, the ASEAN Finance Ministers Meeting, in combination with the ASEAN Central Bank Governors Meeting,[17] supervises cooperation on ASEAN's broad agenda supporting financial market integration. They are supported by relevant deputies' meetings as well as the ASEAN Insurance Regulator's Meeting, ASEAN Capital Markets Forum, and the Senior Level Committee on Financial Integration.

Subsidiary bodies on broad issues of finance include the ASEAN Infrastructure Fund, the ASEAN Forum on Taxation, and the new Working Committee on Financial Inclusion. There are also working committees on financial services liberalization, capital account liberalization, and capital market development.

Subsidiary bodies under the ASEAN Insurance Regulators' Meeting include the ASEAN Insurance Forum, the ASEAN Insurance Training and Research Institute, the AEAN Insurance Council, and the Council of Bureaux. Under the central bank deputies there are subgroupings on banking issues, including on the ASEAN banking integration framework, on payment and settlement systems, and on capacity building.

The ASEAN finance track has been active in managing financial services trade liberalization commitments under AFAS, ASEAN capital market integration through the ASEAN Capital Markets Forum, and the management of currency swap agreements under the ASEAN Memorandum of Understanding on the ASEAN Swap Arrangement.[18] Capital market integration is implemented through the previously mentioned ASEAN Capital Markets Forum consisting of the heads of capital market regulatory bodies in the region. That group has adopted an implementation plan for regional capital market integration that has been adopted by the Finance Ministers.

At a multilateral level, the Finance Ministers have negotiated the Chiang Mai Initiative Multilateralization that manages currency swap agreements among the ten ASEAN Member States as well as China, Japan, and South Korea. As part of the Chiang Mai Initiative Multilateralization, the ASEAN+3 Finance Ministers also have developed and oversee the ASEAN+3 Macroeconomic Research Office.

Other ministerial meetings

While the AEM and the AFMM play a significant role in managing ASEAN economic integration, a range of other ministerial meetings address other sectoral issues. The ASEAN Ministers Meeting on Agriculture and Forestry plays a major role in ensuring food security for the region and helps to manage the agreement on the

17 Sitting together they form that ASEAN Finance Ministers' and Central Bank Governor's Meeting (AFMGM).

18 *See* www.asean.org/storage/images/2012/Economic/AFMM/Agreement_on_Finance/Memorandum%20of%20Understanding%20on%20the%20ASEAN%20Swap%20Arrangement%20(1978).pdf (last accessed 1 June 2020).

region's emergency rice reserve.[19] The ASEAN Ministers on Energy Meeting drives ASEAN's agenda on power production and consumption. It supervises meetings of power utilities and authorities as well as sub-sector networks on renewable energy, energy efficiency and conservation, nuclear energy cooperation, regional energy policy and planning. The ASEAN Telecommunications and IT Ministers Meeting covers telecommunications infrastructure and regulation, the latter through the ASEAN Telecoms Regulators Council. Other ministerial meetings cover Tourism, Transport, Science and Technology, and Minerals.

The ASEAN Charter

In November 2007, the ASEAN Summit in Singapore adopted the ASEAN Charter which went into effect a year later after ratification by all Member States. The Charter enshrines a number of core principles of ASEAN that shape the rules in the rest of the document. Of relevance to ASEAN decision making, the Charter calls for:

> 1. respect for the independence, sovereignty, equality, territorial integrity and national identity of all ASEAN Member States;
>
> …
>
> (e) non-interference in the internal affairs of ASEAN Member States;[20]

These principles significantly limit the kind of central authority and type of decision making that ASEAN can establish.[21] As a result, a core tenet of the Charter is that all decisions of ASEAN should be made by consensus of members not by vote or by decision of some supranational body.[22] The one exception to this is that some decisions on economic matters may be made using an ASEAN Minus X approach as long as there is a consensus to use that approach for that particular matter.[23]

The Charter sets out a hierarchical structure for ASEAN decision making and monitoring above the sectoral body structure discussed above. The highest body in ASEAN is the ASEAN Summit, consisting of all of the leaders of ASEAN. The Charter tasks it with a wide range of activities. Most relevant to this discussion is its responsibility to "provide policy guidance and take decisions on key issues

19 This is under the 2011 ASEAN Plus Three Emergency Rice Reserve Agreement.

20 ASEAN Charter, Chapter I Purposes and Principles, Article 2 Principles.

21 See, e.g., Sukma, Rizal, "ASEAN Beyond 2015: The imperatives for Further Institutional Changes," ERIA Discussion Paper Series, ERIA-DP-2014-01.

22 ASEAN Charter, Chapter VII Decision Making, Article 20 Consultation and Consensus.

23 ASEAN Charter, Chapter VII Decision Making, Article 21 Implementation and Procedure, paragraph 2. The ASEAN Minus X approach allows a subset of ASEAN Member States that are interested in pursuing an economic objective to do so by consensus among the subset rather than all Member States. For example, this was explicitly used in amending the ASEAN Framework Agreement on Services in 2003. www.asean.org/?static_post=protocol-to-amend-the-asean-framework-agreement-on-services-phnom-penh-cambodia-2-september-2003-10-30 (last accessed 1 June 2020).

pertaining to the realization of the objectives of ASEAN"[24] and "authorize the establishment and the dissolution of Sectoral Ministerial Bodies …"[25]

Below the Summit is the ASEAN Coordinating Council consisting of the Foreign Ministers.[26] This body primarily prepares material for Summits and coordinates the actions of the Community Councils. Each of the pillars of the ASEAN Community has its own Community Council. Of relevance to this volume is the ASEAN Economic Community Council which supervises the work of the sectoral bodies under the AEC.[27]

Left out of this discussion are other branches of government. This is because ASEAN is a creature of the executive branches of the governments of the region. This has led to the creation of outside bodies for the other branches. ASEAN legislators and parliamentarians have formed the ASEAN Inter-Parliamentary Assembly (AIPA) to generate greater understanding and cooperation among parliaments and to further advance the ASEAN agenda.[28] Similarly, the ASEAN courts have formed the ASEAN Chief Justices Meeting to support cooperation among ASEAN judiciaries. It is newer than the AIPA and is still working to formalize its structure and objectives. Key objectives are likely to be judicial cooperation and support for ASEAN integration. AIPA is recognized as a body affiliated with ASEAN in Annex 2 of the Charter but as the ACJM was formed after the Charter was ratified, it is not recognized under the Charter.

The Charter also defines the approved sectoral ministerial bodies in Annex 1, which simply memorialized the pre-Charter sectoral structure at least under the AEC. The ministerial bodies are tasked with implementing the directives of the leaders and support cooperation in their respective fields.

The general decision-making process in ASEAN is for broad direction to be given by the leaders to the ministers who then organize subsidiary bodies to develop agreements and proposals for adoption by the higher level bodies. While policy direction flows from top to bottom, technical decisions generally flow from bottom to top. Thus it is unusual for a ministerial meeting to approval an agreement that has not been vetted by technical committees and then the senior officials.

The role of the private sector

The discussion so far has focused on groups of government officials. This is because the ASEAN structure primarily consists of inter-governmental bodies. Annex 2 of the Charter does recognize one capstone business organization, the

24 ASEAN Charter, Chapter IV Organs, Article 7 ASEAN Summit, paragraph 2(b).
25 ASEAN Charter, Chapter IV Organs, Article 7 ASEAN Summit, paragraph 2(f).
26 ASEAN Charter, Chapter IV Organs, Article 8 ASEAN Coordinating Council.
27 ASEAN Charter, Chapter IV Organs, Article 9 ASEAN Community Councils. The composition of the Community Councils is not specified by the Charter. In the case of the AEC Council, it is composed of the ASEAN Economic Ministers.
28 *See* www.aipasecretariat.org (last accessed 1 June 2020).

ASEAN Business Advisory Council (ASEAN-BAC). Other sectoral councils are also included in Annex 2[29] but ASEAN-BAC, whose members are appointed by the governments of ASEAN Member States, has a special role in the ASEAN structure as it has an annual meeting with the ASEAN leaders at the Summit and organizes a parallel ASEAN Business Summit each year. Unfortunately, there is no similar structure to facilitate private sector input into ASEAN decision making at lower levels. While some committees meet regularly with the private sector, others do so seldom or at all.

The lack of interaction between ASEAN committees in the private sector is partially addressed in the AEC Blueprint 2025. The chapter on "A Resilient, Inclusive, People-Oriented, and People-Centered ASEAN" includes a section on "Strengthening the Role of the Private Sector." It begins:

> The role of the private sector in ASEAN integration is important as a key stakeholder in the process. In the AEC 2025 environment, it is recognized that greater involvement of the private sector and more structured participation will be beneficial to the achievement of ASEAN Goals.[30]

The new Blueprint then goes on to call for the development of guidelines for engagement with the private sector by ASEAN sectoral bodies, institutionalization of regular consultations with the private sector to support implementation of ASEAN plans, and private sector bodies to coordinate to coordinate input into the ASEAN process. This is a welcome change but it focuses more on the private sector's input at the implementation stage rather than as a real partner in policy formation. As ASEAN develops the guidelines for engagement with the private sector, it will be critical that the private sector push to be included early in the process.[31]

But ASEAN should consider whether an even more proactive role of the private sector should be supported. As will be discussed at the end of this chapter, cross-sectoral problems may be best addressed through leadership by the private sector with the AEC Council.

ASEAN Community Blueprints

The bulk of the discussion above has focused on the institutional structure of ASEAN. But beginning with the Bali Concord I, ASEAN has worked to develop a coherent set of policy objectives for ASEAN integration into what has now been officially designated the ASEAN Community. Over the years, the policy

29 There are also nine ASEAN+1 business councils and 66 business entities that regularly work with sectoral bodies. ASEAN Economic Community Blueprint 20215, D.2., paragraph 71.

30 ASEAN Economic Community Blueprint 2025, D.2., paragraph 70.

31 The AEC Blueprint 2025 also calls for greater use of public-private partnership, but with a focus on collaboration in the financing of projects. ASEAN Economic Community Blueprint 2025, D.3. The Implementation and Monitoring section of the new Blueprint also calls for establishing partnerships with the private sector and the wider community to "ensure sustained participation of all stakeholders in the integration process." Paragraph 82.x.

documents became ever-more detailed. Following the Bali Concord I was the Framework Agreement on Enhancing ASEAN Economic Cooperation adopted by the leaders in 1992.[32] It provided further guidance on the direction of ASEAN economic integration but was still a fairly basic document.

Starting in 1997, ASEAN policy was guided by the ASEAN Vision 2020[33] which was implemented through the Hanoi Plan of Action for 1999–2004.[34] With the signing by the leaders of the Declaration of ASEAN Concord II (Bali Concord II)[35] in 2003 setting out the ASEAN Community structure, ASEAN created the Vientiane Action Programme[36] for 2004–2010.

With the advent of the Charter, ASEAN formalized the Vientiane Action Programme into a set of blueprints for the three ASEAN Communities. The first three blueprints covering the years 2009–2015 were consolidated into a single document entitled "Roadmap for an ASEAN Community."[37] The AEC Blueprint consisted of both the narrative blueprint and the more detailed strategic action plan. Both documents focused on four objectives for ASEAN economic integration: Single Market and Production Base, Competitive Economic Region, Equitable Economic Development, and Integration into the Global Economy. ASEAN monitored its performance in implementing the many activities laid out in the Strategic Schedule of the ASEAN Community through the ASEAN Scorecard. The ASEAN Economic Community: Progress and Key Achievements report indicates that by October 2015, ASEAN had completed 92.7 per cent of its high priority measures and 79.5 per cent of all measures included in the Strategic Schedule.[38]

Addressing cross-sectoral issues

Much of the work under the 2009–2015 Blueprint was confined to activities that could be implemented by the individual committees that have already been

32 www.asean.org/?static_post=framework-agreement-on-enhancing-asean-economic-cooperation-singapore-28-january-1992 (last accessed 1 June 2020).

33 www.asean.org/?staticpost=asean-vision-2020 (last accessed 1 June 2020).

34 www.asean.org/?staticpost=hanoi-plan-of-action (last accessed 1 June 2020).

35 www.asean.org/?staticpost=declaration-of-asean-concord-ii-bali-concord-ii (last accessed 1 June 2020).

36 www.asean.org/storage/images/archive/VAP-10th%20ASEAN%20Summit.pdf (last accessed 1 June 2020).

37 www.asean.org/storage/images/ASEANRTK2014/2RoadmapforASEANCommunity20092015.pdf (last accessed 1 June 2020). The Roadmap also includes the Initiative for ASEAN Integration (IAI) Strategic Framework and the IAI Work Plan II. This document is ASEAN's effort to address the challenges faced by the newer, and poorer, ASEAN Member States, Cambodia, Laos, Myanmar, and Vietnam. The IAI focuses on providing training and other technical support to the governments and people of Cambodia, Laos, Myanmar, and Vietnam. The program is supervised by the IAI Task Force and covers all aspects of ASEAN integration, not just the AEC. In addition, the CLMV countries are often provided additional time to meet commitments under the AEC Blueprint 2009–2015.

38 See, www.asean.org/storage/images/2015/November/aec-page/AEC-2015-Progress-and-Key-Achievements.pdf, pp. 9–10 (last accessed 1 June 2020).

described. This simplified the process for ASEAN. Cases where significant cross-sectoral coordination was required, for instance in the logistics priority integration sector, were more difficult and results were often not achieved.

Moving forward with the post-2015 agenda will require that ASEAN begin to face this challenge. As one observer noted,

> as the region's economic integration deepens and also broadens, the cross-sectoral linkages are becoming important within the system of ASEAN institutions and processes and require increased coordination and coherence among the ten sovereign nations on issues and policies. ... To deal with the issue at its core must therefore require coordination between the different pillars and sectors to promote development that is sustainable – both for good economics and the environment. The pillars must not act in "silo".[39]

This has been rhetorically addressed in the new Blueprint. In November 2015, the ASEAN leaders adopted a new set of blueprints under the title "ASEAN 2025: Forging Ahead Together."[40] This document sets out the broad outlines of ASEAN's plans to expand the ASEAN Community from 2016 to 2025. The AEC Blueprint identifies five characteristics and elements for the AEC: A highly integrated and cohesive economy, a competitive, innovative, and dynamic ASEAN, enhanced connectivity and sectoral cooperation, a resilient, inclusive, people-oriented and people-entered ASEAN, and a global ASEAN. While the new AEC Blueprint is mostly a logical extension of the 2009–2015 Blueprint, it does include some new items. There is a significantly expanded focus on monitoring and evaluation, a greater role for the private sector in ASEAN policymaking and a focus on some new cross-cutting issues like e-commerce, good governance, good regulatory practices, and financial inclusion. The AEC 2025 Blueprint will be supplemented by strategic action plans for each of the main areas included in the new Blueprint.

Case Study: e-Commerce – A challenge for the future

The AEC Blueprint 2025 calls for the development of an ASEAN Agreement on e-Commerce to facilitate cross-border e-Commerce in the region. The Blueprint proposes that the agreement should cover rules for consumer rights, cross-border dispute resolution, electronic signatures, and personal data protection.[41] These issues already will require agreements

39 Singapore Institute of International Affairs, 2015, "Policy Brief, Strengthening ASEAN Institutions for AEC 2015 and Beyond", pp. 4–5.

40 www.asean.org/storage/2016/01/ASEAN-2025-Forging-Ahead-Together-2nd-Reprint-Dec-2015.pdf (last accessed 1 June 2020).

41 AEC Blueprint 2025, paragraph 53, p. 82.

across a range of topics covered by different ASEAN sectoral bodies. But these are only a few of the issues that a strong agreement on e-commerce would need to cover. Additional issues relating to data localization, nationality of e-commerce vendors, facilitation of shipments of both physical and digital goods, and cross-border financial transactions should be part of a comprehensive agreement. It is difficult to see how any single committee could tackle this issue. For instance, TELMIN conceivably covers some of the issues regarding ICT infrastructure and regulation, data localization, and data privacy, but this is a small part of what needs to be covered. The ASEAN Central Bank Governors Meeting covers banking payment systems but electronic payment systems raise issues beyond normal banking matters. Trade ministers may have authority over some of the trade facilitation matters. Ministries of investment would have inputs on issues like the nationality of e-commerce operations. The Coordinating Committee on Services includes a telecommunications and ICT services sub-group that could cover some issues. With issues covering such a broad spectrum of sectoral bodies, it is hard to see how the ASEAN process, as currently structured, can address the issue.

One solution would be the creation of an e-Commerce Steering Committee similar to the ASEAN Single Window Steering Committee. But in the case of the ASW, the customs authorities are the central body that ultimately must verify that licenses exist and provide final clearance of goods. Thus there is a history of working together and a reason for customs to take the lead. No similar organization exists for e-commerce. Another solution would be to take advantage of the private sector's deep interest in this issue. The chairman of ASEAN-BAC in 2015 suggested that the private sector could take a stronger role in helping guide ASEAN policy on e-commerce. It is hard to see how a private-sector-led process could lead to a comprehensive e-commerce agreement, but it could identify key policy issues to be handled by individual sectoral bodies. If ASEAN then accepted that e-commerce is inherently cross-sectoral and not easily handled in a single agreement, individual agreements supporting e-commerce could be developed across a range of sectoral bodies. ASEAN-BAC could report on the progress directly to the Summit in its regular dialogue and seek policy support at that level.

The addition of a range of cross-sectoral activities in the new Blueprint presents a challenge to the ASEAN process. Interestingly, while the ASEAN Political Security and ASEAN Social Cultural Community Blueprints both explicitly recognize the need to address cross-sectoral issues more effectively, the AEC Blueprint does not. This highlights the challenge facing the ASEAN in implementing the new Blueprint given the existing sectoral structure.

Master Plan for ASEAN Connectivity

The original ASEAN blueprints were supplemented in 2010 by the Master Plan for ASEAN Connectivity (MPAC).[42] A core purpose of the MPAC was to identify how best to accelerate ASEAN integration by setting priorities for the implementation of various ASEAN objectives. In a sense this was an attempt at cross-sectoral coordination. However, the original MPAC was not successful in establishing clear priorities within ASEAN or providing significant levels of coordination as it did not have a strong institutional home within the ASEAN structure. A special committee was established to implement the MPAC and a special staff was created within the ASEAN Secretariat to support implementation, but in the end it falls to sectoral bodies to implement various initiatives and the sectoral bodies are driven by their own agendas and interests.

With the advent of the post-2015 Blueprints, an effort to develop a new program of ASEAN Connectivity has been launched. That program seeks to focus on key areas where cross-sectoral coordination is required to implement ASEAN integration. But it faces many of the same challenges as the MPAC.

Recommendation on cross-sectoral cooperation – the private sector and the ASEAN Economic Community Council

Time and again, ASEAN has demonstrated that cross-sectoral cooperation is a significant challenge. As in many governments, coordination across sectoral bodies fails as there is no body other than the Summit within ASEAN that has sufficient authority to direct sectoral bodies to collaborate and coordinate on challenging issues. And the Summit has a very limited ability to provide detailed management of issues. As a result, one must consider alternatives outside of the ASEAN structure.

As discussed in the box on e-commerce, another approach to addressing cross-sectoral coordination in the AEC would be to more fully embrace private sector cooperation. While finding common ground among private sector actors is also difficult, it would be possible to develop advisory bodies on key cross-sectoral issues like e-commerce or trade facilitation.[43] If those bodies could be led by an activist private sector, they could provide recommendations for ASEAN policy changes across sectoral bodies. If the advisories bodies were tied to the ASEAN Business Advisory Council with its direct access to the ASEAN leaders at the Summit, then the policy recommendations could become part of the annual review by the leaders and possibly provide true direction across sectors.

Many challenges exist with this approach. First, ASEAN has shown little ability in the past to effectively work with the private sector. Second, the private sector

42 www.asean.org/storage/images/ASEAN_RTK_2014/4_Master_Plan_on_ASEAN_Connectivity.pdf (last accessed 1 June 2020).

43 ASEAN did establish an ASEAN Trade Facilitation Joint Consultative Committee but it was led by the government bodies and not the private sector.

is often unwilling to be overly critical of ASEAN and thus provide true leadership to suggest direction to ASEAN. Third, in the past there has really not been a regional private sector to engage with ASEAN. Most companies focused on national level policy. And finally, ASEAN integration has often not been viewed as important by the private sector and there has been limited willingness to invest in promoting change at that level.

With the advent of the ASEAN Community some of these factors are changing. More companies are developing regional business plans and are thus more invested in the success of regional policy approaches. This has led to the establishment of groups like the ASEAN Business Club that seek to promote an ASEAN business agenda. Moreover, groups like the ASEAN Business Club and its related CIMB ASEAN Research Institute, along with other regional research bodies, are generating policy recommendations at the regional level that can be embraced or improved by the private sector, thus providing an intellectual basis for promoting regional agendas in key cross-sectoral areas. Finally, ASEAN is beginning to show a greater interest in engaging with the private sector, opening the door to an advisory committee strategy.

Conclusion

ASEAN is often criticized for talking a lot but doing little. It is certainly the case there is a lot of talk at the over 1,000 ASEAN meetings held each year. But as shown above, ASEAN has accomplished a lot in the economic sphere. But it needs to do much more. Clearly the institutional structure of ASEAN limits its ability to address many of the key challenges for 2015 and beyond. But there is a growing recognition of this fact. This chapter has suggested an approach to addressing one aspect of ASEAN's post-2015 challenges: cross-sectoral coordination. If the ASEAN governments are willing to embrace the AEC and the economic and institutional changes that it represents, new opportunities exist to expand the dialogue on ASEAN policy and more effectively address the difficult issues that face ASEAN today.

Appendix 1

Case study: promoting trade facilitation through automation and information sharing

Trade facilitation is a core objective of the ASEAN Economic Community. Early agreements, like the ASEAN Free Trade Area[44] that was signed in 1992, significantly lowered tariffs in the region. But requirements for licenses and other permits for cross-border transactions can create significant barriers to trade.

44 www.asean.org/storage/images/2012/Economic/AFTA/CommonEffectivePreferentialTariff/Agreement%20on%20the%20Common%20Effective%20Preferential%20Tariff%20Scheme%20for%20the%20ASEAN%20Free%20Trade%20Area.pdf.

Moreover, as the information needed for various licenses and permits is often the same or quite similar, traders spend too much time filling out and filing at different locations information for a wide range of government agencies.

Before computer networks became ubiquitous, some governments sought to address this problem in part by providing a single physical window for submission of documents for all agencies at the border. This at least minimized the amount of time that it took for traders to file their documents but did not particularly simplify the process as separate forms were still filled out and they were processed manually by different agencies.

Today documents can be filled in electronically and submitted over the internet or through other systems, further simplifying the process. But there is still the problem of filing multiple documents, all of which may require much of the same data, for instance company name, address, tax number, HS Codes, and invoices. A computerized and networked "single window" at the national level can address this problem. A well-designed National Single Window can permit the single submission of documents for all needed licenses without having to fill in the same data multiple times.[45] This reduces errors and simplifies matching of documents with shipments. In addition, electronic filing reduces personal interaction with government officials which limits opportunities for collusion. Finally, once all of the data is entered electronically, much of the decision making can be automated as well, with only difficult or unusual cases needing to be reviewed by a government official, further reducing opportunities for corruption.

Over ten years ago, ASEAN recognized the range of benefits that could accrue from an automated National Single Window. But there are even more benefits that can be obtained if information is shared among trading partners. This led to the concept of the ASEAN Single Window. The core idea of the ASEAN Single Window is to link ten National Single Windows in ASEAN into a single network and further leverage the information that is being collected in each Member State.[46] In its most expansive version, the ASEAN Single Window provides business to business, business to government, government to business and government to government linkages in trade for ASEAN. One could imagine that once an exporter enters her information for a transaction, that information could be forwarded to the intended importer and used to begin to populate the import declaration in the receiving country as well as any necessary license applications. The information could also be transmitted to receiving customs authorities and ports to allow for faster and more efficient pre-arrival clearance by incorporating that information into the risk management systems of customs and other bodies. This would permit pre-arrival clearance of most goods and improved targeting

45 The Indonesia National Single Window brings together 18 licensing and permit processes for 16 different ministries and agencies.

46 For a more detailed, though slightly dated, description of the ASW program, see Benjelloun, Pantastico, and Wong, 2012, "Cross-border E-Trade: The ASEAN Single Window," UN ESCAP Trade an Investment Division, Working Paper 03/12, www.unescap.org/sites/default/files/swp0312_0.pdf (accessed February 2016).

of questionable assignments. Furthermore, this information can provide end-to-end supply chain tracking for manufacturers and others. That is the potential of a regional single window and this could then be expanded to a global scale as other major countries and regions develop similar systems.[47]

This was the vision that was embraced by ASEAN at the ASEAN Summit in 2003. At that meeting the leaders agreed to develop the ASEAN Single Window to reduce bureaucratic burdens at the border. Two years later the ASEAN Trade Ministers adopted the Agreement to Establish and Implement the ASEAN Single Window.[48] Through this agreement, the ASEAN Member States committed to establish National Single Windows that enable:

> a. a single submission of data and information; b. a single and synchronous processing of data and information; and c. a single decision-making for customs release of cargoes by the Customs on the basis of decisions, if required, taken by the line ministries and agencies.

In lay terms, Member States are committed to creating a single electronic system for filing and processing all documents needed to import or export goods. Brunei, Indonesia, Malaysia, the Philippines, Singapore, and Thailand committed to establish their National Single Windows by 2008 while the remaining ASEAN Member States were to implement theirs by 2012. By 2008, Singapore – which had a functioning single window in 2005 – Malaysia, Thailand, and the Philippines met those targets and Indonesia was rolling out its system. As of early 2016, National Single Windows are operational in Indonesia, Malaysia, the Philippines, Singapore, Thailand, and Vietnam.

But the agreement goes beyond this national focus to call for the establishment of the ASEAN Single Window (ASW) as a platform for the exchange of trade information between National Single Windows. In essence, the ASEAN Single Window would allow customs authorities to exchange information regarding individual trade transactions electronically, rather than through traditional paper-based transactions. This data can then be used to support risk management and pre-arrival clearance for customs and other government agencies. While the Agreement called for the creation of the NSWs (National Single Window) and the ASW, it gave few details as to how the systems should be designed.

The 2005 agreement was subsequently supplemented by the Protocol to Establish and Implement the ASEAN Single Window in 2006.[49] The Protocol and its annexes set forth a relatively detailed plan for the implementation of the ASW system. Importantly, this agreement was signed by the Finance Ministers.

47 The United States is in the process of developing its own national single window. US Executive Order 13659, 19 February 2014.

48 The Agreement to Establish and Implement the ASEAN Single Window can be found at www.asean.org/?staticpost=agreement-to-establish-and-implement-the-asean-single-window-kuala-lumpur-9-december-2005-2 (accessed February 2016).

49 www.asean.org/wp-content/uploads/images/archive/23084.pdf.

This was necessary because within the ASEAN structure and within national governments, the customs function falls under the authority of the Ministry of Finance, not the Ministry of Trade. And the ASW process in many countries was driven by the national customs authorities.[50] This highlights one of the major challenges of implementing the ASW: it requires coordination across a range of ministries and agencies that include customs authorities and trade ministries (often for licensing), but also quarantine authorities that may fall under the ministry of agriculture, port authorities that may fall under the ministry of transportation, and food and drug authorities that may fall under the ministry of health, as well as many other bodies.

With the signing of the Agreement by the trade ministers and the Protocol by the Finance Ministers, the next major issue that arose was which committee would oversee the work of the ASW. Preparatory work had been completed by the Interagency Task Force on the ASEAN Single Window. Once the Protocol was signed, ASEAN established the ASEAN Single Window Steering Committee to supervise the development of the ASW. The Steering Committee reports jointly to the Senior Economic Officials under the ASEAN Economic Ministers and the ASEAN Customs Director Generals under the ASEAN Finance Ministers. This dual reporting structure was in recognition of the cross-sectoral nature of the work.

The ASEAN Single Window is an interesting study in the implementation of not just an agreement but a relatively complex program of ongoing cooperation within ASEAN. Agreements had to be reached on both the technical and legal aspects of the system. For this reason, two working groups were set up under the ASW Steering Committee. The Working Group on Technical Matters for the ASW (ASW-TWG) was established to address the development of necessary software systems and to agree on the detailed rules and formats for data exchange. The Working Group on Legal and Regulatory Matters (ASW-LWG) was created to establish the legal foundation for the exchange of data. These two working groups worked in parallel to establish the ASW for nearly ten years.

As its name suggests, the work of the ASW-TWG is highly technical in nature. It includes addressing key issues like the data structures to be used to exchange data and type of messaging system to be used to implement the ASW. A fundamental technical decision that was made early on was that the system would not involve a central data repository. Instead, messages would be transferred directly from one NSW to another with no copies being maintained at intermediate points. Obtaining agreement on data structures was a significant challenge as countries had implemented their NSWs using different structures. Compromises were required to permit the consistent exchange of data.

But it does not just deal with ICT systems issues. The ASW-TWG had to review procedures for the generation and use of information in both the sending and receiving countries. This meant coming to agreement on business procedures for

50 In Indonesia, it was organized the Coordinating Ministry for Economic Affairs.

the exchange of data. And as these procedures vary from document to document, it was not a one-time process but an ongoing effort as the ASW was expanded.

It is with these business processes that inputs from other groups became critical. For instance, at its launch the ASW only enabled the exchange of certificates of origin, that is, the document that verifies whether or not a shipment is entitled to preferential treatment under ATIGA. This process is regulated by a separate ASEAN committee, the Sub-Committee on ATIGA Rules of Origin (SC-AROO) of the Coordinating Committee on ATIGA. The ASW-TWG had to find ways to implement the operational procedures approved by SC-AROO in the ASW's electronic environment. This created a significant challenge late in the process as the SC-AROO procedures did not recognize electronic certificates of origin.

Modifying the Operational Certification Procedures (OCP) for ATIGA to permit electronic exchange of information required SC-AROO approval and input. The ASW-TWG and SC-AROO were able to work together to address these issues and develop a revised Operational Certification Procedures but has delayed the implementation of the ASW and, at the time that this chapter was written in early 2016, required that paper certificates still be issued until such time as the OCP is fully amended.

Finally, there is the larger institutional question regarding the long-term financing and operation of the ASW. The ASW comprises an IT system that needs to be managed and maintained. There was no existing mechanism within ASEAN for this purpose. The ASW-TWG and the ASW Steering Committee identified what needed to be done by a body to manage the system, but existing bodies had no authority to implement the program. This had to be referred to higher bodies for decision. At the time of this writing, the Steering Committee has recommended to the ASEAN Senior Economic Officials Meeting that additional staff and funding be provided to the ASEAN Secretariat to manage and upgrade the ASW, particularly the operation of its regional services. No final decision has yet been made on how this will be financed.

The basic legal issues for the international exchange of trade data were reasonably well understood and had been set out in Recommendation No. 35 from the United Nations Centre for Trade Facilitation and Electronic Business (UN/CEFACT).[51] Recommendation No. 35 identifies 12 categories of legal issues that must be resolved to permit the establishment of National Single Windows, many of which carry over to the establishment of a regional single window.

The ASW-LWG was tasked with establishing the necessary legal environment for permitting cross-border exchange of trade data. Following the issues in Recommendation No. 35, the ASW-LWG ultimately developed the Protocol on the Legal Framework (PLF) to Implement the ASEAN Single Window. The PLF covers issues like data retention, data integrity and authentication, information security, governance of the ASW, and liability.

51 Recommendation 35 can be found at www.unece.org/fileadmin/DAM/cefact/recommendations/rec35/Rec35_ECE_TRADE_401_EstablishingLegalFrameworkforSingleWindow_E.pdf (accessed February 2016).

The PLF lays the groundwork for the exchange of information but did not settle all legal issues surrounding the ASW. Specifically, for each document to be exchanged under the ASW it is likely that a separate agreement will be required, like the Operational Certification Procedures for certificates origin that was discussed above. And those agreements, like the OCP, will fall under the purview of other sectoral bodies. For instance, some of the next documents that are under consideration to be exchanged through the ASW are sanitary and phytosanitary certificates. That falls under the SPS committee of CCA and will require coordination with that body to enable the exchange.

As of March 2016, the ASEAN Single Window has begun to operate, albeit in a limited form. Two countries are exchanging the live data on certificates of origin but are not yet able to grant preferential tariffs based on that data. This requires the signing of the OCP and the ratification of the PLF. But both of those prerequisites should be met in 2016 and the ASEAN Single Window will be launched.

But that is not the end of the story. To have a greater impact on trade, the ASW will need to cover a wider range of documents and permit the incorporation of the data in those documents into risk management systems of customs and other government agencies. Consideration should also be given to linking the ASW to national and regional single windows outside of ASEAN. Over the next few years, the ASW Steering Committee will need to work with a range of other sectoral bodies and the private sector to realize the full potential of the ASW.

5 ASEAN trade in goods

Edmund W. Sim

Introduction

Trade in goods represents the basic core of economic cooperation in ASEAN. The ASEAN Member States established the ASEAN Preferential Trading Arrangement in 1977 (ASEAN PTA),[1] with related economic cooperation schemes set up in the early 1980s, all related to trade in goods. These agreements ultimately led to the Agreement on Agreement on the Common Effective Preferential Tariff (CEPT) Scheme for the ASEAN Free Trade Area (AFTA) in 1992[2] and the ASEAN Trade in Goods Agreement (ATIGA) in 2010.[3] Without these agreements focusing on trade in goods, there would be no other ASEAN economic agreements on services and investment: there would be no ASEAN Economic Community (AEC).

However, at this core of ASEAN economic cooperation lies a fundamental flaw: the ATIGA and its predecessor agreements do not establish a customs union but instead establish a preferential trading area (PTA). A customs union would involve completely free movement of goods within the union, with a common external tariff applied to goods originating outside the union. The European Union (EU) is the most well known, but far from the only, example of a customs union. Yet a customs union in ASEAN is not feasible because two of its members, Brunei and Singapore, are free ports with little-to-no import duties applied on goods. Forming an ASEAN customs union would either require the other eight ASEAN members to lower their duty rates to this very low level, or for Brunei and Singapore to raise their duty rates. Neither is going to happen.

That the AEC is based on a PTA is not a fatal flaw, as PTAs operate effectively and efficiently in other parts of the world, particularly in the North American Free Trade Agreement (NAFTA) countries. It does mean, however, that national borders still have a great influence on intra-ASEAN trade, unlike in the EU. This means that rules of origin, customs, trade remedies and other issues will continue

1 Agreement on ASEAN Preferential Trading Arrangements, Manila, February 24, 1977.
2 Agreement on the Common Effective Preferential Tariff Scheme for the ASEAN Free Trade Area, Singapore, January 28, 1992.
3 ASEAN Trade in Goods Agreement, Cha-Am, February 26, 2009.

to be potential sticking points for cross-border trade given that national borders still have meaning inside the AEC.

The continuing influence of national borders in the AEC also affects the creation of a single market in ASEAN. Non-tariff barriers such as industrial standards and other market access issues adversely affect the competitiveness of goods after they cross borders. Trade in services, investment flows and movement of natural persons are also affected by national policies. ASEAN's relative lack of a unified policy on competition, government procurement, subsidies, taxation, labor mobility and other issues accordingly present challenges to the formation of a single market in ASEAN. These gaps in the AEC's coverage are beyond the scope of this chapter on trade in goods, but they should be noted.

Any assessment of ASEAN trade in goods must therefore be grounded in the continued primacy of national borders, owing to its foundation in a PTA and not a customs union. We start with the ATIGA.

Elimination of tariffs

Under ATIGA, each ASEAN Member State may impose tariffs on goods entering from outside ASEAN based on its national schedules. However, for goods originating within ASEAN, ASEAN members are to apply a preferential tariff rate of 0 to 5 percent. These preferential tariff rates are the core of the CEPT scheme.

Virtually all goods are covered by the CEPT scheme. All duties on items covered by the so-called "inclusion" list of the ASEAN-6 countries (Brunei, Indonesia, Malaysia, Philippines, Singapore and Thailand) have been eliminated. Cambodia, Laos, Myanmar and Vietnam (the CLMV countries) were given additional time to implement the reduced tariff rates.

The few remaining items on the so-called "exclusion" list consist mainly of sensitive items such as rice and sugar, with negotiations continuing for these products. ATIGA also eliminates tariff rate quotas and quantitative restrictions but notably does not prevent ASEAN members from imposing trade remedies (antidumping/countervailing duties and safeguard measures). General exceptions to the CEPT are applied to products which an ASEAN member deems necessary for the protection of national security, public morals, the protection of human, animal or plant life and health and protection of articles of artistic, historic or archaeological value.

Obligations of ASEAN Member States

Neither the preambles of ATIGA nor its articles make an explicit reference to Article XXIV of GATT 1994, which authorizes PTAs as consistent with the WTO agreements if they cover "substantially all the trade" in the PTA.[4] Rather, ATIGA

4 GATT 1994: General Agreement on Tariffs and Trade 1994, April 15, 1994, Marrakesh Agreement Establishing the World Trade Organization, Annex 1A, THE LEGAL TEXTS: THE RESULTS OF THE URUGUAY ROUND OF MULTILATERAL TRADE NEGOTIATIONS 17 (1999), 1867 U.N.T.S. 187, 33 I.L.M. 1153 (1994) [hereinafter GATT 1994].

(and its predecessor agreements) are couched entirely within the Enabling Clause that allows developing countries to establish free trade agreements.[5] Without the Enabling Clause, much of how ASEAN implemented its trade liberalization in the AFTA and ATIGA would not be WTO-consistent.

For instance, the original ASEAN PTA contained a rather unprecedented feature in such kind of agreements where it instituted a clause that obligated ASEAN Member States to apply the preferential tariffs on a reciprocal basis.[6] Thirty years later Article 22 of ATIGA includes the same reciprocity clause contained in the original ASEAN PTA. The progressive phase out of duties under CEPT and progressive most-favored nation (MFN) rate reductions may have largely made this article redundant in terms of impact on the relevant tariff concessions. Nevertheless, the ASEAN Member States felt it necessary to retain the reciprocity clause as insurance against future breaches of tariff liberalization commitments by other ASEAN Member States.

Article 5 of ATIGA also contains language mandating MFN treatment among the ASEAN Member States. This means that if an ASEAN Member State grants better treatment to goods from a non-ASEAN member, that same treatment should be accorded to the other ASEAN Member States as per the ATIGA. A general MFN obligation was necessary because most ASEAN Member States also have free trade agreements with non-ASEAN members, such as the US-Singapore Free Trade Agreement. This MFN clause thus reassures the ASEAN Member States that their ATIGA benefits will not be adversely impacted should another ASEAN Member State give better treatment under another trade agreement. This may not be a major issue for tariffs, but it is a major issue for other trade issues, such as non-tariff barriers. In any event, the MFN obligation in the ATIGA is relatively weak because it only calls for consultations if requested, and not for automatic MFN treatment. The aforementioned reciprocity principle also limits the impact of the ATIGA's MFN clause.

Article 6 of ATIGA requires that ASEAN Member States accord national treatment to ASEAN-origin goods. That means that ASEAN Member States should treat ASEAN-origin goods and domestic goods equally. Again, the national treatment obligation is more critical for non-tariff measures, for example, regulations and legislation that affect market access for goods after they have crossed national borders.

Rules of origin

All of ASEAN's preferential trade agreements – the ASEAN PTA, AFTA and ATIGA – incorporated rules of origin to limit the applicability of preferential

5 GATT Contracting Parties, Decision of November 28, 1979 on Differential and More Favourable Treatment, Reciprocity and Fuller Participation on Developing Countries, GATT B.I.S.D. 926th Supp. at 203 (1980) ("Enabling Clause"). The AFTA was notified to the WTO under the Enabling Clause; see WTO document L/4581.

6 ASEAN PTA at Article 8, paragraph 4 ("The effective ASEAN margin of tariff preferences to be accorded to the selected products should take into account existing levels of tariffs in the respective Contracting States in its article").

trade only for goods of "ASEAN" origin.[7] Because the AEC does not establish a customs union, qualifying goods for the ASEAN agreements under these rules of origin and maintaining that qualification becomes vitally important to those wishing to avail themselves of the tariff preferences.

To qualify for ASEAN origin, the general rule is that either: 1) local ASEAN content must be at least 40 percent of the FOB value of the good (known as the regional value content (RVC) methodology) or 2) the product has been subjected to processing so as to change the tariff classification at the four-digit level of the harmonized system (HS) customs classification code for the product (e.g., from plastic resin to plastic bags) (known as the change in tariff classification (CTC) methodology). There are also product-specific rules for certain types of goods such as textiles.

The exporter must obtain a "Form D" paper certification from its national government attesting that the good has met the 40 percent requirement or the change in tariff classification. The Form D must be presented to the customs authority of the importing government to qualify for the CEPT rate. There have been recurring documentary problems that have plagued Form D processing in ASEAN since its inception. Form D documentation has been rejected repeatedly for a variety of apparently trivial reasons:

- The paper was 1–2 millimeters too big or too small (e.g., as not being "A4" size).
- The paper was the wrong shade of color (e.g, for not being sufficiently "violet" or being too "light").
- The specimen signature was not updated.
- The authorized signatory was not updated.
- The signature was slightly different from the specimen signature (e.g., a dot was missing from an "i") or in a slightly different location from specimen signature).
- The document used the wrong font type.
- The document used the wrong font size.
- The exporter's name did not match the invoice documentation, or some other typographical error.

ASEAN customs authorities would thus routinely prevent the importer from clearing customs under the CEPT, forcing the importer either to litigate the matter (a time-consuming process) or pay the MFN rate. A single error for one item covered by a Form D would result in denial of benefits for the entire shipment. Nor have ASEAN customs authorities made compliance easy for the importer. For example, although most ASEAN customs authorities will accept attached annexes to the Form D documentation (such as Excel files or other such compilations) the Thai Customs authorities do not. They require the importer

7 See S. Inama and E. Sim, *Rules of Origin in ASEAN, A Way Forward* (Cambridge 2015).

to input all information into the Form D document itself, a practice that has continued under the ATIGA. This requires importers to submit multiple Form D pages (sometimes hundreds of pages), using the small amount of space available in the form.

In an effort to reduce or eliminate the problems caused by reliance on Form D paperwork, the ASEAN Member States agreed to adopt self-certification for use in ATIGA by 2012 (this has been delayed, as will be explained later). Under self-certification, instead of submitting a form, the exporter would self-certify in its invoices and other sales documentation that the goods are of ASEAN origin. Instead of verifying a paper form, the customs authorities would subject the exporter to post-entry audit should the self-certification be later questioned.

Exporters would be allowed to use either self-certification or the Form D process during initial implementation. This "dual regime" approach allows self-certification for those who can, and the Form D process for those who cannot. However, the initial choice for a scheme will be the exporter's. If the exporter is authorized by ASEAN authorities in the exporting country to act as a "Certified Exporter," the customs authorities in the importing country will have to accept that and will not be able to insist on a conventional certificate to be submitted. The hope is that eventually self-certification will be used for all transactions under the ATIGA, with Form D becoming a document of history.

To test how self-certification would work, Brunei, Malaysia and Singapore initiated their pilot program in late 2010, allowing their exporters to obtain approved status and self-certify their exports. This included manufacturers and trading companies. Thailand joined the pilot program in 2011. The current participants indicate that they believe the program is a great success. The number of transactions covered by the program has increased during its operation, and both companies and governments have been quite happy.

Yet other ASEAN Member States have expressed extreme skepticism of self-certification. Indonesia publicly stated that it would participate in the pilot program only if participating companies were limited to manufacturers. This reflects a general suspicion among certain ASEAN customs authorities that companies, and in particular trading companies, could abuse the system to obtain ASEAN origin wrongly.

Trading companies are particularly suspect, in the view of Indonesia and other ASEAN Member States, because of the difficulty in conducting post-entry audit of documentation. The trading company did not manufacture the goods, so it would not have direct access to the underlying cost data (for RVC) and manufacturing information (for CTC) to confirm that the goods qualify as ASEAN origin. This would not be the case for the manufacturer. Hence allowing trading companies to self-certify would require the ASEAN authority granting the trading company approved exporter status either to rely on second-hand information obtained by the trading company from the manufacturer, which may not be accurate, or worse, not to examine any documentation at all when giving the company approved exporter status. These suspicions are particularly prevalent because the authority for conferring approved exporter status would in most cases rest with the trade ministries in the ASEAN Member States whereas the post-entry inspection authority would rest with the customs agencies in the ASEAN Member States. Customs authorities are traditionally suspicious of trade ministries, even those in their own countries!

Furthermore, some of the skepticism about trading companies arises from the different corporate income tax rates within ASEAN as follows (before credits and deductions, e.g., on a gross basis):

ASEAN Member	*Maximum Rate*
Brunei	23.5%
Cambodia	20.0%
Indonesia	25.0%
Laos	35.0%
Malaysia	25.0%
Myanmar	30.0%
Philippines	30.0%
Singapore	17.0%
Thailand	30.0%
Vietnam	25.0%

For example, a company located in western Indonesia could elect to sell directly to a customer located in eastern Indonesia. The profit generated from the sale would be booked in Indonesia and subject to the 25 percent tax rate. However, the western Indonesian company could alternatively elect to transship the goods through Singapore and onwards to eastern Indonesia (for most ocean shipments this occurs anyway). Then the western Indonesian company could sell through an affiliated Singaporean trading company, which could self-certify the goods as ASEAN origin and thus qualify the goods for the ATIGA duty preference. The profits from the resulting sale would be booked in Singapore at the 17 percent rate instead of in Indonesia at the 25 percent rate. This approach would not be available under the Form D process because either the trading company would be unable to get Form D from the Singapore authorities, or a back-to-back Form D would have been used, which would immediately alert Indonesian customs authorities about the true nature of the sale. Hence the self-certification process could encourage tax evasion, in the eyes of Indonesia.

Thus self-certification skeptics Indonesia, the Philippines and Laos have started their own pilot program for self-certification, for which only manufacturers can participate. Which of the two pilot programs will eventually be adopted by all of ASEAN remains to be seen.

In any event, the potential for abuse of FTA preferences has always existed, with or without self-certification. The current Form D scheme places too much emphasis on form over substance, as an unscrupulous exporter could obtain a certificate of origin using subterfuge anyway. Inspecting individual paper certificates for compliance does not really prevent such abuse. A self-certification scheme, backed by vigorous post-entry audit by customs authorities, will actually target such behavior more efficiently. Trading companies can be subject to additional scrutiny, as they are currently.

SPS and TBT and non-tariff measures (NTMs)

Non-tariff measures (NTMs), including sanitary and phytosanitary measures (SPS) and technical barriers to trade (TBT), represent some of the more difficult areas for the AEC. Unlike tariff measures, which are applied by definition only at the border, NTMs can be applied after the goods have crossed the border. The potential for discrimination against imported goods through NTMs that are actually non-tariff barriers (NTBs) is thusly persistent, and can involve all aspects of government policy, not just border measures.

As a matter of administration, NTMs present three fundamental problems:

1. Identifying the NTMs that are actually NTBs. This includes both existing NTBs and NTBs that have been newly created.
2. Rectifying the NTBs so that the barriers to trade are eliminated.
3. Sanctioning in cases where the rectification efforts have not been satisfactorily undertaken.

Unlike the EU or NAFTA, however, ASEAN is attempting to tackle the complex issues of NTBs without strong regional institutions that could take sufficiently effective measures against the nonconforming behavior. In the EU, the European Commission has broad powers to investigate internal market conditions and to identify NTBs. The Commission and private actors can also seek dispute resolution through the European courts against an EU Member State not in compliance with the EU treaty. NAFTA's NTBs have been largely addressed at the intergovernmental level, but the possibility that regulatory measures can be brought before an arbitration panel under the NAFTA treaty also helps ensure compliance.

The ASEAN Secretariat has none of these powers, nor does the private sector have the ability to invoke ASEAN dispute resolution in case of a breach. In other words, there are relatively detailed commitments on NTB, SPS and TBT measures in ASEAN, but insufficient authority or opportunities to enforce those commitments. Hence the ASEAN experience with regard to NTBs has been somewhat mixed, particularly with regard to the three issues raised earlier.

First, the identification of existing NTBs has been an extended process in ASEAN, involving both self-reporting by ASEAN Member States and original inquiries by the ASEAN Secretariat. Without coercive authority, the ASEAN Secretariat has had difficulties in its investigations. Although there exists a mechanism for the private sector to complain about alleged NTBs, the process is slow and the mechanism hampered by the ASEAN Secretariat's relative lack of authority. As a result, NTBs which were supposed to have been already eliminated by 2010 for most of the ASEAN-6 (2012 for the Philippines) and by 2015 for the CLMV countries still exist, and new NTBs are being created and conceived.

Second, the process of eliminating NTBs through harmonized standards can be very lengthy. The ASEAN Cosmetics Directive was issued in 2002, itself the result of years of cosmetic industry lobbying of the ASEAN Member States and the ASEAN Secretariat. Yet without any legal authority to force the ASEAN Member States to adopt the directive in their national regulations, it took almost a decade for region-wide implementation of the directive. In the EU, by comparison, European Commission directives on standards are implemented relatively quickly, as the Commission's directives have much greater force of law.

Third, ensuring compliance with ASEAN standards or that national standards are not used to block the flow of goods is difficult. The AEC Scorecard has the limited force of negative publicity and peer pressure. Dispute resolution is not available to private actors and ASEAN Member States are reluctant to invoke it. As a result, implementation at the national level in ASEAN is relatively haphazard. For example, a company faced with an ASEAN Member State's deviation from the ASEAN Cosmetics Directive has no legal recourse to seek relief.

The complexity of NTBs thus presents ASEAN with major challenges. NTBs go beyond national borders, making investigation and monitoring of ASEAN Member States' internal policies and regulations vital. Furthermore, ensuring compliance and rectifying NTBs also requires ensuring that various levels of ASEAN Member States' government authorities actually understand and follow ASEAN-wide measures. Yet the limited powers of the ASEAN Secretariat, along with ASEAN's long tradition of non-interference in the internal matters of its members, make the challenges of dealing with NTBs that much more difficult. If the AEC is to achieve the single production base, NTBs must be addressed on a continuing, effective basis, and by ASEAN institutions with the proper authority and tools to deal with these issues.

Customs

The WTO Customs Valuation Agreement is generally applicable in ASEAN through the ATIGA. Article 57.1 states that, "[f]or the purposes of determining the customs value of goods traded between and among the Member States, provisions of Part I of Customs Valuation Agreement, shall apply mutatis mutandis." This commitment to fair and transparent customs administration, in fact, had already been in place in the AFTA, in Article 5.D of the AFTA Agreement.

Yet the most well-known formal dispute settlement procedure undertaken after the signing of the ASEAN Charter involved the failure of one ASEAN Member State to administer its customs laws and procedures with regard to ASEAN-origin goods in a fair and transparent manner. This dispute between the Philippines and Thailand demonstrates that despite extensive written commitments in customs matters, the ASEAN Member States are still pursuing disparate policies.

Over a two-year period during 2006–2008, Thai Customs had systematically rejected the transaction values declared by Philip Morris (Thailand) Limited (PMTL) for cigarettes imported from an affiliated manufacturer in the Philippines,

Philip Morris Philippines (PM Philippines). Pending the final assessment of the customs value, Thai Customs also required that PMTL post guarantees to secure clearance of its imports. Under Thai law, PMTL was unable to seek judicial review of either the decision to collect guarantees or the level of the guarantee. When the customs values of the entries were finally assessed, Thai Customs rejected the transaction values and used a deductive method to determine a higher customs value for the goods.[8]

Rather than invoke ASEAN-based legal processes (after having investigated the procedure with the ASEAN Secretariat and external lawyers), the Philippines requested consultations and invoked the WTO dispute resolution procedure. This was done on February 7, 2008, less than three months after the signing of the ASEAN Charter in Singapore. After failing to reach a satisfactory resolution with Thailand, the Philippines requested the establishment of an arbitration panel on September 29, 2008, just before the Charter was fully ratified later that year. The WTO panel issued a ruling on the Philippines' claims on November 15, 2010.[9] Thailand appealed the panel decision to the Appellate Body, and the Appellate Body upheld virtually the entirety of the panel decision in its own report.[10]

In its WTO complaint, the Philippines claimed that Thai Customs improperly rejected the transaction values of the cigarette entries in violation of Articles 1.1 and 1.2(a) of the WTO Customs Valuation Agreement.[11] Under the WTO Customs Valuation Agreement, the main basis for the valuation of imported goods is the transaction value declared by the importer. When the customs authority questions the declared transaction value, it must follow the procedural rules set out in the WTO Customs Valuation Agreement in examining the circumstances of the transaction between the importer and the exporter and respect the sequential order of valuation methods in using another method to establish the valuation.

Thailand replied that Thai Customs acted consistently with its obligations under the WTO Customs Valuation Agreement in rejecting PMTL's declared transaction value. Thailand argued that since the importer and exporter were related, Thai Customs could examine the circumstances of the sale to determine the acceptability of the declared transaction value (i.e. that it was at arm's length). In doing this under the WTO Customs Valuation Agreement, however, the customs authority must follow certain procedural obligations set out in Articles 1.1, 1.2(a) and 16, including the obligation to give the importer a reasonable opportunity to respond to the customs authority's preliminary consideration.[12]

8 This is based on a summary of the dispute by counsel to the Philippines. www.sidley.com/SidleyUpdates/Detail.aspx?news=4611 (last accessed June 1, 2020).

9 *Thailand – Customs and Fiscal Measures on Cigarettes from the Philippines*, WT/DS371/R.

10 *Thailand-Customs and Fiscal Measures on Cigarettes from the Philippines*, AB-2011-1.

11 Agreement on Implementation of Article VII of the General Agreement on Tariffs and Trade 1994, April 15, 994, Marrakesh Agreement Establishing the World Trade Organization, Annex 1A, The Legal Texts: The Results of the Uruguay Round of Multilateral Trade Negotiations 435 (1999) 1868 U.N.T.S. 279 [hereinafter WTO Customs Valuation Agreement].

12 Id.

Thailand argued that the burden of establishing that the relationship did not influence the transaction price was on the importer under the WTO Customs Valuation Agreement. According to Thailand, therefore, the decision by Thai Customs to reject PMTL's declared transaction value was consistent with the obligations under the WTO Customs Valuation Agreement because PMTL had failed to provide Thai Customs with sufficient information to prove that its relationship with the PM Philippines had not influenced the transaction price.

The WTO panel found that Thai Customs had acted inconsistently with Articles 1.1, 1.2(a) and 16 of the Customs Valuation Agreement, as it had not provided adequate reasoning to show that the affiliation between the importer and exporter affected the price.[13]

The Philippines further argued in its WTO complaint that the valuation methodology used by Thai Customs as a result of rejecting the transaction value – the deductive valuation method – was not applied consistently with Articles 5 and 7 of the WTO Customs Valuation Agreement.[14] The Philippines also argued that Thai Customs violated Article 16 of the WTO Customs Valuation Agreement by failing to provide PMTL with a proper explanation of the customs value calculation, and violated Article 10 of the Agreement by disclosing confidential information to the Thai media. The WTO panel agreed with both additional points.[15]

Thailand – Customs and Fiscal Measures on Cigarettes from the Philippines demonstrates that despite commitments made under the AFTA and subsequently ATIGA, incorporating commitments also made under the WTO Customs Valuation Agreement, Thailand administered its customs laws and regulations in a discriminatory manner. It also confirms the value of dispute resolution, as without having gone through dispute resolution, the Philippines would not have been able to obtain relief from Thailand's discriminatory practices. That the Philippines had to resort to non-ASEAN legal mechanisms to deal with customs issues reflects a lack of confidence in the ASEAN legal and institutional process. This will need to be rectified if the AEC is to develop further.

Trade remedies

ATIGA anticipates that ASEAN Member States may wish to take unilateral actions which may affect their ATIGA obligations. These actions go beyond the standard safeguard provisions contained in most free trade agreements (which normally incorporate the WTO safeguards commitments). For example, Article 11 of ATIGA specifically authorizes ASEAN Member States to take measures which otherwise violate ATIGA, so long as sufficient notice is provided to the other ASEAN members, to allow for consultations. Article 23 further allows ASEAN

13 Panel Report on *Thailand – Customs and Fiscal Measures on Cigarettes from the Philippines*, WT/DS371/R, adopted 15 November 2010, ¶ 8.2 [hereinafter *Cigarette Panel Report*].

14 Art. 5 and 7, WTO Customs Valuation Agreement.

15 *Cigarette Panel Report* ¶ 8.2.

Member States to modify or suspend a tariff concession (e.g., the 0 percent rate of ATIGA) temporarily. This authority is above and beyond the usual WTO trade remedies – antidumping, countervailing duties and safeguard measures – which are specifically authorized by Articles 86 and 87 of the ATIGA.

The existence of these additional provisions and the trade remedy provisions would appear to be akin to one's wearing a belt and suspenders at the same time to hold up one's pants, for example, that they are unnecessarily duplicative, particularly when compared with the EU and NAFTA. Again, this is a relic of the ASEAN PTA and AFTA system, in particular the reciprocity obligation that those agreements imposed. This relic also exists because the ATIGA does not establish a customs union, where such measures would not be permissible.

However, the administration of trade remedies by ASEAN Member States is actually a success story in the AEC. In trade remedies, issues about sovereignty are relaxed, with ASEAN government officials routinely crossing borders to conduct investigations. This contrasts with intra-ASEAN customs matters, where ASEAN customs authorities are very sensitive about national sovereignty and arranging for cross-border inspections can be difficult. ASEAN trade ministries conduct hearings with input from the private sector and its representatives, adhering to WTO and domestic obligations of fairness and transparency. Trade remedy procedures result in the application of measures whose implementation can be monitored. This contrasts with the often non-transparent, non-public procedures used by ASEAN Member States in disputes involving customs or other areas of trade. Trade remedy procedures also allow for dispute resolution and judicial or administrative appeal. Again, this contrasts with other areas of ASEAN policymaking where there is no ability for the private sector to invoke dispute resolution or seek appeal. The trade remedies process thus demonstrates how ASEAN government authorities can and should interact with the private sector in the administration and implementation of the AEC.

ASEAN Single Window

The ASEAN Single Window (ASW) is an attempt to present a unified interface between importers, exporters and the ASEAN Member States for cross-border trade in goods. Once the goods clear one ASEAN border at an ASEAN Member State's National Single Window (NSW), the documentation (in electronic form) would be forwarded to the rest of ASEAN through the ASW. This is vital to optimize operation of the ATIGA because it is not a customs union. Only one border entry is necessary to qualify the goods for free movement within a customs union, whereas in a preferential trading area like the ATIGA, it may be necessary to cross national borders multiple times. Hence the ASW would provide virtual border entry, with the linkage accorded by the ASW program obviating the procedural requirements for subsequent movement within ASEAN.

Theoretically then, the ASW would improve administration of the ATIGA tremendously. A good that qualified for ATIGA in one country would be automatically qualified for ATIGA in all other ASEAN Member States. Hence ASEAN has been pushing for the ASW for years. The ASW called for the ASEAN-6 to adopt NSWs by 2009 and for the CLMV countries to implement NSWs by 2012, so that the ASW would be in place by 2012. This goal has been pushed back, with a pilot ASW project currently under way in Brunei, Indonesia, Malaysia, Philippines, Singapore, Thailand and Vietnam, funded by the US government. The pilot project will study whether ether other data, such as phyto-sanitary and veterinary certificates or commercial information like invoices and freight papers, could also be exchanged through the ASW. Theoretically, an ASW system could also be used for the movement of natural persons, such as through a single ASEAN tourist visa.

The ASEAN Member States are still negotiating a legal agreement to cover the operation of the ASW (the framework only covers the establishment of the ASW itself). Several significant legal issues need to be resolved:[16]

- Legal basis in state law for the implementation of an NSW facility;
- Establishment of an appropriate organizational structure for the implementation and operation of an NSW facility;
- Implementation of proper identification, authentication and authorization procedures;
- Legal framework for proper data protection mechanisms, including rules on rights for authorities and market participants to demand data from the NSW facility and on data sharing between governmental agencies and private organizations;
- Procedures for electronic archiving and the creation of audit trails in electronic systems;
- Relevant measures to be put in place in order to ensure the accuracy and integrity of data, for example by electronic signatures, combined with rules designing the responsibility of actors for the accuracy and integrity of such data;
- Rules on electronic contracting and execution of transactions;
- Rules on liability issues derived from activities in the context of NSW operations;
- Rules on database ownership and on other intellectual property issues;
- Measures avoiding of anticompetitive effects of NSW operations; and
- Mechanisms for dispute resolution.

The practical hurdles in implementing NSWs in ASEAN Member States are also formidable from a technology and infrastructure point of view. Given the diverse state of economic development and infrastructure, NSW administration will be problematic for some countries. The ASEAN Member States have thousands of miles of coastline, with many potential entry points. Linking up all of these points

16 See B. Schermer, 'Legal Issues of Single Window Facilities for International Trade,' presentation, www.uncitral.org/pdf/english/congress/Schermer.pdf (2007) (last accessed June 1, 2020).

electronically, even in only one country like Indonesia, will be very difficult. To put this in perspective, consider that neither the EU nor NAFTA have region-wide Single Windows (nor does the US have an NSW). Yet without effective NSWs, the ASW itself will not work.

Changing the mindset of ASEAN Member States with regard to electronic data interchange is another difficulty. For example, most ASEAN members' national ministries impose firewalls that prevent the use of official e-mail addresses for communications outside their country or even outside the government ministries. Officials in these jurisdictions usually use Gmail or other web-based e-mail accounts established under their personal capacities to communicate with officials in other ASEAN governments. Yet on several occasions, such e-mail communications have not been recognized by these officials' own governments as having any binding effect or even recognized as coming from their own ministries because they came from a webmail account. ASEAN connectivity, a priority item for the AEC, could thus be assisted just by adjusting or improving firewalls, or adopting a common IT solution such as a central server or cloud computing.

Finally, if the underlying legal documentation is still cumbersome, the ASW will not really advance the AEC. As explained earlier, ASEAN customs authorities routinely reject Form D documentation. Although self-certification by exporters may help, if ASEAN customs authorities determine to examine such documentation with extra scrutiny, the benefits of self-certification evaporate. In either event, the ASW would simply result in faster denials of ATIGA benefits; faster resolution, perhaps, but still failing to qualify for preferential treatment. All of the above problems, whether real or potential, demonstrate the need for effective monitoring of the ASW and sanctions should the ASW not work as intended. However, the current weak state of the ASEAN institutions brings into question whether they are able to provide the monitoring and sanctioning functions that will be needed for the ASW to work properly.

Dispute settlement

Dispute settlement is a fundamental aspect of any legal system. Without the ability to invoke rights and obligations provided by a legal system, then those rights and obligations are necessarily devalued because economic actors cannot be certain that they can enforce them. In other words, economic actors need dispute settlement procedures to be effective, even if not necessarily to be used, so that they know that their economic and political bargains with both the state and other economic actors will be honored in the breach. Hence the EU, through its supranational court system, and the NAFTA, through its arbitration panels, provide for such dispute settlement.

Yet although the ASEAN framework provides for dispute settlement, it is not fully developed as an institution. This is not for a lack of available dispute settlement forums in ASEAN. ASEAN has non-binding consultative mechanisms for both ASEAN Member States and ASEAN private citizens. The ASEAN Consultation to Solve Trade and Investment Issues (ACT) was created to provide an informal, non-legally binding, dispute resolution mechanism for businesses encountering operational problems on cross-border issues related to the implementation of ASEAN agreements in trade and investment. The ACT created an online network of government agencies, where complaints can be submitted directly by business operators through a website or through a national ACT office. Once the complaint is lodged, the "Host ACT" (i.e., the ASEAN Member State where the complainant is registered) will review the complaint and submit it to the ACT office of the ASEAN Member State where the issue arose (the "Lead ACT"). The matter will be solved by the two ASEAN Member States involved. In effect, the ACT is a formalized complaint box, allowing for private citizens and companies to express their issues with ASEAN and its Member States, but without any guarantee that the process will provide relief. The effectiveness of the ACT is questionable; some report that the ACT website was inoperable for more than a year because of technical issues.

Another non-binding dispute settlement procedure is the ASEAN Compliance Monitoring Body (ACMB). The ACMB is a non-legally binding consultative dispute settlement mechanism, modeled after the WTO Textiles Monitoring Body. When a dispute is referred to the ACMB, ACMB members from countries not involved in the dispute will, upon request, review and issue findings within an agreed timeframe. Such findings are not legally binding. An opinion pointing to non-compliance should lead to the Member States(s) found to be non-compliant to seriously consider rectifying the non-compliance. ACMB's findings would be tabled as inputs to the Protocol for Enhanced Dispute Settlement Mechanism (EDSM), should the case be raised according to such procedure.[17] Again, this is an attempt to provide non-confrontational means of resolving the dispute.

The primary mechanism for dispute resolution regarding economic agreements in ASEAN is the EDSM. The EDSM is modeled after the WTO Dispute Settlement Understanding (DSU), and indeed many parts of the EDSM appear to have been taken verbatim from the DSU. Unfortunately, this causes some difficulty as the EDSM also adopts a procedural timeline that is even more expedited than the WTO DSU, which the WTO itself has difficulty following, such as having the EDSM panels issue a report within 30–40 days. These deadlines would be impossible to meet even in the best of circumstances, much less in the heady days of any initial dispute. The EDSM also applies the language of "shall" in mandating the procedural steps and deadlines, rather than the WTO DSU's relatively looser "should" for the corresponding steps. This unfortunate choice of language imposes stricter obligations for the EDSM that either cannot be met in an actual dispute procedure or would require extra-legal approaches to administer, such as applying an artificial time schedule (e.g., "ASEAN time") or agreeing to abrogate the terms of the EDSM itself. Hence the EDSM by its own text establishes a dispute resolution procedure that cannot be followed.

17 Protocol for Enhanced Dispute Settlement Mechanism, Vientiane, November 29, 2004.

EDSM follows the same patterns of the DSU, with provisions for consultations, good offices, conciliation and mediation, as well as arbitration by a panel. Most importantly, once a panel is formed by the Senior Economic Officials Meeting (SEOM), the parties to the dispute cannot invoke other dispute processes, such as the WTO DSU. Parties would present their arguments to the panel, which is to rule on the dispute. The panel's decision is automatically adopted by the SEOM of the most senior bureaucrats in the ASEAN Member States' ministries, unless it has a consensus *not* to adopt the decision. The panel's decision can be appealed to the ASEAN Appellate Body, a doppelganger for the WTO Appellate Body. Finally, SEOM administers the compliance with the EDSM panel's decision.

The role of SEOM is particularly problematic. SEOM only meets in person four times a year, which could adversely impact the EDSM's ability to meet its own schedule. SEOM does apply a consultations process whereby SEOM members communicate amongst themselves during the interim. Yet as noted earlier, communication among the ASEAN members is not without difficulties. The role of SEOM is problematic in that the body also monitors implementation of panel decisions and administers compliance measures if necessary, yet has had no experience in doing so.

In addition, the ASEAN Secretariat is supposed to support the EDSM process with administrative and logistical support. However, currently the ASEAN Secretariat only has five trained lawyers in its legal staff. Although if an EDSM dispute were to arise, the ASEAN Secretariat has organized a virtual network of other Secretariat staff who have some experience in disputes who could help, the fact remains that this type of dispute would require tremendous amounts of time and resources from legally trained staff. Funding of the process is also an issue. ASEAN Member States have set aside funding for the EDSM, yet many of the steps necessary to implement the EDSM administratively have not taken place, such as naming full-time members of the ASEAN Appellate Body (who would be compensated). Again, this does not evoke much confidence in the system.

Finally, the EDSM contains certain lacuna. Although the EDSM ostensibly is to assist in the resolution of disputes in ASEAN, the EDSM protocol does not require that the panel actually resolve the dispute in a manner consistent with the principles of ASEAN contained either in the agreement subject to the underlying dispute or elsewhere in ASEAN (e.g., the Charter). Disputes regarding the EDSM protocol itself are not subject to the EDSM protocol. Nor does the EDSM protocol define what constitutes an economic agreement, but instead only provides a list of covered agreements. It is also possible, under the current language of the ASEAN Charter, for an ASEAN Member State to refuse to cooperate with the EDSM process in the panel process, appellate procedure or compliance proceedings and thus create an unresolved dispute subject to Article 26 of the Charter. If that were to happen, conceivably the dispute would be subject to the final review and decision by the ASEAN Summit, providing for a political resolution of the dispute.

Therein lies the tragedy of the EDSM. On paper, it strongly resembles the WTO process and should have all of its advantages. Yet because of the institutional deficiencies and bureaucratic inertia, EDSM remains unused and underdeveloped. This undermines investor confidence in the AEC. Until parties are comfortable enough to entrust their disputes to EDSM, the AEC will not reach its full potential.

Conclusion

Despite all of the institutional difficulties in the AEC, one must be reminded that ASEAN's regional economic integration is arguably the most successful regional economic integration project in the developing world. ASEAN actually operates much better than similar efforts in the Middle East, Africa, South Asia, Central Asia, South America and Central America. Hence to its credit, the AEC's primary comparisons are with regional economic integration projects led by developed countries, for example, the EU and NAFTA. It is only with the EU and NAFTA that the AEC suffers by comparison, and those regional economic projects have had years of prior experience.

Nevertheless, ASEAN should continue to improve itself. The AEC represents the major deliverable of the ASEAN Community for peoples of the region, and trade in goods is the major core of the AEC. ASEAN's leaders need to address the deficiencies in that core or otherwise risk the continued effectiveness of the AEC.

6 ASEAN trade in services

Pasha L. Hsieh

Introduction

Trade in services is critical to economic development and modernization. Sufficient provision of services energizes countries at diverse stages of growth and often serves as a prerequisite for development.[1] Trade in services is also positively correlated with trade in goods, as a 10 percent increase in the former results in a 6 percent growth in the latter.[2] Notably, global services trade has outgrown labor-intensive sectors such as agriculture and manufacturing and hence has led to a substantial impact on productivity and poverty reduction.[3]

The ten-country bloc, the Association of Southeast Asian Nations (ASEAN), is Asia's third largest economy and will move towards the ASEAN Economic Community (AEC) by the end of 2015.[4] Recognizing the importance of the services trade, ASEAN commenced services negotiations in 1995 with the aim of liberalizing the services sector beyond the General Agreement on Trade in Services (GATS) level and to accomplish "a free trade area in services."[5] Trade in services constitutes the core of the AEC because it accounts for 40–60 percent of ASEAN states' gross domestic product (GDP), 58 percent of foreign direct investment (FDI) inflows and more than 50 percent of total employment.[6] Strengthening the provision of services will galvanize ASEAN's transition to a

1 Zakariah Rashid et al., Regional Market for Goods, Services, and Skilled Labor, *in* Realizing the ASEAN Economic Community: A Comprehensive Assessment 20, 44 (Michael G. Plummer & Chia Siow Yue eds. 2009); ASEAN 2030: Toward a Borderless Economic Community [ASEAN 2030] 120 (2014).

2 Juan Blyde & Natalia Sinyavskaya, The Impact of Liberalizing Trade in Services on Trade in Goods: An Empirical Investigation, 11:3 Rev. Dev. Econ. 566, 573 (2007).

3 ASEAN Integration Monitoring Report: A Joint Report by the ASEAN Secretariat and the World Bank [ASEAN Integration Monitoring Report] 93 (2013); Joy Abrenica et al., The Future of Trade in Services for Developing Countries, *in* Trade and Poverty Reduction in the Asia-Pacific Region: Case Studies and Lessons from Low-Income Communities 341, 347 (Andrew L. Stoler et al. eds. 2009).

4 ASEAN Matters for America/America Matters for ASEAN (2014), at 2.

5 ASEAN Framework Agreement on Services (1995) [AFAS], art. I(c).

6 Liberalization of Services, http://aec2015.miti.gov.my/index.php/pages/view/30 (last accessed 1 June 2020); ASEAN Integration Monitoring Report, supra note 3, at 92.

higher value-added economy by circumventing the middle-income trap and fortifying its competitiveness to be on par with China and India.[7]

This chapter provides an up-to-date overview of ASEAN trade in services. The second section discusses the legal framework governing services negotiations and commitments. It will focus on the evolution of the ASEAN Framework Agreement on Services (AFAS) in the context of the AEC. The third section explores the movement of skilled labor by explaining the progress of the ASEAN Agreement on the Movement of Natural Persons (ASEAN MNP Agreement) and the mutual recognition arrangements (MRAs). The fourth section examines the impact of ASEAN+1 free trade agreements (FTAs) and the prospective RCEP on services liberalization in ASEAN. The fifth section offers regulatory reform proposals for intensifying services integration according to the goal of the AEC. The final section concludes this chapter.

The legal framework for ASEAN trade in services

Signed in 1995, the AFAS provided a legal basis for ASEAN's services negotiations.[8] ASEAN states' conclusion of the AFAS took place merely 1.5 years after signing the multilateral GATS and two years subsequent to ASEAN's launch of the Common Effective Preferential Tariff Scheme for the ASEAN Free Trade Area that liberalizes trade in goods.[9] The timeframe illustrates the understanding that liberalizing services trade is crucial to ASEAN's integration.

Services negotiations under the AFAS

The AFAS adopts a successive package structure, under which schedules of services commitments arising from subsequent rounds of negotiations "form an integral part of" the AFAS.[10] As the AFAS is non-self-executing, each ASEAN state is required to sign the protocol, which implements its annexes embodying specific commitments, following domestic ratification procedures to enable each "package of commitments" to take effect.[11] From 1997 to 2014, ASEAN states signed nine packages of commitments (AFAS 1 to 9), and the tenth package of commitments (AFAS 10) will be the final package that realizes the AEC by the end of 2015.[12]

7 Ben Shepherd & Gloria Pasadilla, Services as a New Engine of Growth of ASEAN, the People's Republic of China, and India, ADBI Working Paper Series, No. 349 (2012), at 3; The Work Bank: Economic Premise, No. 98 (2012), at 2.

8 ASEAN Integration in Services (2013), at 3.

9 Id.; ASEAN Integration in Trade in Services: Development, Challenges, and Way Forward, ASEAN Secretariat Paper (2011), at 1.

10 ASEAN Framework Agreement on Services (1995), art. VIII.

11 E.g., Protocol to Implement the Ninth Package of Commitments under the ASEAN Framework Agreement on Services (2014), arts. 4–5.

12 Deunden Nikomborirak & Supunnavadee Jitdumrong, An Assessment of Services Sector Liberalization in ASEAN, *in* ASEAN Economic Community Scorecard: Performance and Perception 47, 53 (Sanchita Basu Das ed. 2013); The Effective of Protocol to Implement the 9th

The fragmented legal framework resulted in complex ASEAN services trade commitments. While ASEAN economic ministers negotiated and signed the packages of AFAS commitments, the liberalization of financial services and air transport services was carried out by finance and transport ministers, respectively.[13] There have been six packages of financial services commitments, and the seventh package is expected to conclude in 2016.[14] Air transport services are implemented through eight packages of commitments and various ASEAN multilateral instruments on aviation services.[15] These general and sector-specific packages of commitments are incorporated into services commitments under the AFAS.

Based on the practice of the GATS, AFAS commitments cover four modes: Mode 1 (cross-border supply), Mode 2 (consumption abroad), Mode 3 (commercial presence) and Mode 4 (presence of natural persons).[16] Importantly, ASEAN states concluded the ASEAN MNP Agreement in 2012.[17] "Upon entry into force of this Agreement," it will "supersede" prior AFAS commitments on Mode 4 and will therefore complement Modes 1–3 commitments under AFAS 9 and AFAS 10.[18] Furthermore, ASEAN countries concluded MRAs to expedite the movement of skilled labor by facilitating the recognition of qualifications for eight professions.[19] The current goal is to materialize the comprehensive ASEAN Trade in Services Agreement (ATISA) to consolidate fragmented services commitments into a single undertaking.[20] This approach was modeled after the 2009 ASEAN Trade in Goods Agreement.[21] The instruments that constitute the framework for ASEAN trade in services are illustrated in Table 6.1 below.

Negotiation modalities towards the ASEAN Economic Community

ASEAN has followed varies modalities for services trade negotiations. The first two packages of AFAS commitments were the result of the request-and-offer approach based on the GATS-like positive list formula.[22] Under this formula,

Package of Commitments under the ASEAN Framework Agreement on Services and Thailand's Schedules of Specific Commitments [9th Package of Commitments], http://en.fap.or.th/index.php?lay=show&ac=article&Id=539847072&Ntype=1 (last accessed June 1, 2020).

13 ASEAN Integration in Services, supra note 8, at 13–14.

14 Id.; Joint Statement of the 1st ASEAN Finance Ministers' and Central Bank Governors' Meeting (AFMGM) [AFMGM Joint Statement], Mar. 21, 2015, para. 15.

15 ASEAN Transport Instruments and Status of Ratification (2015), at 3–5.

16 General Agreement on Trade in Services (GATS), art. I:2.

17 ASEAN Agreement on the Movement of Natural Persons (2012) [ASEAN MNP Agreement].

18 Id., art. 6:2.

19 Yoshifumi Fukunaga, Assessing the Progress of ASEAN MRAs on Professional Services, ERIA Discussion Paper Series (2015), at 2–3.

20 Joint Media Statement, The 46th ASEAN Economic Ministers' (AEM) Meeting [2015 AEM Meeting], Aug. 25, 2014, at 5.

21 Stefono Inama & Edmund W. Sim, The Foundation of the ASEAN Economic Community: An Institutional and Legal Profile 127 (2015).

22 ASEAN Integration in Services, supra note 8, at 10.

Table 6.1 Services-related commitments under the ASEAN framework[1]

Year of Signature	*Package of AFAS Commitments*	*Financial Services Commitments*	*Air Transport Services Commitments*	*ASEAN MNP Agreement*	*MRAs*
1995	AFAS				
1997	1st package (including air transport services)				
1998	2nd package (including air transport & financial services)				
2001	3rd package (including air transport services)				
2002		2nd package			
2004	4th package		4th package		
2005		3rd package			Engineering services
2006	5th package (consolidated commitments)				Nursing services
2007	6th package		5th package		Architectural services; Surveying qualifications
2008		4th package			
2009	7th package		6th package		Accountancy services; Medical practitioners; Dental practitioners
2010	8th package				
2011		5th package (consolidated commitments)	7th package (consolidated commitments)		

2012				Signed; not yet effective	Tourism professionals
2014	9th package; not yet effective		8th package; not yet effective		
2015	10th package (scheduled)	6th package			
2016		7th package (scheduled)			

[1] Nikomborirak & Jitdumrong, supra note 12, at 52–53; 9th Package of Commitments, supra note 12; ASEAN Integration in Services, supra note 8, at 13–15; AFMGM Joint Statement, supra note 14, para. 15; ASEAN Transport Instruments and Status of Ratification, supra note 15, at 3–5; Yoshifumi Fukunaga & Hirari Ishido, Values and Limitations of the ASEAN Agreement on the Movement of Natural Persons (2015), at 2; Fukunaga, supra note 19, at 2–3.

Consolidated commitments: Previous commitments consolidated into a single schedule

Not yet effective: due to the incomplete domestic ratification procedure

ASEAN states listed the sectors and modes of supply that they wish to liberalize in the binding AFAS commitments. From AFAS 3 to AFAS 6, ASEAN negotiators introduced the common sub-sector approach to expedite services liberalization.[23] A common sub-sector denotes a sub-sector in which minimum three or four ASEAN states made commitments in the GATS or prior AFAS packages.[24] These concessions would be multilateralized to all ASEAN states, including those making no corresponding commitments.

To avoid a free rider effect, ASEAN ministers adopted the protocol for the ASEAN Minus X modality in 2003.[25] This modality's origin can be traced to the 1992 Framework Agreement on Enhancing ASEAN Economic Cooperation.[26] The agreement permits "two or more Member States" to initiate negotiations and liberalize selected sectors and allows others to join later.[27] Unlike the common sub-sector approach, the concessions would only be granted on a reciprocal basis under the ASEAN Minus X modality. The rationale is that ASEAN integration would not be dragged down to the pace of countries unwilling to cooperate and that the benefits of liberalization would incentivize these states to open their services markets.[28]

The AEC Blueprint, adopted in 2007, has governed the negotiations of AFAS 7 and subsequent packages of commitments.[29] The AEC expects to transform ASEAN into a "single market and production base" by 2015.[30] The services trade-related target is to achieve a free flow of services and skilled labor within the bloc.[31] The AEC Blueprint set specific actions. First, "substantially all restrictions on trade in services for" entire services sectors should be eliminated by 2015.[32] In particular, Modes 1 and 2 will be subject to no limitation.[33] Second, it is noteworthy that the AEC will not become a unified market like the European Union

23 Id.

24 Id.

25 Based on the Protocol to Amend the ASEAN Framework Agreement on Services (2003), Article IV bis (ASEAN Minus X modality) was added to the AFAS. Id. at 18; David Chin Soon Siong, ASEAN's Journey towards Free Trade, *in* Economic Diplomacy: Essays and Reflections by Singapore's Negotiations 209, 216 (C. L. Lim & Margaret Liang eds. 2011) [Economic Diplomacy].

26 Rodolfo C. Severino, Southeast Asia in Search of an ASEAN Community: Insights from the Former ASEAN Secretary-General 352 (2006).

27 Framework Agreement on Enhancing ASEAN Economic Cooperation (2012), art. I:3.

28 Severino, supra note 26, at 352.

29 ASEAN Integration in Services, supra note 8, at 19; Nikomborirak & Jitdumrong, supra note 12, at 53.

30 ASEAN Economic Community (AEC) Blueprint (2007), sec. I.

31 Id. sec. II.A.

32 Four priority services sectors, including air transport, e-ASEAN, healthcare and tourism services, as well as logistics services, are subject to earlier deadlines. Also, financial services integration expects to be completed by 2020. Id. sec. II.A.2. For information on the specific sub-sectors of these priority sectors, refer to Appendix 1: CPC Definition for the Services Priority Integration Sector (PIS) and Logistics Services (LOG), Dionisius Narjoko, AEC Blueprint Implementation Performance and Challenges: Services Liberalization, ERIA Discussion Paper Series (2015), at 16.

33 AEC Blueprint, supra note 32, sec. II.A.2.

(EU) because of the limited scope of the Modes 3 and 4 liberalization. A pivotal Mode 3 issue is foreign equity participation for ASEAN corporations. The AEC's compromise is to allow 70 percent rather than 100 percent of ASEAN equity participation by 2015.[34] Through various MRAs, Mode 4 liberalization, which will facilitate labor mobility, applies to professional services.[35] Due to political sensitivity, the movement of low-skilled and unskilled labor is excluded from the AEC framework. Finally, the AEC Blueprint permits a 15 percent overall flexibility that enables ASEAN states to exclude selected services sectors from commitments.[36] The ASEAN Minus X formula will also continue to apply to services liberalization.[37]

In the past 20 years, ASEAN has undergone liberalization on trade in services through successive AFAS packages. The initial packages were marginally GATS-plus.[38] As if they were negotiating the GATS, many ASEAN states considered domestic restrictions as bargaining chips that can be used in exchange for further concessions from others.[39] AFAS commitments may also compromise their positions in services negotiations under the World Trade Organization (WTO).[40] Nonetheless, the AEC has promoted more progressive liberalization of services trade. In addition to the liberalization of air transport services and financial services, which are implemented under separate tracks, general AFAS packages cover more than 140 services sectors.[41] The overall liberalization rate of AFAS 8 achieves 72.9 percent of the AEC targets, thus making services commitments substantially GATS-plus.[42] Compared with other modes, the low Mode 3 liberalization rate was a result of states' failure to meet foreign equity targets in certain sectors such as logistics services.[43]

The business community should be cautious that the liberalization rate above demonstrates national commitments in respective schedules rather than the actual extent of liberalization, which predominantly depends on domestic regulations. For the banking industry, a breakthrough is the ASEAN Banking Integration Framework (ABIF) implemented by the 2015 Protocol to Implement the Sixth

34 Id.; notably, the delays for the Seventh and Eighth packages of commitments were partially due to ASEAN states' reluctance to exceed 50 percent of foreign equity participation. ASEAN Integration Monitoring Report, supra note 3, at 95–96.

35 AEC Blueprint, supra note 32, sec. II.A.2.

36 Id.

37 Id.

38 Siong, supra note 25, at 215.

39 Severino, supra note 26, at 232.

40 Siong, supra note 25, at 215.

41 Broad categories include business services, communication services, construction and engineering-related services, distribution services, education services, environmental services, health-related and social services, tourism and travel-related services, recreational, cultural and sporting services, and road and maritime transport services. Singapore – Schedule of Commitments for the 8th Package of Commitments under the ASEAN Framework Agreement on Services.

42 Narjoko, supra note 32, at 11; Sirisena Dahanayake, Implications of Liberalizing Professional Services: Legal, Accountancy, and Engineering Services in Lai PDR (2012), at 12.

43 Narjoko, supra note 32, at 10–11; Shepherd & Pasadilla, supra note 7, at 23.

Packages of Commitments on Financial Services.[44] Under the ABIF platform, an ASEAN bank that attains Qualified ASEAN Bank (QAB) status will be accorded equal treatment in other ASEAN states.[45] Yet, as the ABIF does not create a supra-national institution like the European Central Bank, the QAB criteria will be determined by two central banks in a reciprocal bilateral agreement.[46] Each state thus retains flexibility in agreeing to the arrangements. The ABIF is expected to enhance financial services integration under the AEC and enhance ASEAN bank's pan-regional operations.

The movement of skilled labor

Recognizing the impact of the mobility of professionals on ASEAN's competitiveness to attract FDIs, the AEC's objective to be a single market and production base includes a free flow of skilled labor.[47] The Mode 4 liberalization is paramount to narrow ASEAN's development gap because skilled workers in the least developed CLMV countries (Cambodia, Laos, Myanmar and Vietnam) can benefit from a 14–20 percent wage increase.[48] The ASEAN framework that expedites the movement of skilled labor includes MRAs and Mode 4 concessions in AFAS packages, to be superseded by the ASEAN MNP Agreement.[49] Mode 3 obligations under the ASEAN Comprehensive Investment Agreement (ACIA) also contribute to Mode 4 progress. The ACIA obliges states to allow entry, temporary stay and work of "investors, executives, managers and members of the board of directors" to facilitate the operation of ASEAN corporations.[50] The preferential treatment under the ASEAN MNP Agreement applies to these key positions identified in the ACIA.[51]

ASEAN MNP Agreement

The commitments for Mode 4 in the WTO and FTAs are far more restrictive than other modes of supply and thus have great potential for improvement.[52] Until

44 Protocol to Implement the Sixth Packages of Commitments on Financial Services under the ASEAN Framework Agreement on Services (2015), art. 5.

45 Charles Small, Indonesia-Malaysia Financial Agreement a Model for Bilateralism, Jan. 9, 2015, www.aseanbriefing.com/news/2015/01/09/indonesia-malaysia-financial-agreement-model-bilateralism.html (last accessed June 1, 2020).

46 Id.; Rajiv Biswas, ASEAN Banking Accord "A Key Step towards Economic Integration," Mar. 23, 2015, www.dw.com/en/asean-banking-accord-a-key-step-towards-economic-integration/a-18333763 (last accessed June 1, 2020).

47 AEC Blueprint, supra note 32, sec. II.A.5.

48 Simon Feeny & Mark McGillivray, The Role of ASEAN Connectivity in Reducing the Development Gap, *in* Narrowing the Development Gap in ASEAN: Drivers and Policy Options 84, 113 (Mark McGillivray & David Carpenter eds. 2013); ASEAN Community 2015: Managing Integration for Better Jobs and Shared Prosperity 72 (2014).

49 AFAS packages includes AFAS 1–10, and financial services and air transport services commitments.

50 ASEAN Comprehensive Investment Agreement (2009) [ACIA], art. 22.

51 ASEAN MNP Agreement, art. 12:2.

52 WTO Secretariat, GATS, Mode 4 and the Pattern of Commitments: Background Information, Apr. 11–12, 2012, at 3; Presence of Natural Persons (Mode 4), Background Note by the Secretariat,

the implementation of the prospective ATISA, the ASEAN MNP Agreement is the key instrument to enable the movement of service providers in the bloc. In line with the AEC Blueprint, the agreement applies to skilled workers rather than all "natural persons."[53] Furthermore, the agreement, which will supersede all AFAS commitments, extends only to services sectors. Although the agreement stipulates that it covers persons engaged in trade in services, goods and investments, none of the ASEAN countries made commitments in non-services sectors.[54] For instance, the cross-border transfer of a sales manager of a regional manufacturing or agricultural plant falls outside the scope of the agreement because manufacturing and agriculture *per se* are not services sectors. Nevertheless, the manager's entry to other ASEAN states for business trips is guaranteed under the ACIA, which covers "services *incidental to*" these non-services sectors.[55]

Like the GATS, the coverage of the ASEAN MNP Agreement is confined to the services provision on a non-permanent basis. The agreement will facilitate intra-ASEAN "temporary entry or temporary stay of" service providers.[56] The term "temporary" is negatively defined in the agreement, based on the model of the GATS "Annex on Movement of Natural Persons Supplying Services."[57] Moreover, the ASEAN MNP Agreement will "not apply to measures affecting natural persons seeking access to the employment market of another Member State" or "measures regarding citizenship, residence or employment on a permanent basis."[58] ASEAN states are allowed to maintain visa requirements for public purposes, so long as benefits under the agreements are not nullified or impaired.[59] Arguably, the potential for skilled worker migration within the region is curtailed because the agreement does not apply to the permanent entry of natural persons.[60] Because of the ambiguity as to what length of time "temporary" entails, ASEAN states' commitments in their schedules vary significantly across different categories of natural persons.[61]

The ASEAN MNP Agreement encompasses four categories of natural persons, including intra-corporate transferees (ICTs), business visitors, contractual service

S/C/W/301, Sept. 15, 2009 [Presence of Natural Persons (Mode 4)], at 25; Sherry Stephenson & Gary Hufbauer, Labor Mobility, *in* Preferential Trade Agreement Policies for Development: A Handbook 275, 281 (Jean-Pierre Chauffour & Jean-Christophe Maur eds. 2011).

53 ASEAN MNP Agreement, preamble.

54 Id. preamble & art. 1(b); Fukunaga, supra note 19, at 5.

55 Emphasis added. Fukunaga, supra note 19, at 5; ACIA, art. 3:3(f).

56 ASEAN MNP Agreement, art. 2:1.

57 Id. art. 2:2; Annex on Movement of Natural Persons Supplying Services Under the Agreement, General Agreement on Trade in Services (GATS), art. 2.

58 ASEAN MNP Agreement, art. 2:2.

59 Id. art. 2:3; Under the GATS, "the operation of visa requirements only for natural persons of certain Members but not for others is not *per se* regarded as nullifying or impairing such benefits." Presence of Natural Persons (Mode 4), supra note 52, at 6.

60 ASEAN 2030: Toward a Borderless Economic Community, supra note 1, at 163.

61 Rupa Chanda, Mobility of Less-Skilled Workers under Bilateral Agreements: Lessons for the GATS, 43:3 J. World Trade 479, 497 (2009); Stephenson & Hufbauer, supra note 52, at 276.

providers and other categories as defined in schedules of commitments.[62] The ICTs under the agreement denote executives, managers and specialists employed by enterprises, whereas investors are covered under the ACIA.[63] As most Mode 4 entries in the GATS' horizontal commitments are related to ICTs (64.1 percent) and business visitors (23.5 percent), there is a close link between Mode 4 commitments and FDI through commercial presence.[64] The commitments under the ASEAN MNP Agreement follow the same trend with the purpose of easing employee movement for ASEAN corporations.[65]

All ASEAN states made ICT commitments, but only seven and three countries made commitments in business visitors and contractual service suppliers, respectively.[66] Business visitors are allowed to stay in the host country from 30 to 90 days and the duration of stay for ICTs ranges between one month and three years.[67] The maximum periods of stay for natural persons under the ASEAN MNP Agreement do not go beyond those in GATS commitments. As for the liberalization coverage in sub-sectors, one may contend that the Mode 4 commitments under the agreement are GATS-plus. Yet, the commitments of seven ASEAN countries fail to show significant improvement in comparison with those made under AFAS 8 and the ASEAN-Australia-New Zealand Free Trade Area (AANZFTA).[68] This reinforces ASEAN's lack of forward-looking liberalization over Mode 4 and its making of more extra-regional than internal concessions.

Mutual recognition arrangements

Other than Mode 4 commitments, the MRAs that facilitate the recognition of qualifications advance the AEC's services trade. MRAs are outside the WTO framework and are rarely addressed in FTAs.[69] Under the AFAS, mutual recognition

62 ASEAN MNP Agreement, art. 2:1. Some GATS commitments include independent professionals. Under the ASEAN MNP Agreement, a number of ASEAN countries made commitments in professionals under "other categories." E.g., Annex 1 Schedules of Commitments: Malaysia, ASEAN Agreement on MNP, at 3–4.

63 E.g., Annex 1 Schedules of Commitments: Brunei Darussalam, ASEAN Agreement on MNP, at 2–3; Fukunaga, supra note 19, at 4.

64 Presence of Natural Persons (Mode 4), supra note 52, at 20–21. Business visitors are corporate employees who enter another state for purposes of establishing commercial presence or of negotiating business. Id. at 7. Also refer to the analysis in Fukunaga, supra note 19, at 23–24.

65 Sarah Huelser & Adam Heal, Moving Freely? Labour Mobility in ASEAN, Asia-Pacific Research and Training Network on Trade, No. 40 (2014), at 4.

66 Table 1: Summary of National Commitments of the ASEAN MNP Agreement, *in* Fukunaga, supra note 19, at 8–9.

67 Id.; Under the GATS, "while business visitors are generally allowed to stay up to 90 days, the presence of intra-corporate transferees … tends to be limited to periods of between two and five years." Presence of Natural Persons (Mode 4), S/C/W/75, Dec. 8. 1998, at 1 & 28.

68 The seven countries include Brunei, Cambodia, Malaysia, Myanmar, the Philippines, Singapore and Vietnam. Fukunaga, supra note 19, at 16–30.

69 The only requirements for mutual recognition arrangements (MRAs) are set forth in Article VII of the GATS.

of licenses and certifications will be based on states' respective agreements.[70] The AEC Blueprint mandates that MRAs for all professional services be completed by 2015.[71] Nonetheless, ASEAN states have only concluded MRAs that apply to eight professions and these MRAs cover less than 2 percent of ASEAN's 300 million-person workforce.[72] Against the conventional understanding, MRAs merely provide a scheme of regulatory cooperation rather than accord direct recognition.[73] A key challenge is the divergence of national legislation governing various professions. To facilitate comparisons of qualifications across the ten ASEAN states, the ASEAN Qualifications Reference Framework will be developed under a capacity-building initiative of the AANZFTA.[74]

Based on different objectives, the eight ASEAN MRAs can be categorized as two major types: MRA frameworks and MRAs. MRAs aim to enhance the movement of designated professionals. Nevertheless, MRA frameworks, which govern accountancy services and surveying services, only identify broad principles and facilitate information exchange with the purpose of negotiating final MRAs.[75] For the other six professions, implementation methods at the national and regional levels vary across MRAs. First, the MRAs on engineering services and architectural services created the ASEAN Chartered Professional Engineer Coordinating Committee (ACPECC) and the ASEAN Architecture Council.[76] These ASEAN-level institutions and national regulatory bodies form a three-step registration system.

An engineer who meets the MRA's educational and experience requirements should be first certified by the domestic regulatory body, which submits the application to the ASEAN committee.[77] After the ACPECC approves and accords the title "ASEAN Chartered Professional Engineer," the engineer is eligible to apply to be a "Registered Foreign Professional Engineer" in another ASEAN country.[78] The final MRA on accountancy services will follow this model.[79] Second, without involving a regional mechanism, the MRAs on nursing services,

70 AFAS, art. V.
71 AEC Blueprint, supra note 32, sec. II.A.2.
72 Fukunaga, supra note 19, at 3; Giovanni Capannelli, ASEAN Labouring under Outdated Migration Policies, East Asia Forum, Dec. 19, 2014, www.eastasiaforum.org/2014/12/19/asean-labouring-under-outdated-migration-policies/ (last accessed June 1, 2020); ASEAN Economic Integration Monitor (2014), at 33.
73 Presence of Natural Persons (Mode 4), supra note 52, at 19.
74 Labor Migration, Skills & Student Mobility in Asia (2014), at 36; Fukunaga, supra note 19, at 27.
75 E.g., ASEAN Mutual Recognition Arrangement (MRA) Framework on Accountancy (2009), art. 1; Chia Siow Yue, Free Flow of Skilled Labour in ASEAN, *in* ASEAN Economic Community Scorecard: Performance and Perception 107, 118–19 (Sanchita Basu Das ed. 2013).
76 ASEAN MRA on Engineering Services (2005), art. 3.1; ASEAN MRA on Architectural Services (2007), art. 3.1.
77 ASEAN MRA on Engineering Services (2005), art. 3.
78 Id.; Deunden Nikomborirak & Supunnavadee Jitdumrong, ASEAN Trade in Services, *in* The ASEAN Economic Community: A Work in Progress 95, 104–05 (Sanchita Basu Das ed. 2013); Dahanayake, supra note 42, at 28.
79 Fukunaga, supra note 19, at 24–25; Final Draft, ASEAN MRA on Accountancy Services (2014), art. 4.

medical practitioners and dental practitioners require a two-step registration process. Certified by the country of origin, a medical doctor with sufficient qualification and without ethics violations may register as a Foreign Medical Practitioner in the host state.[80]

Last, the eighth and most recent agreement, the MRA on Tourism Professionals (MRA-TP) was concluded in 2012.[81] Unique among ASEAN MRAs, the MRA-TP governs unregulated professions because there are no international standards for "tourism professionals."[82] As tourism is central to ASEAN's economic development due to the sector's contribution to GDP and employment, promoting the mobility of tourism professionals will substantially benefit the region.[83] The MRA-TP matures the regional tourism industry by developing common curriculum and competency standards for 32 job titles such as butcher and travel consultant.[84] A person who possesses a tourism certificate issued by a national agency in compliance with MRA requirements can be recognized as a "Foreign Tourism Professional" in another state.[85] Also distinct from prior MRAs, the MRA-TP will create a Web-based regional database to help registered professionals seek employment in ASEAN countries.[86]

The AEC Blueprint treats MRAs as pivotal instruments to accomplish a free flow of services and skilled labor within the bloc. The earlier MRAs on engineering services and architectural services have resulted in 533 engineers and 195 architects being registered and accredited with ASEAN-level regulatory bodies.[87] However, ASEAN MRAs are generally conceived to achieve limited mobility for designated professions.[88] In practice, the provision of MRAs that mandates minimum years of experience (ranging from three to ten years) restricts the number of eligible professionals.[89] Even fulfilling the MRA criteria does not guarantee

80 ASEAN MRA on Medical Practitioners (2009), art. 3.1.
81 ASEAN MRA on Tourism Professionals (2012).
82 As tour guides are subject to regulatory requirements in certain ASEAN countries, they are not covered under an MRA. Fukunaga, supra note 19, at 26.
83 For instance, the revenues of the tourism sector contribute to 10 percent of the Gross Domestic Product (GDP) in Cambodia and 10 percent of employment in the Philippines. Trade Policy Review, Report by the Secretariat, Cambodia, Revision, WT/TPR/S/253/Rev.1, Nov. 24, 2011, at 79; Trade Policy Review, Report by the Secretariat, the Philippines, Revision, WT/TPR/S/261/Rev.2, May 9, 2012, at 93.
84 ASEAN MRA on Tourism Professionals, art. II; ASEAN Mutual Recognition Arrangement on Tourism Professionals (MRA) – Handbook (2013) [MRA-TP Handbook], at 18.
85 ASEAN MRA on Tourism Professionals, art. III.
86 MRA-TP Handbook, supra note 84, at 45–46.
87 ASEAN MRA on Engineering Services, www.acpecc.net/list.php?module=mra (last accessed June 1, 2020); ASEAN Architect Register, http://site.aseanarchitectcouncil.org/main/3000/index.asp?pageid=167531&t=asean-architect-register (last visited June 1, 2020).
88 ASEAN Integration Monitoring Report, supra note 3, at 113; Sukti Dasgupta & Sanchita Basu Das, The Limited Impact of the ASEAN Economic Community on Skilled Labour Migration, ISEAS Perspective, No. 48 (2014), at 6.
89 Guntur Sugiyarto & Dovelyn Rannveig Agunias, A "Freer" Flow of Skilled Labour within ASEAN: Aspirations, Opportunities and Challenges in 2015 and Beyond, Issues in Brief, No. 11 (2014), at 3.

employment because of additional requirements set by the host states. The labor market test exemplifies the obstacle. For example, a Malaysian company that plans to recruit a foreign engineer must demonstrate the absence of qualified local engineers for the specific project.[90]

The nationality and residency restrictions, as well as the language requirements, often render MRAs futile.[91] Thailand is a key case. While the country technically allows foreign nurses, none have been admitted because the licensing examination is conducted in Thai.[92] While MRAs can be important policy tools to promote the regional mobility of professionals, domestic regulations hinder the effectiveness of the MRAs.

Services commitments under ASEAN's external FTAs

ASEAN's services negotiations pursue inward- and outward-looking strategies. The AFAS packages, the ASEAN MNP Agreement and MRAs provide the major impetus for services liberalization within the AEC. To ensure ASEAN's centrality in the global supply chain, internal commitments should exceed those made under external FTAs. ASEAN has concluded five ASEAN+1 FTAs with China, Korea, Japan, India, Australia and New Zealand.[93] A new initiative that was launched in 2012 is to negotiate the Regional Comprehensive Economic Partnership (RCEP), which includes the ten ASEAN countries and six FTA partners.[94] The ASEAN-centered RCEP and the US-led Trans-Pacific Partnership (TPP) will be dominant Asia-Pacific mega FTAs that shape the global trade governance.[95]

The RCEP will harmonize rather than replace the ASEAN+1 FTAs, and these FTAs will set the benchmarks for the services commitments under the RCEP.[96] Although the RCEP will be finalized after the formation of the AEC in 2015, the

90 Nikomborirak & Jitdumrong, supra note 78, at 130. The Philippines imposes the labor market test requirement for foreign nationals in its Labor Code. Rafaelita M. Aldaba, ASEAN Economic Community 2015: Labor Mobility and Mutual Recognition Arrangements on Professional Services, Discussion paper Series No. 2013-04 (2013), at 4.

91 See Aldaba, supra note 90, at 3–4 (explaining that the Philippines' Constitutional and Foreign Investment Law requirements); Nikomborirak & Jitdumrong, supra note 78, at 130 (stating that a foreign architect must reside in Malaysia for 180 days in a year).

92 Fukunaga, supra note 19, at 20–21.

93 The ASEAN-Australia-New Zealand Free Trade Agreement (AANZFTA) is a trilateral agreement. For information on the five FTAs, see ASEAN 2030, supra note 1, at 35.

94 Regional Comprehensive Economic Partnership (RCEP), www.mfat.govt.nz/Trade-and-Economic-Relations/2-Trade-Relationships-and-Agreements/RCEP/ (last accessed June 1, 2020).

95 Four of the 12 participating countries (Brunei, Malaysia, Singapore and Vietnam) of the Trans-Pacific Partnership are ASEAN countries that will also participate in the RCEP. Ian F. Fergusson et al., The Trans-Pacific Partnership (TPP) Negotiations and Issues for the Congress, CRS Report (2015), at 2.

96 Guiding Principles and Objectives for Negotiating the Regional Comprehensive Economic Partnership (2012), principle 5 & sec. II.

RCEP progress will inevitably energize the AEC's services integration.[97] Among the five ASEAN+1 FTAs, the AANZFTA is the only "single undertaking" FTA that covers goods, services, investment, and the dispute settlement mechanism.[98] Following the model of the ASEAN-China FTA (ACFTA), other ASEAN FTAs have been negotiated under a framework agreement that allows key components of FTAs to be separately negotiated and concluded.[99]

The conclusion of the trade in services agreements of the ACFTA and the ASEAN-Korea FTA (AKFTA) took place in 2007.[100] Similar to the AFAS modality, the ACFTA and the AKFTA adopted the package structure for services commitments.[101] As for the ACFTA, the first package of commitments constitutes part of the TIS Agreement and the second package that increases GATS-plus commitments was signed in 2011.[102] In 2014, almost a decade after the framework agreement, ASEAN and India completed agreements on services and investment.[103] Because the negotiations for services and investment agreements between ASEAN and Japan will not be finalized until the end of 2015, the bilateral Closer Economic Partnership (AJCEP) remains an ASEAN FTA that solely covers trade in goods.[104]

The positive-list-based services commitments under ASEAN+1 FTAs are mostly related to Mode 2 and Mode 4 is the least committed mode of supply.[105] The fact that the current degree of AFAS 8's services commitments exceeds that of ASEAN+1 FTAs demonstrates the positive step towards the AEC.[106] Among

97 The negotiators decided to postpone the initially envisioned 2015 deadline for completing the pact. Id. sec. VIII; RCEP Agreement: Ministers of 16 Nations to Finalise Modalities on August 24 in Malaysia [RCEP Agreement], The Eco. Times, Aug. 16, 2015, http://economictimes.indiatimes.com/news/economy/foreign-trade/rcep-agreement-ministers-of-16-nations-to-finalise-modalities-on-august-24-in-malaysia/articleshow/48499795.cms (last accessed June 1, 2020).

98 Free Trade Agreements with Dialogue Partners, www.asean.org/communities/asean-economic-community/category/free-trade-agreements-with-dialogue-partners (last accessed June 1, 2020); The ASEAN Economic Community: A Work in Progress, supra note 78, at 357.

99 The ASEAN Economic Community: A Work in Progress, supra note 78, at 349–62; Economic Diplomacy, supra note 25, at 221.

100 Free Trade Agreements with Dialogue Partners, supra note 98.

101 Yoshifumi Fukunaga & Hikari Ishido, Assessing the Progress of Services Liberalization in the ASEAN-China Free Trade Area (ACFTA), ERIA Discussion Paper Series (2013), at 14.

102 The third package of commitments is under negotiation. Id. at 1 & 14.

103 ASEAN-India Free Trade Area, www.asean.org/news/item/asean-india-free-trade-area-3 (last accessed June 1, 2020).

104 ASEAN-Japan Dialogue Relations, www.asean.org/news/item/asean-japan-dialogue-relations (last accessed June 1, 2020); ASEAN 2030, supra note 1, at 35.

105 Hikari Ishido, Harmonization of Trade in Services by APEC Members, IDE Discussion Paper, No. 410 (2013), at 24; Trade Policy Review, Report by the Secretariat, Indonesia, WT/TPR/S/278, Mar. 6, 2013, at 109–110; 2nd Package of ASEAN-China Services Commitments under the ASEAN-China Agreement on Trade in Services (2011). Note that Ishido's survey does not include the ASEAN-India Agreement on Trade in Service and the ASEAN-Japan Closer Economic Partnership Agreement, which lacks service commitments.

106 Based on the Hoekman Index that measures the degree of service comments, the levels of commitments by ASEAN countries under AFAS 8, the AANZFTA, the ASEAN-Korea FTA and the ASEAN-China FTA are 0.42, 0.23, 0.19 and 0.12, respectively. Id. at 8–15.

the ASEAN+1 FTAs, the AANZFTA, which includes a separate chapter on the movement of natural persons (MNP), is the strongest in its GATS-plus services commitments.[107] The inclusion of the MNP annex in the recent ASEAN-India Agreement on Trade in Services also indicates the RCEP's further liberalization in Mode 4.[108] Although none of the ASEAN+1 FTAs provides for MRAs, the RCEP participating countries expect to include MRAs in the pact and ASEAN MRAs can direct the RCEP's approach.[109] The coverage of the RCEP and ASEAN+1 FTAs will influence the AEC's degree of consolidation and is therefore critical to service-oriented business in ASEAN.

Regulatory reform

The AEC is a milestone for services liberalization that will lead to a single market and production base. Yet, ASEAN governments should not only target at services integration according to the AEC Blueprint, but should also envision the post-2015 roadmap. Regulatory reform is necessary to energize ASEAN's global competitiveness in the services-oriented market. First, reshaping the fragmented nature of ASEAN's services commitments is critical to attract potential foreign investors. The prospective ATISA should consolidate general AFAS packages, two sector-specific packages and Mode 4 commitments under the ASEAN MNP Agreement in a single schedule of commitments. Similarly, the ATISA should strengthen its linkages with Mode 3 commitments under the ACIA to avoid Mode 4 limitations from obstructing commercial presence.[110] A related transparency problem is the lengthy process for ASEAN to publish concluded agreements. The fact that AFAS 9 was concluded in 2014 but has yet to be published prevents ASEAN service businesses from adopting a progressive strategy based on recent commitments.[111] Stakeholders often need to rely on the ASEAN agreement-related information provided by the Economic Research Institute for ASEAN and East Asia (ERIA). The ASEAN Secretariat is therefore advised to promptly update the status of negotiations and agreements on its website.

Second, reform is required for the modality of services negotiations. To ease the difficulty of reaching a consensus, the AEC Blueprint allows for the ASEAN Minus X formula and the 15 percent flexibility option in ASEAN states' services commitments.[112] In reality, neither principle is clear. The ASEAN Minus X approach makes commitments fragmented and opaque. It is ambiguous whether

107 Id.; The ASEAN Economic Community: A Work in Progress, supra note 78, at 363; AANZFTA, Ch. 9.
108 India Formally Signs Trade in Services & Trade in Investments Agreement with ASEAN, Sept. 9, 2014, http://pib.nic.in/newsite/PrintRelease.aspx?relid=109489.
109 RCEP Agreement, supra note 97.
110 See Fukunaga, supra note 19, at 31 (analyzing the risk of disconnections between Modes 3 and 4 in ASEAN services commitments).
111 2015 AEM Meeting, supra note 20; Services, www.asean.org/communities/asean-economic-community/category/services (last accessed June 1, 2020).
112 AEC Blueprint, supra note 32, sec. II.A.2; Narjoko, supra note 32, at 12.

a state can opt out of the commitments to which it initially agreed if it cannot meet the commitment threshold at the implementation stage.[113] Also, no ASEAN agreements elaborate principles governing the 15 percent flexibility proviso, and it became impossible to understand whether a country decided not to commit certain services sectors based on the rule. It is vital for ASEAN states to remove these exemptions in the post-2015 agenda. More importantly, the commitments under AFAS 1 to 9 have followed the positive list approach. The AEC is advised to switch the current mode to the more progressive negative list approach, which can ensure transparency and cover newly developed services.[114]

Third, forming a more unified ASEAN services market entails deepening commitments in Modes 3 and 4. An increasingly difficult hurdle in Mode 3 negotiations is the foreign equity restrictions, which led to the AEC Blueprint's conservative target of the 70 percent foreign equity participation rule. While some ASEAN countries have increased the foreign equity threshold to 100 percent, four states (Indonesia, the Philippines, Thailand and Vietnam) fail to meet the AEC target even with the exercise of the 15 percent flexibility option.[115] Consequently, a key step for AFAS negotiations is to minimize market access and national treatment limitations for Mode 3, so that the effectiveness of the foreign equity commitments will not be undermined by domestic rules.[116] Moreover, Mode 4 commitments under the ASEAN MNP Agreement should substantially improve. It is important to delink Mode 4 commitments from Mode 3, allowing for greater mobility of independent professionals in the region. To keep ASEAN's consolidation in the RCEP, it is recommended that ASEAN states increase the duration of temporary stays for natural persons and the coverage of services subsectors. The benchmark for such commitments should be based on ASEAN+1 FTAs such as the AANZFTA.

Fourth, the AEC Blueprint is confined to skilled labor, but in reality more than 87 percent of intra-ASEAN migrants are low-skilled workers.[117] In other words, ASEAN's Mode 4 liberalization falls short of benefiting the majority of the workforce. Nevertheless, allowing the temporary movement of low-skilled or unskilled workers demonstrates "the greatest absolute and poverty-related gains for developing countries" and can efficiently narrow ASEAN's development gap.[118] For example, remittances account for 10 percent of the Philippines'

113 Severino, supra note 26, at 352–53; Nikomborirak & Jitdumrong, supra note 12, at 59–60.

114 Christopher Findlay, Services Trade Liberalization in ASEAN, *in* Roadmap to an ASEAN Economic Community 172, 186–87 (Denis Hew 2005); Aaditya Mattoo & Pierre Sauve, Services, *in* Preferential Trade Agreement Policies for Development: A Handbook 235, 251–52 (Jean-Pierre Chauffour & Jean-Christophe Maur eds. 2011).

115 Dahanayake, supra note 42, at 12; Narjoko, supra note 32, at 14; ASEAN Integration Monitoring Report, supra note 3, at 96.

116 Philippa Dee, Does AFAS Have Bite? Comparing Commitments with Actual Practice (2013), at 21. Note that the AEC Blueprint mandates only "[n]o restrictions for Modes 1 and 2." AEC Blueprint, supra note 32, sec. II.A.2.

117 Sugiyarto & Rannveig Agunias, supra note 89, at 1 & 4.

118 Joy Abrenica et al., The Future of Trade in Services for Developing Countries, *in* Trade and Poverty Reduction in the Asia-Pacific Region: Case Studies and Lessons from Low-Income

GDP, and the spending of remittances on household consumption had a poverty-alleviating effect for rural families.[119] Notwithstanding the substantial economic impact, ASEAN has dealt with non-skilled workers as a political instead of trade issue.[120] The most recent regional instrument is the ASEAN Declaration on the Protection and Promotion of the Rights of Migrant Workers in 2007.[121] Although the Declaration identifies ASEAN commitments and obligations of receiving and sending states, its absence of enforcement mechanisms limits its practical value.[122] To protect migrant workers, some ASEAN states have concluded binding bilateral labor agreements and similar memoranda of understanding.[123] Liberalizing the temporary movement of non-skilled workers and enhancing their labor rights ought to be developed in tandem. To this end, ASEAN states should incorporate a liberalized yet managed system on migrant workers into the AEC and the RCEP.

Finally, the full implementation of MRAs will enable the AEC to be an integrated professional services market and provide best practices for the RCEP. Increasing the transparency and coverage of MRAs is essential. For instance, although accountants in Thailand constitute the largest proportion of the ASEAN accounting profession, 83.7 percent of Thai accounting professionals neither know nor understand the MRA Framework on Accountancy Services.[124] Built on the MRA-TP model, prospective MRAs should extend to other unregulated professions such as information systems (IT) technicians and financial analysts, so that the scope of skilled workers covered by MRAs can be significantly enlarged.[125] Harmonizing the implementation process will lead to better utilization of MRAs. ASEAN states should restrictively apply the "subject to domestic laws and regulations" provisions in MRAs and accord professionals the right of independent practice by removing nationality, residency and language requirements.[126]

Communities 341, 354 (Andrew L. Stoler et al. eds. 2009); Feeny & McGillivray, supra note 48, at 113; Chanda, supra note 61, at 1.

119 Personal remittances, received (percent of GDP), http://data.worldbank.org/indicator/BX.TRF.PWKR.DT.GD.ZS (last visited August 25, 2015).

120 Mid-Term Review of the Implementation of AEC Blueprint: Executive Summary (2012), at 39; Stephenson & Hufbauer, supra note 52, at 279. Currently, the protection of migrant work is under the auspices of the ASEAN Political-Security Community. ASEAN Political-Security Community Blueprint (2007), sec. II.A.1.5.

121 ASEAN Declaration on the Protection and Promotion of the Rights of Migrant Workers (2007).

122 Id. at arts. 5–22; Huelser & Heal, supra note 65, at 4–5.

123 Huelser & Heal, supra note 65, at 5; Arti Grover Goswami et al., When and Why Should Bilateral Labor Agreements Be Used? *in* Let Workers Move: Using Bilateral Labor Agreements to Increase Trade in Services 39, 50–53 (Sebastian Saez ed. 2013).

124 Current Status of the Accounting and Auditing Profession in ASEAN Countries (2014), at 16–17; Tiyadah Pichayasupakoon, The Impact of the ASEAN Economic Community (AEC) on the Recruitment of Accountants: A Case Study of Listed Firms on the Stock Exchange of Thailand, 14:2 Silpakorn Univ. J. Soc. Sciences, Humanities, and Arts 1, 5–7 (2014).

125 Fukunaga, supra note 19, at 28; Huelser & Heal, supra note 65, at 8.

126 E.g., ASEAN Mutual Recognition Arrangement on Nursing Services (2006), arts. 3.2; ASEAN MRA on Engineering Services (2005), art. 3.3. See Fukunaga, supra note 19, at 16 ("The ASEAN

More fundamentally, ASEAN should align MRAs with domestic immigration rules. Unlike EU workers' freedom of movement, the mobility of ASEAN professionals is subject to respective states' immigration policy. The action under the AEC Blueprint to "[f]acilitate the issuance of visas and employment passes" is hardly implemented.[127] It is suggested that ASEAN look to the experiences of the North American Free Trade Agreement (NAFTA) and the US-Singapore FTA (USSFTA). While retaining contracting parties' border control, the NAFTA and the USSFTA created special visa categories for workers and the numbers of visas are subject to agreed upper limits.[128] The improved and integrated visa regime will enhance the effectiveness of ASEAN MRAs.

Conclusion

Trade in services propels economic development by modernizing the trade structure and alleviating poverty. The AEC's target to transform ASEAN to a single market and production base is intertwined with services integration that leads to a free flow of services and skilled labor within the bloc. Against this background, this chapter provides an up-to-date comprehensive overview of ASEAN trade in services form law and practice perspectives.

By examining the evolution of AFAS negotiations, it explains that while average services concessions are GATS-plus, lower Modes 3 and 4 commitments prevent the AEC from becoming a more unified market. Restrictions on Mode 3 lie in foreign equity participation, and obstacles to Mode 4 are due to domestic implementations of the ASEAN MNP Agreement and MRAs. To reinvigorate ASEAN trade in services, the AFAS structure and commitments should be developed in tandem with ASEAN+1 FTAs and the RCEP. Regulatory reform that intensifies the AEC's services integration will be critical to ASEAN's global competitiveness and provide best practices for the multilateral trading system.

MRA in principle does not give a right for independent practice [and] Vietnam is the only ASEAN country that allows independent practice").

127 AEC Blueprint, supra note 32, sec. II.A.5.

128 Fukunaga, supra note 19, at 29; Arti Grover Goswami & Sebastian Saez, How Well Have Trade Agreements Facilitated Temporary Mobility *in* Let Workers Move: Using Bilateral Labor Agreements to Increase Trade in Services 17, 30–32 (Sebastian Saez ed. 2013); Sherry Stephenson & Gary Hufbauer, supra note 52, at 281–82.

7 Horizontal embeddedness, business, and human rights

Fostering the corporate responsibility to respect human rights within the ASEAN Community

Michelle Staggs Kelsall

Introduction

In 2015, the Association of Southeast Asian Nations ('ASEAN') reached another major milestone toward regional integration by formally establishing the ASEAN Community ('AC'). The AC brought with it a renewed agreement from ASEAN Member States ('AMS') to implement ASEAN's common vision of a 'politically cohesive, economically integrated, socially responsible and truly rules-based, people-oriented, people-centred ASEAN'.[1] The newly adopted ASEAN Economic, Socio-Cultural and Political Security Blueprints (2015–2025) provide an ambitious agenda for ASEAN over the next decade to achieve these ends.[2]

In this chapter, I consider regional integration in one of the most contested areas of AMS' commitments under the ASEAN Charter – the promotion and protection of human rights – as it relates to one of AMS' most significant constituencies – the business community. I contend that although the regional human rights system in ASEAN is still in a nascent stage of its development, if the business and human rights agenda is taken seriously within ASEAN, then ASEAN stands to contribute significantly toward the ongoing development of corporate human rights responsibilities under international law. This is because the horizontal application of human rights obligations to transnational corporations and other business enterprises has, until very recently, remained unsettled in international law, with the international human rights system primarily relying on states (via the treaty-based system) to ensure corporate compliance with international human rights norms. As will be explained in further detail in this chapter, the

1 *Kuala Lumpur Declaration on ASEAN 2025: Forging Ahead Together*, preamble, at paragraph 6. (Jakarta: The ASEAN Secretariat, 2015) Available online at: www.asean.org/storage/2015/12/ASEAN-2025-Forging-Ahead-Together-final.pdf. (accessed 1 June 2020) (hereafter 'Forging Ahead').
2 Ibid., at pp. 19–103.

United Nations Guiding Principles on Business and Human Rights (the 'UNGP Framework'),[3] which were unanimously endorsed by the Human Rights Council in June, 2011, marks a significant departure from this approach, by affirming the corporate responsibility to respect human rights as a stand-alone responsibility above and beyond corporate compliance with national laws.[4]

In this context, ASEAN's approach to integration via cooperation and coordination at the inter-ministerial and inter-agency level – what Diane Desierto has aptly described as a system of 'horizontal embeddedness'[5] – stands to become an important example of how the corporate responsibility to respect human rights can be integrated into the regulation of the private sector in Asia. This is particularly the case because ASEAN has defined corporate social responsibility as a 'cross-cutting issue'[6] which, although traditionally housed under its socio-cultural pillar, has more recently been included as part of the agenda of both the ASEAN Political-Security Community ('APSC')[7] and the ASEAN Economic Community ('AEC').[8] In particular, the AEC blueprint clearly aligns ASEAN's efforts at economic integration with the United Nations 2030 Agenda for Sustainable

3 *Guiding Principles on Business and Human Rights: Implementing the Protect, Respect and Remedy Framework*, HR/PUB/11/04 (New York and Geneva: United Nations, 2011), available online at: www.ohchr.org/Documents/Publications/GuidingPrinciplesBusinessHR_EN.pdf. (accessed 1 June 2020).

4 As noted by the Special Representative to the Secretary General of the United Nations in explaining this responsibility: '[T]he corporate responsibility to respect human rights exists independently of state duties and variations in national law. There may be situations in which companies have additional responsibilities … but the responsibility to respect has become the baseline norm for all companies in all situations.' See Human Rights Council, Eleventh Session, Agenda Item 3, 22 April 2009, Report of the Special Representative of the Secretary General on the Issue of Human Rights and Transnational Corporations and Other Business Enterprises, A/HRC/11/13, para 47 (accessed 1 June 2020) [hereafter '2009 HRC Report']. See also UNGPs, General Principles, paragraph (b), whereby the responsibility to respect human rights exists in addition to corporate compliance with national laws.

5 Diane A. Desierto, *ASEAN's Constitutionalization of International Law: Challenges to Evolution Under the New ASEAN Charter* 49 Columbia Journal of Transnational Law (2011) pp. 268–320, at p. 280.

6 Email communication with Assistant Director-General ASEAN Socio-Cultural Community Pillar, 10 July 2013 (on file with the author).

7 See Section A.2.2 (Instill the culture of good governance, the rule of law, promotion and protection of human rights and fundamental freedoms as well as combat corruption) at paragraph (v): 'Support the ASEAN Foundation to strengthen its collaboration with the private sector and other relevant stakeholders to instill corporate social responsibility'). See *ASEAN Political-Security Blueprint 2015–2025* in Forging Ahead (supra, note 1) at p. 24.

8 See Section D.5 (Contribution of stakeholders on regional integration efforts), at paragraph 78: 'Strategic measures include the following: (i) Continuing to enhance engagement with stakeholders on economic issues to promote a better understanding of ASEAN integration initiatives; (ii) *Work closely with stakeholders towards promoting corporate social responsibility (CSR) activities*; and (iii) Enhance consultation with stakeholders on new initiatives.' [Emphasis added]. See *ASEAN Economic Community Blueprint 2015–2025*, in *Forging Ahead* (supra, note 1) at p. 93.

Development, which itself makes reference to the UNGP Framework.[9] This is a significant departure from the previous AEC Blueprint, which provided less emphasis on stakeholder engagement and which did not explicitly create a nexus between ASEAN's integration efforts and the United Nations' policy agenda.

As a result, ASEAN's proposed integration of CSR into the AC has the potential to provide important insights for other regional coordination efforts in this respect, both within Asia and beyond. However, ASEAN will need to evince a stronger commitment toward integrating the international legal norms subsumed in the ASEAN Charter into its implementation process in order for concrete measures ensuring the responsibility to respect human rights to take shape. It will also require greater consensus amongst AMS that CSR is not (or not solely) a philanthropic endeavour but rather, a core part of business operations, which needs to be evinced through business engagement with human rights due diligence, greater transparency and reporting on human rights issues, as well as stronger engagement with civil society in responding to the region's key human rights concerns.

Part I: The regional human rights architecture in ASEAN and its relationship to business & human rights

In Part I of this Chapter, I provide an overview of both the corporate responsibility to respect human rights as embodied in the UNGP Framework and the current regional human rights architecture within ASEAN. I first discuss the UNGP Framework and the shift that it seeks to bring about, in international human rights law, toward recognizing the responsibility of transnational corporations and other business enterprises to respect human rights, independent of the domestic legal obligations with which they have to comply. I assert that this shift is significant for understanding any evolution of CSR within ASEAN, because it seeks to re-cast what was traditionally a voluntary responsibility as one which is a generally accepted 'baseline norm' amongst transnational corporations and other business enterprises. If ASEAN takes a leadership role in strengthening corporate engagement with this norm, Southeast Asia could become an important example of how to further promote and develop the corporate responsibility to respect human rights for other regional bodies.

Business and human rights, international law and ASEAN's role in international agenda-setting

On the 16 June 2011, in an unprecedented step, the United Nations Human Rights Council unanimously endorsed the Guiding Principles on Business and

9 Transforming Our World: The 2030 Agenda for Sustainable Development A/RES/70/1 (New York: United Nations 2015), at para 68. Available online at: https://sustainabledevelopment.un.org/content/documents/21252030%20Agenda%20for%20Sustainable%20Development%20web.pdf. (accessed 1 June 2020).

Human Rights ('UNGPs'). The UNGPs and the 'Protect, Respect and Remedy Framework' which preceded them, were developed over the course of six years by Professor John Ruggie, who in 2005 was appointed the Special Representative to the United Nations Secretary General on the issue of 'Human Rights and Transnational Corporations and Other Business Enterprises' ('SRSG').[10] They comprise 31 principles and supporting commentary, ten of which relate to the state duty to protect human rights; 14 to the corporate responsibility to respect human rights; and six pertaining to both state and business responsibility to provide access to remedies for victims of human rights harms, through state-based judicial and non-judicial, as well as operational-level, grievance mechanisms. It was unprecedented for governments in the UN to unanimously endorse a normative standard (albeit non-legal) developed by an individual expert, without negotiation or amendments. This was possible due to a broad consultative process that had built support among all key constituencies over the course of the SRSG's six-year mandate.

ASEAN Member States played a key role in shaping the agenda of the UNGPs from the very start of the SRSG's mandate. Representatives of government and civil society from Indonesia, Singapore and Thailand helped to facilitate Asia's contribution to the research and consultations that led to their adoption in 2011. In particular, Ambassador Makarim Wibisono was Chair of the (then) UN Commission on Human Rights when it adopted the resolution that established the mandate of the SRSG on Business and Human Rights in 2005. In 2006, the SRSG's second regional multi-stakeholder consultation was held in Bangkok and focused on the toy industry. Later consultations on the development of the Guiding Principles were held in Singapore in liaison with the ASEAN CSR Network. Additionally, the Lee Kuan Yew School of Public Policy at the National University of Singapore collaborated with the SRSG's mandate in research on access to remedy for corporate-related human rights impacts in Southeast Asia.

Although the UNGPs themselves did not claim to create new international legal obligations, they did recognize 'the role of business enterprises as specialized organs of society performing specialized functions, required to comply with all applicable laws *and to respect human rights*'[11] (emphasis added). This latter obligation – to respect human rights – was characterized by the SRSG not as a duty but instead as a pre-existing responsibility, and one which was both distinct from and held in addition to compliance with domestic law.[12]

The UNGPs set out the corporate responsibility to respect human rights as, first and foremost, meaning that companies have a responsibility to refrain from harming others. As the SRSG noted, 'To respect human rights essentially

10 *See* Commission on Human Rights, Human Rights Resolution 2005/69, page 1 at paragraph 1, available online at: www.ohchr.org/EN/Issues/Business/Pages/ResolutionsDecisions.aspx (last accessed 1 June 2020).

11 UNGPs, General Principles, paragraph 1(b), at 1.

12 The distinction between a state's duty to protect human rights and the corporate responsibility to respect human rights will be further discussed in Chapter 2 which follows.

means not to infringe on the rights of others – to do no harm.'[13] This definition is consistent with the meaning of 'respect for human rights' as determined by the Economic, Social and Cultural Rights Committee in General Comment No.12 (1999), which underpins much of the international legal thinking on the obligations of states to respect human rights under human rights conventions, and which extends this responsibility to corporations.[14] The SRSG affirmed through his research that it is, as a result, almost universally accepted that corporations have a negative responsibility to refrain from harming individuals and to refrain from being complicit in human rights violations committed by states.[15] This included acceptance of a responsibility to respect from 'nearly every company and CSR initiative, endorsed by the world's largest business associations, affirmed in the UN Global Compact and enshrined in soft law instruments such as the ILO Tripartite Declaration and OECD Guidelines'.[16]

The SRSG, however, further asserted that, in addition to having a negative obligation (to refrain from harming an individual's human rights), the responsibility to respect human rights includes additional *positive* obligations, whereby businesses 'should act with *due diligence* to avoid infringing on the rights of others and to address the adverse impacts with which they are involved'[17] (emphasis added). According to the UN Guiding Principles, these positive obligations include: 1) taking adequate measures for the prevention, mitigation and where appropriate, remediation of adverse human rights impacts;[18] 2) avoiding causing or contributing to such impacts through their own activities;[19] 3) preventing or mitigating adverse human rights impacts directly linked to business operations, even if the businesses in question have not directly contributed to these impacts;[20] and 4) conducting human rights due diligence – a process that should include 'assessing actual and potential human rights impacts, integrating and acting upon the findings, tracking responses and communicating how impacts are addressed'.[21] David Karp has noted that as a result, the UNGPs established 'in an entirely separate sphere – not one that can be signed up for or opted out of – what exactly respect for human rights would need to mean in practice, in order for a company to live up to this commitment or obligation to do so'.[22]

13 'Protect, Respect, Remedy Framework (note 15), at 9.
14 Committee on Economic, Social and Cultural Rights, Twentieth Session, Geneva, 26 April–14 May 1999, Agenda Item 7, General Comment 12: The Right to Adequate Food (E.C12./1999/5), available online at: www.fao.org/fileadmin/templates/righttofood/documents/RTF_publications/EN/General_Comment_12_EN.pdf (last accessed 1 June 2020). See also Karp (note 6), at 64–65.
15 SRSG Report.
16 Ibid.
17 Protect, Respect and Remedy Framework at para 6.
18 UNGPs Guiding Principle 11.
19 UNGPs Guiding Principle 13.
20 UNGPs Guiding Principle 13.
21 UNGPs Guiding Principle 17.
22 Karp, at 83.

Hence, although claiming not to have created new international law, by creating positive duties on business to institutionalize the responsibility to respect human rights, the UNGPs did, in fact, herald a departure from previous understandings of the duties of corporations (as non-state actors) within the international human rights system. They did so by attempting to create a direct international obligation upon corporations to engage in positive measures to implement this responsibility. And while the UN Guiding Principles remain a 'soft law' instrument, their implementation in several domestic jurisdictions, in addition to their uptake by several international standard-setting bodies, has caused some scholars to claim that they have succeeded in 'entrenching the notion of the existence of a corporate responsibility to respect human rights'[23] in a way that did not previously exist.

Since 2011, the Human Rights Council has established two working groups to foster stronger corporate accountability for human rights within the international human rights system. The first comprises the Working Group on the Issue of Human Rights and Transnational Corporations and other business enterprises (UNGP Working Group), and the second comprises an Open-ended Intergovernmental Working Group on Transnational Corporations and Other Business Enterprises with respect to Human Rights (the 'OEIWG'). The OEIWG is tasked with elaborating 'an internationally legally binding instrument to regulate, in international human rights law, the activities of transnational corporations and other business enterprises'. The OEIWG, which was established by resolution in 2015, is still in the process of defining the scope of this instrument. The UNGP Working Group, which was established by resolution in 2011, is tasked with promoting the use of the UNGPs globally; conducting country visits (at the invitation of host governments); and guiding the work of an annual Forum on Business and Human Rights (Annual Forum), held in Geneva, where companies, civil society, academia and government convene to discuss the business and human rights agenda.

ASEAN governments and peoples have continued to have an ongoing influence over these intergovernmental working groups, with the prominence of ASEAN officials and civil society at the Annual Forum being one notable example of this. Over the past four years, representatives of the AICHR have attended the annual forum every year, and for the past two years have been joined by representatives from the ASEAN CSR Network. Government delegates from Indonesia, the Philippines and Singapore, as well as representatives from the Thai, Indonesia, Philippine and Malaysian human rights commissions, have also attended. In 2016, the Working Group held its first regional forum for Asia in Doha, Qatar, and the ASEAN CSR Network's Mr Thomas Thomas played a leading role in facilitating the plenary sessions for discussions. Additionally, during the first term of the UNGP Working Group's mandate (2011–2016),

23 Justine Nolan, 'Refining the Rules of the Game: The Corporate Responsibility to Respect Human Rights', (2014) 30:78 Utrecht Journal of International and European Law, 7.

Dr Puvan Selvenathan (Malaysia), Head of the International Trade Centre in New York, was the Working Group Member for Asia.

ASEAN's support of the UNGP Framework, as well as the AICHR's ongoing engagement with the intergovernmental process further promoting it, may signal a commitment toward instituting the corporate responsibility to respect human rights within the ASEAN region. Before turning to consider how the AICHR may begin to lead efforts in this respect, I look first at the history of the institutionalization of human rights and CSR in ASEAN, as well as the mandate of each human rights body as it pertains to business and human rights. This provides an important background through which to understand how the ASEAN is likely to consider the regulation of any such responsibility in the future.

A brief history of the institutionalization of human rights and CSR in ASEAN

Any recent engagement from ASEAN governments and civil society in support of a corporate responsibility to respect human rights needs to be considered in ASEAN's historical context. For much of its early history, the protection and promotion of human rights rarely surfaced in official ASEAN discourse. As John Ciorciari notes, the original members of ASEAN (Indonesia, Malaysia, the Philippines, Singapore and Thailand) established the Association in 1967 in large part 'to manage neighbourly feuds and ward off communist advances'.[24] Both the Bangkok Declaration (1967) and the Treaty of Amity and Cooperation (1976) clearly provided for a loosely integrated agenda in order to secure economic, political and sociocultural cooperation through consensus vote. As a result, in addition to containing political and security tensions through the pacific settlement of disputes, the primary goal of ASEAN for much of the Cold War period appears to have been to foster stronger ties between Member States in support of increasing economic prosperity. This led to what Desierto articulates as the development of ASEAN institutions via 'a gradual accretion process, created through piecemeal bilateral, trilateral and multilateral negotiations, formalized in separate international treaties, instruments, protocols and communiques'.[25] Much of this was consolidated by adopting an approach that came to be known as 'the ASEAN Way', whereby intergovernmental relationships in ASEAN were grounded in mutual respect for the independence and sovereignty of all nations and non-interference in the internal affairs of other states. This regional context has 'shaped the promotion of human rights norms across the region and continues to influence the evolution of a regional human rights system within ASEAN'.[26]

24 John D. Ciorciari, *Institutionalizing Human Rights in Southeast Asia* 34 Human Rights Quarterly (2012), pp. 695–725 at p. 697.

25 Desierto, supra, note 5, at p. 284.

26 Kelsall and Sperfeldt, supra, note 5 at p. 116.

From 1993 to 2008: Beyond the 'Asian values' debate?

During the 1990s, however, a notable shift took place with regard to governments' support for the international human rights system. The developments during this decade would act as an important precursor to both the eventual adoption of a CSR platform and the institutionalization of the regional human rights bodies, both following on from the adoption of the ASEAN Charter in 2008. Table 7.1 provides a brief overview of key events and legal instruments developed from 1993 onwards.

Momentum toward the development of a regional human rights system appears to have been spurred on by the 1993 Vienna World Conference on Human Rights and the discussions in the region that preceded it. Yet perhaps evincing the regional body's propensity to view its commonality as one of economic development, ASEAN's interest in human rights seemed to be largely mobilized by a concern to promote economic, social and cultural rights at the expense of civil and political rights. In what came to be known as the 'Asian values' debate, several ASEAN governments rejected the universality of human rights in favour of a culturally relative view of rights, in which ASEAN (as well as other Asian) governments sought to reassert the right to development as 'the precondition of liberty, progress, justice and creativity'. Any subordination of this right to so-called Western values (which considered the rule of law as paramount) was seen as further evidence of the post-colonial nature of international law and its ability to relegate any assertion of rights which originated in the developing world as subordinate to those agreed by the West.[27] The Bangkok Declaration, signed by several Asian (and ASEAN) governments in the lead-up to the World Conference, provided a platform through which Asian governments could align their values ahead of the global discussions and further entrench this perspective.

At the World Conference itself, however, despite voicing further criticism of the culturally relativist nature of rights, ASEAN governments seemed to firmly reject the 'Asian values' argument in support of universalism. All 171 Member States present in Vienna expressly agreed that human rights are not subject to national and regional particularities and that 'it is the duty of States, regardless of their political, economic and cultural systems, to promote and protect all human rights and fundamental freedoms'.[28] This commitment toward the universality of human rights was further affirmed at the 26th ASEAN Ministerial Meeting in Singapore later that year. At that meeting, the ASEAN Foreign Ministers adopted a joint communiqué in which they 'welcomed the international consensus achieved during the World Conference on Human Rights in Vienna' and 'reaffirmed ASEAN's commitment to and respect for human

27 Diane A. Desierto, 'Universalizing Core Human Rights in the New ASEAN: A Reassessment of Culture and Development Justifications against the Global Rejection of Impunity', Goettingen Journal of International Law, (2009), pp. 77–114 at p. 102 (hereafter, 'Desierto (2009)').

28 See in particular, Vienna Declaration and Programme of Action, Distr. GENERAL A/CONF.157/23, 12 July 1993, at paragraph 5. Available online at: www.ohchr.org/EN/ProfessionalInterest/Pages/Vienna.aspx (last accessed 1 June 2020) as quoted in Desierto 2009 at p. 81.

Table 7.1 Key developments in ASEAN for the institutionalization of CSR and human rights

1993–	**Bangkok Declaration of the Regional Meeting for Asia of the World Conference for Human Rights** (preceding the Vienna World Conference on Human Rights): Asian governments (including the then ASEAN Member States) reaffirm their commitment to the United Nations Charter, the International Bill of Rights and the Universal Declaration of Human Rights, but emphasize the principles of national sovereignty and territorial integrity. **Vienna World Conference on Human Rights:** 171 States (including ASEAN Member States) adopt Vienna Declaration and Programme of Action, which commits governments to 'promote and protect all human rights and fundamental freedoms, regardless of their political, economic and cultural systems' and further, 'to consider establishing regional and sub-regional arrangements for the promotion and protection of human rights where they do not already exist'. **26th ASEAN Ministerial Meeting (Singapore)**: in support of the establishment of a regional human rights mechanism.
1995	Viet Nam becomes a member of ASEAN July: Working Group for an ASEAN Human Rights Mechanism (Working Group) is formed.
1997	Laos PDR and Burma/Myanmar becomes a member of ASEAN.
1998	Cambodia becomes a member of ASEAN. Working Group becomes an official ASEAN dialogue partner.
2005	Indonesia chairs the Human Rights Council; approves the appointment of the Special Representative for Human Rights and Transnational Corporations and Other Business Enterprises.
2007	The ASEAN Charter is signed. Declaration on the Protection and Promotion of Migrant Workers is adopted.
2008	ASEAN Charter is ratified. ASEAN Foundation partners with the Asian Institute of Management (AIM) to establish the 'Network of ASEAN Corporate Foundations'. Human Rights Council approves the 'Protect, Respect and Remedy Framework' for the United Nations Guiding Principles on Business & Human Rights.
2009	ASEAN Intergovernmental Commission on Human Rights (AICHR) is established.
2010	ASEAN Commission on the Promotion and Protection of the Rights of Women and Children (ACMW) is established.
2011	United Nations Guiding Principles on Business & Human Rights is unanimously endorsed by the Human Rights Council. ASEAN CSR Network is inaugurated and registered as a company limited by guarantee in Singapore.
2012	ASEAN Human Rights Declaration is adopted.
2013	ASEAN Declaration on the Prevention of Violence Against Women and Violence Against Children is adopted.
2015	31 December – ASEAN Community is formally established, and ASEAN Vision 2025 (Forging Ahead, Together) is launched.

rights and fundamental freedoms as set out in the Vienna Declaration of 25 June 1993'. It was also further announced in Singapore that ASEAN 'should consider the establishment of an appropriate regional human rights mechanism', further entrenching the call made at Bangkok.

This decade would also be characterized by the emergence of a vibrant civil society within ASEAN, advocating and promoting the rights of ASEAN peoples – a fact which ASEAN itself would acknowledge in two important ways. First, it accepted the Regional Working Group for an ASEAN Human Rights Mechanism as dialogue partner to ASEAN in 1998.[29] The Working Group, which comprised human rights advocates, academics and civil servants from throughout the region, actively engaged with the Senior Officials Meetings on the sidelines of the ASEAN summit and would become pivotal in institutionalizing human rights in ASEAN. Second, it established the ASEAN Foundation in 1997 – a philanthropic arm whose aim would be to both promote 'greater interaction amongst the peoples of ASEAN' and 'contribute to the evolution of a development cooperation strategy that promotes mutual assistance, equitable economic development, and the alleviation of poverty'.[30]

Finally, the 1990s would prove further significant because ASEAN would acquire four new members in Laos PDR, Viet Nam, Burma/Myanmar and Cambodia. Much of the 'Asian values' debate, seemingly put to rest in 1993, would resurface in later discussions regarding human rights, as both former and current socialist states (in Viet Nam, Laos PDR and Cambodia) would seek to re-emphasize their significance for the region. Hence, by the time the Vientiane Programme of Action (2004) ('VAP 2004') was agreed, the emphasis on human rights had become much more about their *promotion* through the 'political evolution' of AMS, as opposed to their *protection* through a regional system. ASEAN governments did further commit, however, through VAP 2004 to elaborate 'an instrument on the protection and promotion of the rights of migrant workers' and to 'establish an ASEAN Commission on the Promotion and Protection of the Rights of Women and Children'. The former became the precursor to the Declaration on the Protection of the Rights of Migrant Workers (2007) and the subsequent establishment of a Committee on Migrant Workers tasked with implementing the Declaration through the creation of a legally binding instrument in support of it. The latter could be agreed because all ten Member States had ratified the Convention on the Elimination of Discrimination against Women ('CEDAW') and the Convention on the Rights of the Child ('CRC'), and would

29 Han Duy Phan, 'Evolution Towards an ASEAN Human Rights Body', 9 Asia-Pacific Journal on Human Rights and the Law 1 (2008) pp. 1–12 at 5. See also ASEAN, 'Joint Declaration of the 33rd Ministerial Meeting' at paragraph 33. Available online at: www.asean.org/?static_post=joint-communique-of-the-33rd-asean-ministerial-meeting-bangkok-thailand-24-25-july-2000 (last accessed 1 June 2020).

30 See ASEAN Foundation website, at: http://aseanfoundation.org/organisation/about-asean-foundation (last accessed 1 June 2020). See also the ASEAN Charter, Article 15, which refers to the ASEAN Foundation's mandate to 'collaborate with relevant ASEAN Bodies to support ASEAN Community Building'.

subsequently lead to the establishment of the ACWC in 2010, shortly after the ASEAN Intergovernmental Commission on Human Rights was established in accordance with the ASEAN Charter.

The tensions prevalent in the evolution of the human rights system prior to the ASEAN Charter evince an on-going disagreement within ASEAN (post-Charter) as to the extent to which economic development should be prioritized over the protection and promotion of human rights.[31] As will be discussed in greater detail below, as a result, any institutionalization of a corporate responsibility to respect human rights within ASEAN is likely to remain open to diverse interpretation within AMS. Nevertheless, it is precisely because of its links with the sustainable development agenda that securing support from AMS for institutionalizing this responsibility may prove easier than for other rights-based protections, at least in the near future.

The ASEAN Charter, CSR and the ASEAN Human Rights Declaration

The ratification of the ASEAN Charter in 2008 was a major turning point for human rights in ASEAN, in that AMS formally agreed to institutionalize human rights within ASEAN. Article 2(i) explicitly states that ASEAN shall act in accordance with the following principles: 'respect for fundamental freedoms, the promotion and protection of human rights and the promotion of social justice' and 'adherence to the rule of law, good governance, and the principles of democracy and constitutional government'. Perhaps even more significantly, and as Desierto points out, 'Member States are expressly obligated to "take all necessary measures to effectively comply with all obligations, including the enactment of appropriate domestic legislation, to effectively implement the provisions" of the Charter and "to comply with all obligations of membership".' Together with ASEAN's commitment to establish an ASEAN Human Rights Body under Article 14, the Charter appeared to secure an ASEAN human rights system. As such, the Charter seemed to shift the more fluid commitment of promoting human rights, as articulated in VAP 2004, toward the protection of human rights, by committing ASEAN, once and for all, to ensuring that governments were held accountable to their international human rights obligations.

The Charter would also further institutionalize ASEAN's philanthropic arm – namely, the ASEAN Foundation. Article 15 of the ASEAN Charter established the ASEAN Foundation as supporting ASEAN's community building agenda

31 Evidence of this is most clearly seen in the negotiations toward the ASEAN Human Rights Declaration. Although no official *travaux preparatoires* is available for this document, some of the iterative drafts discussed over the three-year period in which it was developed have been analysed by Renshaw. See 'The ASEAN Human Rights Declaration 2012', *Human Rights Law Review* [2013] pp. 1–23. See also Michelle Staggs Kelsall and Christoph Sperfeldt, *Chapter 5: Not Nudging, Embracing: The ASEAN Human Rights Declaration as a Catalyst for Reinforcing a Rights-based Approach to Constitutionalism* in International IDEA (ed.) The Rule of Law and Constitution-building: The Role of Regional Organizations (Stockholm: Institute for Democracy and Electoral Assistance, 2014), pp. 113–138.

through, *inter alia*, promoting 'greater collaboration amongst the business community, academia, civil society and other stakeholders in ASEAN'.[32] This would soon prove significant from the perspective of ASEAN's CSR mandate, because the Foundation would establish, as one of its first projects post-Charter, a 'Network of ASEAN Corporate Foundations', in which a regional network for CSR would begin to be conceptualized for the region. Initially in partnership with the Asian Institute of Management ('AIM') in the Philippines, the ASEAN Foundation would host a number of workshops and meetings through which growing agreement on a regional network for CSR would emerge within ASEAN. This would eventually lead to the development of the ASEAN CSR Network ('ACN'), a registered company limited by guarantee on 10 December 2010 in Singapore. A 'network of networks', the ACN would subsequently increase its membership to CSR organizations in 7 out of 10 ASEAN countries.[33]

Despite its promise to further safeguard the protection of human rights within the region, the establishment of the AICHR in 2009 and the 'Terms of Reference' instituting the body would, however, prove to weaken the more robust provisions of the Charter and revert ASEAN's commitment to human rights to a more facilitative and consultative role. This is perhaps not surprising, given AMS' more general reluctance to engage with the treaty body monitoring system, outside of a few notable exceptions. Rather than instituting a system of accountability, the AICHR would instead be conceived of as a consultative body, hence reducing its role to one of advising Member States (if called upon to do so) and mainstreaming human rights within ASEAN itself.

Nevertheless, the AICHR has since proven significant in consolidating ASEAN's regional human rights identity. Perhaps the AICHR's most important achievement to date has been securing the adoption of the ASEAN Human Rights Declaration ('AHRD') in 2012, ASEAN's first agreed regional human rights instrument since becoming an independent legal entity through the Charter in 2008. The AHRD itself has been heavily critiqued and criticized as a regional human rights instrument by United Nations offices, as well as academia and civil society. This is, in large part, because what some had hoped would culminate in ASEAN entrenching a shared normative commitment to international human rights law regionally, has more readily been identified as reflecting the tension in Southeast Asia between the 'aspiration on the part of some Southeast Asian States to endorse universal human rights and an on-going reluctance on the part of others to cede sovereignty.'[34]

Yet the AHRD should not be mistaken as being a simple reaffirmation of the 1993 Bangkok Declaration and a return to 'Asian values' within ASEAN. As Catherine Renshaw has pointed out,

32 ASEAN Charter, Article 15.

33 See ASEAN CSR Network website, www.asean-csr-network.org/c/about-us/our-journey-to-inauguration (accessed 1 June 2020).

34 Catherine Shanahan Renshaw, 'The ASEAN Human Rights Declaration 2012', *Human Rights Law Review* [2013] pp. 1–23 at p. 22.

> The Bangkok Declaration was framed as a protest against a world order perceived as perpetuating injustices against developing countries: the practice of human rights was projected as an instrument of the West, selectively utilized to suit the West's purposes. This sentiment is not present in the AHRD. The focus of the Declaration is squarely on the region, and on the challenge of mapping human rights onto the political landscape of Southeast Asia. *The problem is that there is no unanimity among the States of the region about how this might best be done.*[35]
>
> (Emphasis added)

Part II: Mandate and function of ASEAN's key human rights bodies as it relates to CSR and business and human rights

As this brief history illustrates, by 2012 ASEAN had established three primary regulatory bodies through which to channel the regional promotion and protection of human rights. It had also secured, within civil society, the establishment of the ACN, a vehicle for further enhancing cooperation within the ASEAN business community toward coordinating the CSR agenda. In addition, it had secured a strong regional commitment toward the protection and promotion of human rights through the ASEAN Human Rights Declaration, albeit with limited agreement as to what form ensuring a commitment to human rights protection should take.

In this section, I turn to focus on the extent to which each body explicitly interprets its mandate vis-à-vis the regulation of transnational corporations and other business enterprises. What becomes apparent from this overview is that the AICHR is currently the primary standard-setting body within ASEAN tasked with directing the combined CSR and business and human rights agenda, but that as yet, AICHR's role remains largely limited to working with civil society – and in particular, the ASEAN CSR Network – in these efforts.[36] Stronger engagement between the AICHR, ASEAN ministries, and the ASEAN business community within AMS could, in fact, prove to be a way forward in securing the corporate responsibility to respect human rights, and one for which AICHR has already made some progress.

Structure of ASEAN's human rights bodies

In keeping with ASEAN's approach of horizontal embeddedness, each of the ACMW, ACWC and AICHR is comprised of officials from ASEAN Member

35 Ibid., at p. 21.

36 See ASEAN Intergovernmental Commission on Business and Human Rights, *Thematic Study on Business and Human Rights: Synthesis Report* (Jakarta: ASEAN Secretariat, June 2014), available online at: file:///Users/michellekelsall/Dropbox/Michelle's%20Docs/Desktop%20April%202015/ASEAN/AICHRs_Thematic_Study_on_CSR_and_Human_Rights_in_ASEAN.pdf (accessed 1 June 2020). See also, Press Release 'Workshop on CSR and Human Rights in ASEAN: Outcomes of the AICHR Thematic Study', 14 June 2014, available online at: http://aichr.org/press-release/workshop-on-csr-and-human-rights-in-asean-outcomes-of-the-aichr-thematic-study/#more-1496 (accessed 1 June 2020).

States, selected by the AMS themselves, who act in a consultative capacity, both for ASEAN and each AMS.[37] There is no uniform process by which AMS select officials to represent them in these rights bodies, and as a result, each comprises a mix of civil society advocates, academics and government officials from within ASEAN. Consistent with its policy of ensuring cooperation through inter-Ministerial coordination, none of the ASEAN human rights bodies currently have a mandate to monitor AMS' adherence to the international human rights conventions to which they are a party, nor are there complaints mechanisms established whereby ASEAN nationals can formally petition any of the ACWC, ACMW or the AICHR with regard to specific human rights cases. Both the Commissions and the Committee report to a different inter-Ministerial body within ASEAN, all of which are tasked with drafting the terms of reference governing the relevant body, overseeing their respective work-plans and agreeing the instruments (or facilitating the execution of instruments) drafted by them.

The AICHR reports to the ASEAN Foreign Ministers Meeting (or 'AMM') and all of AICHR's work to date has fallen under the ASEAN Political-Security Community Blueprint. This makes the AICHR the most strategically placed of the three rights bodies, in that its mandate is clearly aligned with ASEAN's efforts to constitutionalize human rights at the regional level through the development of both policies and legally binding instruments in support of the human rights and fundamental freedoms contained in the ASEAN Charter.[38] The ACMW, on the other hand, reports to the ASEAN Senior Labour Officials Meeting, whose work falls primarily under the ASEAN Socio-Cultural Community Blueprint. However, the work of the ACMW in developing a legally binding instrument for the promotion and protection of the rights of migrant workers is further acknowledged in the Political-Security Community Blueprint, hence providing it with a discrete mandate to help secure a binding agreement within ASEAN on this specific set of rights. The ACWC, on the other hand, reports to the ASEAN Social Welfare and Development Ministers, whose work is housed solely under the ASEAN Socio-Cultural Community Pillar. As will be discussed in greater detail in Section 2.2.2 below, despite the fact that the ACWC's mandate arose from the ratification by all ten ASEAN Member States of CEDAW and the CRC, the strength of its protection mandate has been somewhat reduced by its limited engagement with ASEAN's Political-Security pillar.

What emerges from a review of the mandate and functions of each body is that, to date, only the AICHR has readily engaged with CSR and instituting the corporate responsibility to respect human rights within ASEAN. This is despite

37 In the case of the ACWC, this includes one elected official each representing the rights of women and the rights of children, hence making the body comprise 20 ASEAN officials in total.

38 See in particular Section II of the APSC (2009–2015), 'Characteristics and Elements of an ASEAN Political-Security Blueprint', particularly at sub-section 7, whereby the political-security aspects of ASEAN integration are fundamentally tied to implementing the ASEAN Charter, ensuring the ratification of legally binding instruments within ASEAN, and further securing a rules-based community. See also *Forging Ahead*, supra, note 1 at pp. 22–23.

the fact that strengthened engagement with the private sector would assist both the ACWC and the ACMW to secure rights-based protections for women, children and migrant workers and their families, and would further help ensure the prevention of human rights abuses against these groups. An obvious lacuna to ASEAN's policy approach in this respect has been the fact that, to date, none of ASEAN's human rights bodies have been explicitly acknowledged in ASEAN's Economic Community Blueprint, hence limiting the capacity of each body to engage with existing inter-Ministerial cooperation efforts directly targeting the private sector through the regulation of trade and investment. Similarly, up until 2015, there had been no explicit acknowledgement within the AEC Blueprint of CSR, despite ASEAN itself claiming that CSR was a 'cross-cutting issue'.

This, however, may be changing. Particularly pertinent is the inclusion in the new AEC Blueprint of a commitment to 'working closely with stakeholders towards promoting corporate social responsibility activities' as part of an ongoing process of strengthening the contribution of non-state actors to its integration efforts.[39] Although there is no explicit linkage created to the work of ASEAN's human rights bodies in this respect, it does create an avenue through which strengthened engagement on CSR from those bodies may be seen as a welcome development by the inter-Ministerial bodies engaged with integration efforts for the AEC.

ASEAN Committee on the Implementation of the ASEAN Declaration on the Protection and Promotion of the Rights of Migrant Workers ('ACMW')

Despite the significance of the ASEAN Charter in securing the establishment of a regional human rights system, discussions to establish ASEAN's first human rights 'body' in fact pre-dated this development. The ASEAN Declaration on the Protection and Promotion of the rights of Migrant Workers (2007) set forth an ambitious agenda for cooperation between states within ASEAN that both send and receive migrant workers. The Declaration sought to bring into effect a rights-based approach, which ASEAN had first adopted in VAP 2004, and to apply it to the issue of migrant labour across the region. It confirmed the shared responsibility, of both sending and receiving states, to intensify efforts to protect and promote the rights of migrant workers and their families. It also further called upon ASEAN governments to take concrete measures to prevent and curb trafficking in persons.

The ACMW's primary tasks are: 1) to develop an ASEAN instrument on the protection and promotion of the rights of migrant workers; and 2) to foster intergovernmental cooperation in ASEAN on the issues of the rights of migrant workers, labour migration governance and the prevention of human trafficking. The ACMW in fact pre-dated the establishment of ASEAN's two commissions: the first meeting of the ACMW took place on 15–16 September 2008 in Singapore. Although provided with the less formal status of being a 'Committee' (as

39 Ibid.

opposed to being a Commission), no substantive distinction is made with regard to the ACMW as a body. To date, negotiations on a legally binding instrument to secure stronger protections for migrant workers has 'reached deadlock': as at April 2016, and nearly eight years after the ACWC was formed, ASEAN appears no closer toward reaching agreement on protecting and promoting the rights of migrant workers in the region. As will be discussed further below, given the challenges of this mandate, adopting a stronger focus in support of the regulation of the private sector, through CSR, may prove a short-term avenue upon which the ACMW may wish to focus its efforts.

ACWC: A focus on the elimination of violence against women and violence against children

Although established six months after the AICHR, in April 2010, the ACWC was in fact conceived of first and acknowledged in pre-Charter ASEAN through VAP 2004. At the time, reform-minded ASEAN officials and ASEAN civil society advocates saw the institutionalization of a Women and Children's Commission as 'easier sell' to ASEAN's newer members than that of a regional human rights body. However, somewhat ironically, it was the establishment of the AICHR that became the catalyst for restarting relatively dormant discussions for the ACWC.

The ACWC specifically links its mandate to the CEDAW and the CRC and the treaty bodies that support their implementation. Ciorciari notes that the ACWC also appears to have a stronger protection mandate within AMS: amongst other things, its Terms of Reference provide for it to advocate on behalf of women and children, promote the implementation of relevant laws, and propose to AMS governments policies and processes for the protection of the rights of women and children. This seems likely to be because all ten AMS have ratified the CEDAW and the CRC, hence theoretically providing for a stronger basis from which ACWC members can agree uniform strategies to engage with the domestic level actors in the promotion and protection of the rights of women and children. In reality, however, reservations entered by some AMS (most notably, Brunei Darussalam, Malaysia and Singapore, in relation to CEDAW) make it challenging to reach consensus on an approach to the ACWC's protection mandate.

To date, the ACWC has not focused its efforts on engaging specifically with CSR or the corporate responsibility to respect human rights. The Commission identified as a key priority during its first term in office the elimination of violence against women ('VAW') and violence against children ('VAC'). Although cursory mention is made of engaging with the private sector in this respect, the ACWC's current Work-Plan (2012–2016) primarily focuses on the Commission engaging in awareness-raising efforts, the development of performance standards in relation to VAW and VAC (namely, disability rights, access to justice, non-violent approaches to child-rearing), as well as strengthening engagement within AMS to implement the recommendations of the CEDAW and CRC Treaty Body committees. The 2014 Declaration on the Elimination of Violence Against Women and Violence Against Children does make mention of the ACWC strengthening partnerships with external parties, including the private sector, in eliminating VAW and VAC. However, to date, ACWC's engagement with both the private sector and the UN UNGP Working Group on the corporate responsibility to respect human rights remains largely non-existent.

AICHR, CSR and business and human rights

Despite some initial controversy as to its role as a standard-setter for human rights in the region, the AICHR has been given the broadest human rights mandate of the three human rights bodies within ASEAN. With its drafting of the AHRD, the AICHR continues to play the overarching leadership role within ASEAN with regard to mainstreaming the organization's approach to human rights. This is clearly evidenced in the AICHR's consecutive work-plans (2010–2015 and 2016–2020),[40] in which there is a strong emphasis on strengthening the promotion and protection of human rights in alignment with the building of the AC;[41] working towards the further development of regional human rights instruments;[42] coordinating with ASEAN sectoral bodies to ensure the implementation of the AHRD;[43] and advising ASEAN bodies on human rights issues (upon request).[44] The Commission is tasked with meeting at a minimum twice a year, but in reality meets much more often. Despite not being remunerated for their role as Commissioners, AICHR delegates (or their nominees) met on average at least once a month in 2015, predominantly to engage with the UN, civil society and interested foreign governments (such as the EU and Japan) on implementing discussion forums and training programs relating to human rights issues.[45]

The AICHR is undoubtedly taking a leadership role in relation to the corporate responsibility to respect human rights within ASEAN. It is strongly supported in these efforts by the ACN. In 2014, the AICHR launched its first baseline study, which focused on the relationship between corporate social responsibility ('CSR') and human rights (the 'Study'). The Study argued that the period of rapid economic development underway in Southeast Asia mandated a 'strong focus on corporate governance and accountability, transparency and legitimacy'

40 See Five Year Workplan of the ASEAN Intergovernmental Commission on Human Rights (2010–2015) (hereafter, 'AICHR Workplan 2010–2015'), available online at: http://aichr.org/about/ (accessed 29 April 2016); and Five Year Workplan of the ASEAN Intergovernmental Commission on Human Rights (2016–2020) adopted by the 48th ASEAN Ministers Meeting on 3 August 2015 (hereafter, 'AICHR Workplan 2016–2020'), available online at: http://aichr.org/about/ (accessed 29 April 2015).

41 AICHR Workplan 2010–2015, at section 4.1; AICHR Workplan 2016–2020, at section 4.1.

42 AICHR Workplan 2010–2015, at section 4.2, paragraph 4; AICHR Workplan 2016–2020, at section 4.2, paragraph 4.

43 AICHR Workplan 2010–2015, at section 4.6; AICHR Workplan 2016–2020, at section 4.6.

44 AICHR Workplan 2010–2015, at section 4.7; AICHR Workplan 2016–2020, at section 4.7.

45 See archive of the AICHR calendar for 2015, available online at: www.aichr.org (last accessed 1 June 2020).

within the ASEAN business community.[46] Furthermore, while acknowledging the regional particularities of countries in the ASEAN region, in reaching its conclusions it made 'strong reference to established internationally recognized frameworks, particularly the United Nations "Protect, Respect and Remedy Framework" for business and human rights, the subsequent Guiding Principles on Business and Human Rights, and other relevant internationally relevant tools and measurements to regulate corporate conducts (*sic*).'[47] The goal of the Study was to 'provide a comprehensive assessment of CSR as it relates to the promotion and protection of human rights in the ASEAN region'.[48]

The Study highlights the significant differences in approach to CSR and human rights taken across the region. It links these divergent approaches to the differing stages of economic development ASEAN countries have reached, grouping countries into higher-income (Singapore; Brunei Darussalam), middle-income (Indonesia, Malaysia, the Philippines, Thailand, Viet Nam) and lower-income (Cambodia, Lao PDR and Myanmar) countries.[49] It argues that a divergence in governments' approach to the institutionalization of both CSR and a corporate responsibility to respect human rights can be explained by the extent to which a government exercises regulatory control over the economy, with lower-income countries still primarily relying on development agencies to foster engagement with international standards and norms.[50]

The Study further asserts that for the most part, countries in the lower- and middle-income brackets tend to see CSR as a form of corporate philanthropy, with governments largely relying on corporations to voluntarily engage in a responsibility to respect human rights, rather than creating a regulatory environment that would facilitate it or make doing so mandatory. The Study does, however, recommend that ASEAN develop both a comprehensive CSR strategy for the region, as well as develop an ASEAN-wide CSR Human Rights Guideline that 'is in line with internationally accepted human rights principles, such as the UNGP'.[51] This suggests the willingness within the AICHR to further drive efforts toward consolidating alignment with the UNGPs amongst AMS and within ASEAN, and, to date, is one of the strongest shows of support from within the ASEAN intergovernmental bodies of aligning ASEAN's emerging regional human rights system with international law – albeit soft law – as it relates to the regulation of corporate human rights responsibilities. As will be discussed in greater detail below, because the corporate responsibility to respect human rights can be so clearly linked to the sustainable development agenda within ASEAN, instituting this responsibility

46 Study Team on Business and Human Rights in ASEAN, 'Thematic Study on Business and Human Rights in ASEAN – Summary and Recommendations' (AICHR, Jakarta/Singapore, 21 June 2014) available online at: http://business-humanrights.org/en/business-human-rights-in-asean (last accessed 1 June 2020), at p. 2 (hereafter, 'AICHR BHR Study').

47 Ibid.

48 Ibid.

49 Ibid., at pp. 12–18.

50 Ibid., at p. 18.

51 Ibid., at p. 21.

may be one core area in which ASEAN's inter-Ministerial forums can agree to make progress. AICHR would therefore do well to further develop its mandate in this regard.

Part III: Further developing CSR and business and human rights in ASEAN

I now turn to consider three priority areas which may be considered paramount to ASEAN's current CSR and business and human rights agenda: namely, 1) moving ASEAN's agenda for CSR from corporate philanthropy to securing a core obligation amongst businesses to respect human rights; 2) ensuring greater transparency and reporting on human rights impacts from the corporate sector; and 3) further focusing on the regulation of irregular labour within ASEAN. I place these priorities in the context of the UNGP Framework and the corporate responsibility to respect human rights as articulated therein, and consider how the AICHR might begin to undertake the challenging task of addressing these priority areas.

Moving from corporate philanthropy to core business

Although significant progress has been made toward securing both a regional human rights system and a network of CSR organizations within ASEAN, to date, the intersection between these two parallel initiatives within has remained somewhat 'ad hoc'. This is at least in part due to the fact that, to date, AMS hold diverse views as to the significance of CSR and its relationship (if any) to human rights. According to the AICHR Study, several AMS still consider any social responsibilities undertaken by corporations to be largely philanthropic and outside of the core business operations of companies.

This, however, appears to be changing. Since the release of its Study in 2014, several members of the AICHR have engaged with the ACN in support of its work throughout the region. This has included through participating in several regional and international events in which the ACN has continued to raise awareness with regard to the responsibility to respect human rights and how it should now form part of core business operations. In 2015, this included an event at which representatives of three ASEAN governments subsequently publicly committed to pursue the adoption of a National Action Plan in support of the UNGP Framework. National Action Plans provide a policy commitment from governments toward the implementation of the UNGP Framework, including the corporate responsibility to respect human rights and, as such, may be seen as an important 'first step' toward securing strengthened engagement from companies to adhere to this responsibility. To date, the National Human Rights Institutions in Malaysia, Indonesia and the Philippines have each stated that they are in varying stages of developing these plans. Malaysia's National Human Rights Institution, SUHAKAM, has released a Framework for the Development of a National Action Plan, hence making Malaysia the first country in Asia to evince a commitment toward developing this policy commitment.

As the AICHR itself has already identified, an important next step may be to strengthen engagement with a comprehensive CSR strategy within ASEAN. Given its own engagement with the ACN, ensuring the development of any such strategy clearly delineates the corporate responsibility to respect human rights as being core to business operations should remain a key priority for the AICHR.

Transparency and reporting on human rights impacts

The AICHR itself has identified increasing transparency within the ASEAN business community as a high priority for its CSR and human rights agenda. The AICHR Study indicated that this was most significant in Singapore and Brunei Darussalam; however, there have been notable efforts from within ASEAN civil society to further encourage companies in other countries to increase the transparency of their operations, as well as to undertake greater internal and external reporting with regard to actual and potential adverse human rights impacts.

Perhaps most notable is the work of the Myanmar Centre for Responsible Business' initiative to promote Transparency in Myanmar Business Enterprises ('TiME'). With TiME, the Centre ranked Myanmar's 100 largest businesses with regard to the level of transparency companies exhibited about their corporate governance and business practices, particularly concerning anticorruption, organizational transparency, human rights, health, safety and the environment. The goal of TiME is not to score companies on their performance in these areas, but rather, to score the level of transparency about these issues, hence further incentivizing companies to publicly disclose information about their operations. Additionally, from 2013–2015 the Human Rights Resource Centre conducted a series of consultations throughout the ASEAN region in support of the development of the United Nations Guiding Principles Reporting Framework ('UNGP Reporting Framework'). Through these consultations, ASEAN companies, civil society and government officials were the first to participate in consultations to develop a series of 'smart' questions which companies could utilize to show their company's alignment with the UN Guiding Principles. The resulting framework is the first comprehensive guidance for companies to report on human rights issues in line with their responsibility to respect human rights. It has since been endorsed by over 80 investors representing US$4.8 trillion in assets under management as an essential tool for human rights reporting.

Ensuring greater transparency amongst companies within ASEAN with regard to their human rights impact has at least two advantages. First, it provides more information upon which civil society can understand the extent to which companies within ASEAN are attempting to address adverse human rights impacts. Although companies have assumed that such disclosure places them in a more compromising position vis-à-vis civil society, the evidence in several instances in fact suggests the contrary. Such disclosure can facilitate important partnerships between companies and CSOs. In this respect, several multi-stakeholder initiatives now rely on this capacity for collaboration. Second, transparency also provides ASEAN governments with access to information about the extent to which the private sector is having an impact on human rights in a particular AMS. Such disclosure can be of benefit for a number of bilateral relationships in addition to the region as a whole. As such, strengthened engagement on transparency initiatives within the private sector are likely to be of benefit to ASEAN governments as a whole.

Private sector due diligence on migrant labour and labour in supply chains

Labour migration has been a significant feature of the ASEAN economy for several decades. Stefan Rother and Nicola Piper note that the ASEAN region contributes 12.8 million (or 6 per cent) of the total 215 million labour migrants across the world; 3.9 million (or 30 per cent) of which comprise intra-ASEAN labour migration. Singapore and Malaysia are the largest migrant receiving, whereas Indonesia and the Philippines are the largest migrant sending countries in the region.

A key feature of migration flows in ASEAN has been that they are predominantly fuelled by low-wage, temporary labour, with many migrants being employed in so-called low-skilled jobs. As has been noted by Rother and Piper, this often results in 'an inherently problematic form of public-private partnership' forming, whereby government migrant agencies within AMS regulate the flow of migrant labour but typically outsource recruitment of migrant workers to private contractors. This has resulted in several reported instances of low-skilled labourers being sold into debt bondage, and in the worst cases, to an ongoing cycle of human trafficking being instigated in some of ASEAN's most important industries.[52]

To date, the focus in the ASEAN Economic Community Blueprint on the free movement of skilled labour has created a lacuna within ASEAN's existing policy framework, providing limited space for social policy as it relates to unskilled migrant labour to form part of the AEC's agenda. As has been noted by Jenina Joy Chavez, 'a major absence in the social dimension of ASEAN is the non-recognition of low and unskilled labour in official discussions as a target for regional action'.[53] This is despite the fact that movement of unskilled labour is prevalent in the region, and a lack of regulation is leading to some of the region's most egregious human rights abuses taking place. To some extent, the

52 In a recent prominent example, an Associated Press investigation of the Thai fishing industry from 2013–2015 revealed Burmese fishermen working off the Indonesian island of Benjina for up to 20 hours a day in appalling slave-like conditions. Although the Indonesian government was quick to respond once the story had broken, it revealed the extent to which irregular migrant flows in Southeast Asia's supply chain were fuelling global markets.

53 Jenina Joy Chavez, 'Social Policy in ASEAN: The Prospects for Integrating Migrant Labour Rights and Protection' *Global Social Policy* (2007) vol. 7(3) pp. 358–378 at pp. 363–364.

legal instrument in support of the Declaration being formulated by the ACWC seeks to address the lacuna, but the stasis reached in negotiations is reflective of both the complexity of the issue and ASEAN's inability to reach consensus on an agreed policy approach toward regulating this market.

As a result, the AICHR, together with the ACMW, may wish to consider strengthening engagement with the ACN toward engaging with the private sector to further strengthen human rights due diligence with regard to the use of migrant labour in the region. Several multinational corporations (most notably Flextronics in Malaysia) are already undertaking due diligence in order to ensure that migrants working in their companies are not subject to conditions of bonded labour. Strengthening engagement with the private sector in this regard is likely to avert several potential crises within key industries within ASEAN in the future and would enable ASEAN to maintain its goals in line with the 2030 Agenda for Sustainable Development, which itself makes reference to the UNGP Framework.

Conclusion

The historic establishment of the ASEAN Community in 2015 brings with it an opportunity to strengthen CSR in ASEAN, and in particular, to concretize the corporate responsibility to respect human rights within the ASEAN business community. The inclusion in the AEC Blueprint of a commitment from ASEAN governments to engage with stakeholders to promote CSR provides ASEAN's human rights bodies with a clear mandate to pursue ongoing engagement with the ACN toward institutionalizing both the use of human rights due diligence processes, as well as strengthening transparency and reporting regarding companies' human rights impacts. Furthermore, in light of the significance of labour migration within ASEAN, and in particular, so-called unskilled migrant labour, further engaging with transnational corporations and other business enterprises with regard to their employment policies and practices may begin to bridge what has to date seemed an unbridgeable gap in ASEAN's current policy agenda relating to migrant labour.

For these hopes to become a reality, however, clear leadership and focus will be required. In this respect, the recent partnership between the AICHR and ACN is promising, in that it unites two entities which have a sound institutional basis within ASEAN and whose mandates can be clearly traced back to the ASEAN Charter, which, itself, heralded a new era in intergovernmental relations within the region. One clear concern regarding any focus on a corporate responsibility to respect human rights within ASEAN is that it may lead to less concentration on the duty of states to protect human rights – another key part of the UNGP Framework and, indeed, of the development of ASEAN's human rights system more generally. It could also potentially lead some states to argue in favour of strengthening this responsibility in order to pass the buck to multinational corporations (originating from outside of ASEAN) vis-à-vis the obligation to provide remedies to victims of human rights obligations. This chapter has focused in its discussion on the prevention of human rights violations: yet clearly, for human rights accountability mechanisms to be further strengthened within ASEAN, ensuring adequate remedies for human rights violations to which corporations have caused or contributed is also required. Ultimately, however, if ASEAN's human rights bodies are to live up to the aspirations of the Charter, strengthened engagement with both CSR and the corporate responsibility to respect human rights needs to remain a focus of the ASEAN Community building.

8 ASEAN's foreign investment regime

Diane A. Desierto

Introduction

ASEAN's foreign investment treaties provide much insight into a regional foreign investment policy that seeks to purposely calibrate the demands of freedom of capital flows, with sovereign prerogatives of ASEAN Member States and their external partners to issue domestic regulations to protect public interests.[1] As of this writing, the International Investment Agreements Navigator of the United Nations Conference on Trade and Development (UNCTAD)[2] indicates that ASEAN has 12 regional treaties containing investment provisions (in force), and one still pending entry into force:

ASEAN Investment Treaty	*Date of Entry into Force*	*Date of Signature*
ASEAN-Hong Kong Special Administrative Region Investment Agreement[3]	17 June 2019	12 November 2017
ASEAN-India Investment Agreement[4]	Not yet in force	12 November 2014

1 *See among others* Diane A. Desierto, *ASEAN Investment Treaties, RCEP, and CPTPP: Regional Strategies, Norms, Institutions, and Politics*, 27 Washington International Law Journal 2 (April 2018), pp. 349–406, at file:///C:/Users/diane/Downloads/27WILJ349.pdf (last accessed 1 June 2020); Diane A. Desierto, *Regulatory Freedom and Control in the New ASEAN Regional Investment Treaties*, 16 The Journal of World Investment and Trade (2015), pp. 1018–1057; Sungjoon Cho and Jürgen Kurtz, *Legalizing the ASEAN Way: Adapting and Reimagining the ASEAN Investment Regime*, 66 American Journal of Comparative Law 2 (Summer 2018), pp. 233–266.

2 *See* UNCTAD International Investment Agreements Navigator at https://investmentpolicy.unctad.org/international-investment-agreements/groupings/15/asean-association-of-south-east-asian-nations- (last accessed 1 June 2020).

3 Agreement on Investment Among the Governments of the Hong Kong Special Administrative Region of the People's Republic of China and the Member States of the Association of Southeast Asian Nations, full text at https://investmentpolicy.unctad.org/international-investment-agreements/treaty-files/5655/download (last accessed 1 June 2020) [hereafter, "ASEAN-Hong Kong Investment Treaty"].

4 Agreement on Investment under the Framework Agreement on Comprehensive Economic Cooperation between the Association of Southeast Asian Nations and the Republic of India, full text at https://investmentpolicy.unctad.org/international-investment-agreements/treaty-files/3337/download (last accessed 1 June 2020) [hereafter, "ASEAN-India Investment Treaty"].

ASEAN-China Investment Agreement[5]	1 January 2010	15 August 2009
ASEAN-South Korea Investment Agreement[6]	1 September 2009	2 June 2009
ASEAN-Australia-New Zealand Free Trade Agreement Investment Chapter[7]	10 January 2010	27 February 2009
ASEAN Comprehensive Investment Agreement[8]	24 February 2012	26 February 2009
ASEAN-Japan Investment Chapter 7, Article 51[9]	1 December 2008	28 March 2008
ASEAN-US Trade and Investment Framework Arrangement[10]	25 August 2006	25 August 2006
ASEAN-Korea Framework Agreement[11]	1 July 2006	13 December 2006
ASEAN-India Framework Agreement[12]	1 July 2004	7 March 2004
ASEAN-China Framework Agreement[13]	1 July 2003	4 November 2002

5 Agreement on Investment of the Framework Agreement on Comprehensive Economic Co-Operation between the People's Republic of China and the Association of Southeast Asian Nations, full text at https://investmentpolicy.unctad.org/international-investment-agreements/treaty-files/2596/download (last accessed 1 June 2020) [hereafter, "ASEAN-China Investment Treaty"].

6 Agreement on Investment under the Framework Agreement on Comprehensive Economic Cooperation Among the Governments of the Member Countries of the Association of Southeast Asian Nations and the Republic of Korea, full text at https://investmentpolicy.unctad.org/international-investment-agreements/treaty-files/3339/download (last accessed 1 June 2020) [hereafter, "ASEAN-South Korea Investment Agreement"].

7 Chapter 11 (Investment) of the ASEAN-Australia-New Zealand Free Trade Agreement, full text at https://investmentpolicy.unctad.org/international-investment-agreements/treaty-files/2590/download (last accessed 1 June 2020) [hereafter, "ASEAN-Australia-New Zealand FTA Investment Chapter"].

8 ASEAN Comprehensive Investment Agreement, full text at https://investmentpolicy.unctad.org/international-investment-agreements/treaty-files/3095/download (last accessed 1 June 2020) [hereafter, "ACIA"].

9 Agreement on Comprehensive Economic Partnership among Japan and Member States of the Association of Southeast Asian Nations, Chapter 7 (Investment), sole provision Article 51, at https://investmentpolicy.unctad.org/international-investment-agreements/treaty-files/2570/download (last accessed 1 June 2020) [hereafter, "ASEAN-Japan Investment Chapter"].

10 Trade and Investment Framework Arrangement between the United States of America and the Association of Southeast Asian Nations, https://investmentpolicy.unctad.org/international-investment-agreements/treaty-files/2733/download (last accessed 1 June 2020) [hereafter, "ASEAN-US TIFA"].

11 Framework Agreement on Comprehensive Economic Cooperation Among the Governments of the Member Countries of the Association of Southeast Asian Nations and the Republic of Korea, 13 December 2005, full text at https://investmentpolicy.unctad.org/international-investment-agreements/treaty-files/3094/download (last accessed 1 June 2020) [hereafter, "ASEAN-Korea Framework Agreement"].

12 Framework Agreement on Comprehensive Economic Cooperation between the Republic of India and the Association of Southeast Asian Nations, full text at https://asean.org/?static_post=framework-agreement-on-comprehensive-economic-cooperation-between-the-republic-of-india-and-the-association-of-southeast-asian-nations-2 (last accessed 1 June 2020) [hereafter, "ASEAN-India Framework Agreement"].

13 Framework Agreement on Comprehensive Economic Cooperation between ASEAN and the People's Republic of China, 4 November 2002, full text at https://asean.org/?static_post=framework-agreement-on-comprehensive-economic-co-operation-between-asean-and-the-people-s-republic-of-china-phnom-penh-4-november-2002–4 (last accessed 1 June 2020) [hereafter, "ASEAN-China Framework Agreement"].

ASEAN Framework Agreement on Services[14]	30 December 1998	15 December 1995
ASEAN-EU Cooperation Agreement[15]	1 October 1980	7 March 1980

The post-ASEAN Charter treaties with investment provisions arguably describe ASEAN's unique foreign investment policy under Southeast Asia's specific Charter-based vision of narrow economic integration. While there was a previous ASEAN Investment Agreement (1987)[16] under which an investment dispute had been triggered,[17] the purpose of that Agreement was singularly focused on

> creat(ing) favourable conditions for investments by nationals and companies of any ASEAN member state in the territory of the other ASEAN member states and to facilitate the desired flow of private investments therein to increase prosperity in their respective territories.[18]

Creating foreign investment incentives alone used to be the overriding objective of pre-Charter ASEAN's foreign investment regime.

The Charter-based ASEAN's foreign investment regime now has to be read alongside Southeast Asia's broader aspirations to be a "region of lasting peace, security and stability, sustained economic growth, shared prosperity and social progress",[19] that "adher[es] to the principles of democracy, the rule of law and good governance, respect for and protection of human rights and fundamental freedoms".[20] While the ASEAN Economic Community "aims to enhance further [ASEAN's] attractiveness as an investment destination globally through the

14 ASEAN Framework Agreement on Services, full text at https://investmentpolicy.unctad.org/international-investment-agreements/treaty-files/2450/download (last accessed 1 June 2020) [hereafter, "ASEAN Services Agreement"].

15 Cooperation Agreement between Member Countries of ASEAN and European Community, 7 March 1980, full text at https://investmentpolicy.unctad.org/international-investment-agreements/treaty-files/3106/download (last accessed 1 June 2020) [hereafter "ASEAN-EC Cooperation Agreement"].

16 Now terminated. *See* Agreement Among the Government of Brunei Darussalam, the Republic of Indonesia, Malaysia, the Republic of the Philippines, the Republic of Singapore, and the Kingdom of Thailand for the Promotion and Protection of Investments, 15 December 1987, full text at https://investmentpolicy.unctad.org/international-investment-agreements/treaty-files/5554/download (last accessed 1 June 2020).

17 *Yaung Chi Oo Trading Pte Ltd. v. Government of the Union of Myanmar,* ASEAN I.D. Case No. ARB/01/1, Award, 31 March 2003, full text at www.italaw.com/sites/default/files/case-documents/ita0909.pdf (last accessed 1 June 2020).

18 Id. at footnote 16, at third paragraph of the Preamble.

19 Charter of the Association of Southeast Asian Nations, Preamble, sixth paragraph, [hereafter, "ASEAN Charter"], full text at https://asean.org/storage/2012/05/3.-November-2019-The-ASEAN-Charter-27th-Reprint_rev-2711191.pdf (last accessed 1 June 2020).

20 ASEAN Charter, at eighth paragraph of the Preamble.

establishment of an open, transparent and predictable investment regime in the region",[21] it also sought to establish "a more transparent, consistent and predictable [set of] investment rules, regulations, policies, and procedures"[22] that would be consistent with creating "a single market and production base, a highly competitive economic region, a region of *equitable* economic development, and a region fully integrated into the global economy".[23] An examination of ASEAN's post-Charter investment treaties reveal several distinct features, each of which will be discussed in more detail in the subsections following: 1) development-focused investment, acknowledging differentiated development within ASEAN's regional investment environment, and acknowledging regulatory freedom for environmental, public policy or social prerogatives; and 2) ensuring enhanced rules-based protection to foreign investors and providing for alternative modes of investor-State dispute settlement, including conciliation, mediation, consultations, arbitration, and/or local court adjudication.

Development-focused ASEAN's regional investment environment: regulatory freedom for environmental, public policy, or social prerogatives

ASEAN's regional investment treaties often contain provisions for special and differential treatment for newer ASEAN states (Cambodia, Myanmar, Laos, and Viet Nam), almost following the same identical language below:

> Article 18 Special and Differential Treatment for the Newer ASEAN Member States
>
> In order to increase the benefits of this Agreement for the newer ASEAN Member States, and in accordance with the objectives set out in the Preamble, the Parties recognise the importance of according special and differential treatment to the newer ASEAN Member States under this Agreement, through:
>
> (a) technical assistance to strengthen their capacity in relation to investment policies and promotion, including in areas such as human resource development;
> (b) access to information on the investment policies of other Parties, business information, relevant databases and contact points for investment promotion agencies;

21 ASEAN Economic Community Blueprint 2025, at Part A.3., para. 14, at www.asean.org/storage/2016/03/AECBP_2025r_FINAL.pdf (last accessed 1 June 2020).
22 ASEAN Economic Community Blueprint, at para. 28, p. 13, at https://asean.org/wp-content/uploads/archive/5187-10.pdf (last accessed 1 June 2020).
23 Id. at footnote 22, at para. 1, p. 2. Italics added.

(c) commitments in areas of interest to the newer ASEAN Member States; and
(d) recognising that commitments by each newer ASEAN Member State may be made in accordance with its stage of development.[24]

Other ASEAN regional investment treaties emphasize the objective of development – including differentiated levels of development taking into account conditions or circumstances within ASEAN Member States – in either the preamble, initial guiding principles, or in other development cooperation provisions as may have been provided for in these treaties.[25] These provisions are well in line with ASEAN's commitments under its Economic Community Blueprint 2025 to help "narrow the development gap"[26] within ASEAN, consistent with its own development-driven paradigm for Southeast Asia as a foreign investment hub.[27] In particular, the ASEAN Comprehensive Investment Agreement elaborates on building a regional investment environment in Southeast Asia that does not just focus on the usual strategies of investment liberalization, but also maintaining the equal and continuing public interest and public policy prerogatives of ASEAN Member States as Host States for foreign investment:

Article 2 Guiding Principles

This Agreement shall create a liberal, facilitative, transparent and competitive investment environment in ASEAN by adhering to the following principles:

(a) provide for investment liberalisation, protection, investment promotion and facilitation;
(b) progressive liberalisation of investment with a view towards achieving a free and open investment environment in the region;
(c) benefit investors and their investments based in ASEAN;
(d) maintain and accord preferential treatment among Member States;
(e) no back-tracking of commitments made under the AIA Agreement and the ASEAN IGA;

24 ASEAN-Hong Kong Investment Treaty, Article 18. *See similar or nearly identical provisions in* ASEAN-India Investment Treaty, Article 16; ASEAN-South Korea Investment Agreement, Article 16; ASEAN-Australia-New Zealand Investment Chapter, Article 15; ACIA, Article 23.

25 ASEAN-EC Cooperation Agreement, first and third paragraphs of Preamble, and Articles 2(1), 4(1) to 4(5); ASEAN Services Agreement, fifth paragraph of Preamble; ASEAN-Japan Investment Chapter, seventh paragraph of Preamble; ASEAN-South Korea Investment Agreement, fifth paragraph of Preamble; ASEAN-India Investment Treaty, sixth paragraph of Preamble; ASEAN-China Investment Treaty, fourth paragraph of Preamble; ACIA, second, fourth, and fifth paragraphs of Preamble.

26 ASEAN Economic Community Blueprint 2025, at p. 2, para. 6(ii), full text at www.asean.org/storage/2016/03/AECBP_2025r_FINAL.pdf (last accessed 1 June 2020).

27 *See* Sungjoon Cho and Jurgen Kurtz, *The Limits of Isomorphism: Global Investment Law and the ASEAN Investment Regime*, 17 Chicago Journal of International Law 2 (Winter 2017), pp. 341–369, at pp. 363–369.

(f) grant special and differential treatment and other flexibilities to Member States depending on their level of development and sectoral sensitivities;
(g) reciprocal treatment in the enjoyment of concessions among Member States, where appropriate; and
(h) accommodate expansion of scope of this Agreement to cover other sectors in the future.[28]

The above vision of striving for balance between the protection of private investment, with the maintenance of host State public interest prerogatives, finds some parallel resonance as well in the human dignity-based premises of inter-regional and intergovernmental development cooperation established in the ASEAN – European Community Cooperation Agreement. The ASEAN-EC Cooperation Agreement seeks to "contribute to a new phase of international economic cooperation and to facilitate the development of their respective human and material resources on the basis of freedom, equality, and justice".[29] The same Agreement establishes development cooperation between ASEAN and the European Community under the recognition that

> ASEAN is a developing region and [the European Community] will expand its cooperation with ASEAN in order to contribute to ASEAN's efforts in enhancing its self-reliance and economic resilience and social well-being of its peoples through projects to accelerate the development of the ASEAN countries and of the region as a whole.[30]

However, even foreign investment that is undertaken within the framework of development cooperation between ASEAN and its external partners raises questions about the maintenance, improvement, and ratcheting up of environmental and social standards as part of the Charter-based understanding of ASEAN Centrality.[31] As the Asia Foundation reported in detail in 2019:

> Southeast Asia has also been one of the most successful regions in the world in terms of economic development. ASEAN's emergence coincided with a period of remarkable economic expansion, with per capita incomes in the region expanding 33 times from US$122 in 1967 to US$4,021 in 2016.3 When ASEAN was founded in 1967, nearly all of its members were

28 ACIA, Article 2.
29 ASEAN-EC Cooperation Agreement, third paragraph of Preamble.
30 ASEAN-EC Cooperation Agreement, Article 4(1).
31 *See among others* Lukas Maximilian Mueller, *ASEAN Centrality under threat – the cases of RCEP and connectivity*, 8 Journal of Contemporary East Asia Studies 2 (2019), pp. 177–198; Siow Yue Chia and Michael G. Plummer, ASEAN Economic Cooperation and Integration: Progress, Challenges, and Future Directions (Cambridge University Press, 2015), at pp. 167–168; ASEAN Vision 2025: Forging Ahead Together (ASEAN Secretariat, Jakarta, 2015), at p. 13, para. 5, full text at https://asean.org/wp-content/uploads/2015/11/67.-December-2015-ASEAN-2025-Forging-Ahead-Together-2nd-Reprint.pdf (last accessed 1 June 2020).

> low-income economies. Today, the region includes two with high incomes (Singapore and Brunei), two with upper middle incomes (Malaysia and Thailand), and the rest with lower middle incomes. ASEAN has played an important role in this economic improvement by helping to maintain regional stability and facilitating greater regional economic integration. While the key driver of economic growth has been two-way trade between individual ASEAN countries and major economies (US, Japan, South Korea, China, and Europe), recent evidence shows that intra-ASEAN trade is on the rise, and trade and investment from other countries is also increasing. In the last decade, trade and investment from China has become an important contributor to ASEAN countries' economic growth, and China is now the largest trading partner for every ASEAN country.[32]

Significantly, ASEAN's foreign investment growth in recent years – while progressively increasing – has been spread across many sectors taking a dominant role in Southeast Asia's development, from the creation of special economic zones,[33] to the steady buildup of digital economies,[34] as well as to the rapid expansion of services such as health care service sectors.[35] ASEAN's policy focus with respect to investment is clearly diverse and evolving.

The development focus of ASEAN regional investment treaties is also evident from treaty provisions specifically preserving ASEAN Member States and their external partners' regulatory freedoms to legislate and enact measures for public policy, environmental, or social objectives. Thus, in the ASEAN-Hong Kong Investment Treaty,

> [n]on-discriminatory regulatory actions by a Party that are designed and applied to achieve legitimate public welfare objectives, such as the protection of public health, safety, and the environment, do not constitute expropriation [where an action or series of related actions by a Party has an effect equivalent to direct expropriation without formal transfer of title or outright seizure].[36]

The ASEAN-India Investment Treaty contains more extensive provisions preserving such regulatory freedoms, such as: 1) a provision declaring that there is

32 The Asia Foundation, *ASEAN as the Architect for Regional Development Cooperation: Advancing ASEAN Centrality and Catalyzing Action for Sustainable Development* (2019), pp. 2–3, full text at https://asiafoundation.org/wp-content/uploads/2018/09/ASEAN-as-the-Architect-for-Regional-Development-Cooperation_Nov2018.pdf (last accessed 1 June 2020).

33 ASEAN Investment Report 2017, *Foreign Direct Investment and Economic Zones in ASEAN,* full text at https://asean.org/storage/2017/11/ASEAN-Investment-Report-2017.pdf (last accessed 1 June 2020).

34 ASEAN Investment Report 2018, *Foreign Direct Investment and the Digital Economy in ASEAN,* full text at https://asean.org/storage/2018/11/ASEAN-Investment-Report-2018-for-Website.pdf (last accessed 1 June 2020).

35 ASEAN Investment Report 2019, *FDI in Services: Focus on Health Care,* full text at https://unctad.org/en/PublicationsLibrary/unctad_asean_air2019d1.pdf (last accessed 1 June 2020).

36 ASEAN-Hong Kong Investment Treaty, Annex 2, para. 4 in relation to para. 2(b).

no violation of national treatment obligations in the case of "extension of financial assistance or measures taken by a Party in favour of its investors and their investments in pursuit of legitimate public purpose including the protection of health, safety, the environment";[37] 2) a provision declaring there is no expropriation in the case of non-discriminatory regulatory measures by a Party or measures and awards by judicial bodies of a Party that are designed and applied in pursuit of public policy to achieve legitimate public interest or public welfare objectives, such as the protection of public health, safety, and the environment";[38] and 3) safeguard measures in times of crises.[39]

The ASEAN-China Investment Agreement takes a slightly different route, instead prescribing various situations or circumstances of inapplicability of the treaty, such as: 1) the non-retroactivity of the treaty to "any act or fact that took place or any situation that ceased to exist before the date of entry into force of this Agreement";[40] 2) measures on taxation, procurement, subsidies, or grants, services supplied in the exercise of governmental authority, and measures affecting trade in services;[41] 3) inapplicability of the expropriation clause or provision to the issuance of "compulsory licenses granted to intellectual property rights in accordance with the Agreement on Trade-Related Aspects of Intellectual Property Rights in Annex 1C to the WTO Agreement";[42] 4) prevention or delay of transfers

> through the equitable, non-discriminatory and good faith application of its laws and regulations [relating to: (a) bankruptcy, loss of ability or capacity to make payments, or protection of the right of creditors; (b) non-fulfilment of the host Party's transfer requirements in respect of trading or dealing in securities, futures, options or derivatives; (c) non-fulfilment of tax obligations; (d) criminal or penal offences and the recovery of the proceeds of crime; (e) social security, public retirement or compulsory saving schemes; (f) compliance with judgements in judicial or administrative proceedings; (g) workers' retrenchment benefits in relation to labour compensation relating to, amongst others, foreign investment projects that are closed down; and (h) financial reporting or record keeping of transfers when necessary to assist law enforcement or financial regulatory authorities];[43]

and 5) safeguard measures for exchange actions in conformity with the International Monetary Fund (IMF) Agreement,[44] or to safeguard the balance of payments.[45]

37 ASEAN-India Investment Treaty, Article 3(5).
38 ASEAN-India Investment Treaty, Article 8(9).
39 ASEAN-India Investment Treaty, Article 12 in relation to Article 11 (on transfers).
40 ASEAN-China Investment Agreement, Article 3(2).
41 ASEAN-China Investment Agreement, Article 3(4).
42 ASEAN-China Investment Agreement, Article 8(6).
43 ASEAN-China Investment Agreement, Article 10(3).
44 ASEAN-China Investment Agreement, Article 10(5).
45 ASEAN-China Investment Agreement, Article 11.

The ASEAN-South Korea Investment Agreement blends explicit provisions on regulatory freedoms, as well as provisions prescribing treaty inapplicability, such as: 1) treaty inapplicability to measures involving government procurement, subsidies or grants, taxation measures, claims arising out of events which occurred or had been raised prior to the Agreement's entry into force, services supplied in the exercise of governmental authority ("such as law enforcement, correctional services, income security or insurance, social security or insurance, social welfare, public education, public training, health and child care"[46]), and measures covered by other treaties such as the Agreement on Trade in Services under the ASEAN-South Korea Framework Agreement;[47] 2) a provision on reservations preventing the applicability of substantive standards of investment protection to certain sectors with non-conforming measures;[48] 3) prevention of transfers

> through the equitable, nondiscriminatory and good faith application of its laws and regulations [relating to: (a) bankruptcy, insolvency or the protection of the rights of creditors; (b) issuing, trading or dealing in securities, futures, options or derivatives; (c) criminal or penal offences; (d) social security, public retirement or compulsory savings scheme; (e) ensuring compliance with the judgments in judicial or administrative proceedings; (f) severance entitlement of employees; (g) financial reporting or record keeping of transfers when necessary to assist law enforcement or financial regulatory authorities; and (h) taxation];[49]

4) safeguard measures during crises;[50] 5) and the inapplicability of the expropriation clause to "the issuance of compulsory licences granted in relation to intellectual property rights under the TRIPS Agreement".[51] The ASEAN-Australia-New Zealand FTA Investment Chapter follows a similar pattern, with provisions that: 1) explicitly do not apply the investment chapter to government procurement, subsidies or grants, and services supplied in the exercise of governmental authority;[52] 2) prevent or delay a transfer through the equitable, non-discriminatory, and good faith application of its laws and regulations relating to: (a) bankruptcy, insolvency, or the protection of the rights of creditors; (b) issuing, trading, or dealing in securities, futures, options, or derivatives; (c) criminal or penal offences and the recovery of the proceeds of crime; (d) financial reporting or record keeping of transfers when necessary to assist law enforcement or financial regulatory authorities; (e) ensuring compliance with orders or judgments in judicial or administrative proceedings; (f) taxation; (g) social security, public retirement, or compulsory savings schemes; and (h) severance entitlements of employees.

46 ASEAN-South Korea Investment Agreement, Article 2(e).
47 ASEAN-South Korea Investment Agreement, Article 2(2).
48 ASEAN-South Korea Investment Agreement, Article 9.
49 ASEAN-South Korea Investment Agreement, Article 10(2).
50 ASEAN-South Korea Investment Agreement, Article 11.
51 ASEAN-South Korea Investment Agreement, Article 12(5).
52 ASEAN-Australia-New Zealand FTA Investment Chapter, Article 1(2).

In summary, ASEAN regional investment treaties blend strategies of differentiating between the development circumstances of newer ASEAN Member States (the CMLV countries, Cambodia, Myanmar, Laos, and Viet Nam), as well as building in provisions for inapplicability of the investment treaty to specifically identified regulatory objectives or public policies. These are considerably more far-ranging than the current models of bilateral investment treaties in the individual ASEAN Member States.[53] As of this writing, no investor-State dispute has been brought yet under the ASEAN regional investment treaties.

Rules-based protection to foreign investors and alternative modes of investor-state dispute settlement

Most of the ASEAN regional investment treaties contain clauses on the treatment of investment, as well as a diverse configuration of remedies to resolve disputes between foreign investors and the Host States of foreign investment. While the ASEAN-HK Investment Treaty contains provisions on national treatment, most-favoured nation treatment, fair and equitable treatment, full protection and security of investment,[54] these provisions themselves contain exemptions from coverage,[55] as well as specifically narrowed definitions.[56] The same treaty provides only for consultations to resolve disputes, with an agreement to enter into future discussions on the settlement of investment disputes.[57]

Similarly, the ASEAN-China Investment Treaty provides a range of investment protection guarantees but with corresponding carve-outs for each guarantee. Thus, even if the ASEAN-China Investment Treaty contains an expansive definition of covered investments under this treaty (e.g. "every kind of asset invested by investors of a Party"), such investments must be "in accordance with the relevant laws, regulations, and policies of another Party in the territory of the latter".[58] Policies are further defined as "those affecting investment that are endorsed and announced by the Government of a Party, and made publicly available in a written form".[59] Investment treatment protections under this treaty are similarly narrowed. While the national treatment clause maintains the standard

53 See Diane A. Desierto, *Monitoring and Implementing ASEAN Investment Policy in ASEAN's Regional Investment Treaties,* US Agency for International Development (USAID), May 2018, full report at www.nathaninc.com/wp-content/uploads/2018/05/Monitoring-and-Implementing-AEC-Investment-Policy-in-ASEAN-ACTI-15D-003-2018.pdf (last accessed 1 June 2020).

54 ASEAN-Hong Kong Investment Treaty, Article 3 (National Treatment), 4 (Most Favoured Nation Treatment), and 5 (Treatment of Investment).

55 Id. at Article 4(3) to 4(5).

56 Especially for the fair and equitable treatment standard (that which "requires each Party not to deny justice in any legal or administrative proceedings in accordance with the principle of due process of law") and the full protection and security standard (that which "requires each Party to take such measures as may be reasonably necessary to ensure the physical protection and security of the covered investment") under Article 5(1)(a) and 5(1)(b), respectively.

57 Id. at Articles 21 and 22.

58 ASEAN-China Investment Treaty, Article 1(d).

59 Id. at footnote 1 of the ASEAN-China Investment Treaty.

formulation,[60] the most-favoured nation (MFN) treatment clause provides a carve-out:

> if a Party accords more favourable treatment to investors of another Party or third country and their investments by virtue of any *future* agreements or arrangements to which that Party is a party, it shall not be obliged to accord such treatment to investors of another Party and their investments. However, upon request from another Party, it shall accord adequate opportunity to negotiate the benefits granted therein.[61]

The same MFN treatment is not applicable to preferential treatment accorded to investors under other pre-existing investment agreements, as well as "any existing or future preferential treatment accorded to investors and their investments in any agreement or arrangement between or among ASEAN Member States or between any Party and its separate customs territories".[62] The ASEAN-China Investment Treaty also narrows the definition of fair and equitable treatment of investment (e.g. "the obligation of each Party not to deny justice in any legal or administrative proceedings"[63]), as well as full protection and security of investment (e.g. "each Party [should] take such measures as may be reasonably necessary to ensure the protection and security of the investment of investors of another Party"[64]). Finally, the ASEAN-China Investment Treaty provides that parties to investment disputes "shall, as far as possible, resolve the dispute through consultations".[65] If such disputes cannot be resolved through consultations within six months from the date of written request for consultations and negotiations, the investor can choose to submit the dispute to the local courts or administrative tribunals, or to arbitration at the International Centre for Settlement of Investment Disputes (ICSID) or under UNCITRAL rules or other mutually agreed arbitration rules.[66]

The ASEAN-Korea Investment Treaty contains similar language as that of the ASEAN-China Investment Treaty when it comes to the narrowing of investment protections in clauses on most-favoured nation (MFN) treatment,[67] fair and equitable treatment,[68] and full protection and security.[69] Additionally, the

60 Id. at Article 4 (National Treatment): "Each Party shall, in its territory, accord to investors of another Party and their investments treatment no less favourable than it accords in like circumstances, to its own investors and their investments with respect to management, conduct, operation, maintenance, use, sale, liquidation, or other forms of disposal of such investments."
61 ASEAN-China Investment Treaty, Article 5(2).
62 Id. at Article 5(3)(a) and (b).
63 Id. at Article 7(2)(a).
64 Id. at Article 7(2)(b).
65 Id. at Article 14(3).
66 Id. at Artic.e 14(4).
67 ASEAN-Korea Investment Treaty, Article 4(3) and 4(4).
68 Id. at Article 5(2)(a).
69 Id. at Article 5(2)(b).

ASEAN-Korea Investment Treaty clarifies that fair and equitable treatment and full protection and security clauses "do not require treatment in addition to or beyond that which is provided under the customary international law and do not create additional substantive rights".[70] The same treaty contains identical options for investor-State dispute settlement as that provided for in the ASEAN-China Investment Treaty.[71]

In contrast, the ASEAN-Australia-New Zealand FTA Investment Chapter does not contain an MFN treatment clause.[72] The national treatment clause follows standard formulations as in other regional ASEAN investment treaties such as the ASEAN-China Investment Treaty and ASEAN-Korea Investment Treaty,[73] and also contains narrow language on the scope of fair and equitable treatment and full protection and security clauses,[74] similar to those contained in the ASEAN-Korea Investment Treaty. The ASEAN-Australia-New Zealand FTA Investment Chapter primarily prescribes consultations to resolve investment disputes, which may include the use of non-binding third party procedures.[75] The failure to resolve the dispute within 180 days from receipt a State of the investor's request for consultations, would entitle the investor to submit the claim to conciliation or arbitration.[76]

A similar model of narrowly defined investment treatment protections (national treatment, MFN treatment, fair and equitable treatment, full protection and security clause)[77] could also be found in the ASEAN Comprehensive Investment Agreement. Likewise, this Agreement contemplates a broad range of dispute settlement procedures for investment disputes. An investment dispute is deemed to arise between an ASEAN Member State and an investor of another ASEAN Member State "that has incurred loss or damage by reason of an alleged breach of any rights conferred by this Agreement with respect to the investment of that investor".[78] When such a dispute arises, parties must initially seek consultations and negotiations.[79] If such consultations prove unsuccessful, the investor may submit the claim to domestic litigation, administrative tribunals,[80] or arbitration,[81] or conciliation. Conciliation proceedings may be initiated at any time upon agreement of the investor and the Host State, subject to procedures that the parties devise.[82]

70 Id. at Article 5(2)(c).
71 Id. at Article 18.
72 Id. at footnote 7.
73 Id. at Article 4.
74 Id. at Article 6(2).
75 Id. at Article 19.
76 Id. at Article 20.
77 ASEAN Comprehensive Investment Agreement, Articles 5, 6, and 11.
78 Id. at Article 29(1).
79 Id. at Article 31(1)(b) to (f).
80 Id. at Article 33(1)(a).
81 Id. at Article 32.
82 Id. at Article 30.

The ASEAN-India Investment Treaty contains significant qualifications to the scope of investment protection clauses. While the national treatment clause does refer to "treatment no less favorable than that [a State] accords, in like circumstances, to its own investors and their investments",[83] the same clause also contemplates differentiation in treatment according to governmental or administrative unit:

> The treatment to be accorded by a Party [under national treatment] means, with respect to a regional or local level, treatment no less favourable than the most favoured treatment accorded at that regional or local level, in like circumstances, to investors, and investments of the investors, of the Party to which it forms a part.[84]

The same Treaty provides criteria for the determination of "like circumstances" warranting the application of national treatment, requiring

> an objective assessment of all circumstances on a case-by-case basis, including, inter alia: a) the sector the investor is in; b) the location of the investment; c) the aim of the measure concerned; and d) the regulatory process generally applied in relation to the measure concerned. The examination shall not be limited to or biased towards any one factor.[85]

The ASEAN-India Investment Treaty also does not contain an MFN clause, but contains similarly narrowed language on the scope of fair and equitable treatment and full protection and security clauses as those contained in the ASEAN-Korea Investment Treaty.[86] The ASEAN-India Investment Treaty purposely carves out from the expropriation clause

> non-discriminatory regulatory measures by a Party or measures and awards by judicial bodies of a Party that are designed and applied in pursuit of public policy to achieve legitimate public interest or public welfare objectives, such as the protection of public health, safety, and the environment.[87]

Finally, the ASEAN-India Investment Treaty contains virtually identical provisions on investor-State dispute resolution options as those contained in the ASEAN Comprehensive Investment Agreement.

Apart from the above treaties, other ASEAN regional investment agreements as of this writing that contain investment-related provisions do not elaborate on the nature of investment protection standards or investor-State dispute settlement

83 ASEAN-India Investment Treaty, Article 3(1).
84 Id. at Article 3(2).
85 Id. at Article 3(4).
86 Id. at Article 7.
87 Id. at Article 8(9).

options, but instead suggest leaving these aspects to further negotiations in the future, between the treaty parties concerned.[88]

Conclusion

It is worth examining ASEAN's burgeoning program of regional investment treaties to observe the incremental evolution of ASEAN's regional investment policy towards a deeper balancing of investment protection objectives with Host State regulatory prerogatives. Significantly, these regional investment treaties are being concluded *simultaneously* with the ongoing expansion of individual bilateral investment treaty programs of the ASEAN Member States, which suggests that ASEAN Member States are amenable to the layering of multiple international obligations – bilateral as well as regional – to define the region's foreign investment regime. What also bears emphasizing here is Southeast Asia's commitment to incentivizing foreign investment that is *consistent* with the domestic laws of individual ASEAN Member State jurisdictions. This emphasis translates to ensuring that ASEAN Member States do not relinquish or diminish their individual duties under human rights law and public policy and regulatory responsibilities towards their respective populations, while in the process of attracting, promoting, and protecting foreign investments to spur economic growth and contribute to the material dimensions of development. A 2014 report by the Organisation of Economic Cooperation (OECD) concludes that

> there is a slow but steady evolution, among ASEAN Member States towards more convergence of national legislation for the protection of investment … Individual countries have been progressively bringing their domestic legislation in line with common protection standards, on the basis of the ASEAN Comprehensive Investment Agreement (ACIA).[89]

However, there has not been counterpart harmonization when it comes to the human rights obligations, environmental laws, climate change commitments, and labour laws and public policies among ASEAN Member States. One can therefore expect that while the ASEAN foreign investment regime is leading towards regional harmonization of investment protection, it remains fissured on the preservation of host State public policy spaces to protect, respect, and facilitate human rights as these are impacted by foreign investment activities.

88 See ASEAN-Japan Economic Partnership Agreement, Chapter 7 (Investment), Article 51 (Investment); ASEAN-United States Trade and Investment Framework Arrangement, Section Four; ASEAN-Korea Framework Agreement on Comprehensive Economic Cooperation, Article 2.3 (Investment); ASEAN Framework Agreement on Services, Articles IV and VII; ASEAN-European Union Cooperation Agreement, Article 3.

89 Organization for Economic Development and Cooperation (OECD), *Southeast Asia Policy Perspectives: 2014*, at page 31, full text available at www.oecd.org/daf/inv/investment-policy/Southeast-Asia-Investment-Policy-Perspectives-2014.pdf (last accessed 1 June 2020).

9 The rule of law and human rights in ASEAN

Towards a "rules-based" community?

David Cohen

Introduction

As will be seen below, the leaders of ASEAN have promised their citizens a "rules-based community" that is based upon the rule of law, good governance, democracy, and the promotion and protection of human rights.[1] Such a rules-based community, they say, is necessary to ensure peace, prosperity, and sustainable development for the peoples of ASEAN. This rules-based community, they further promise, will thus be people-centered and people-oriented, and it will be achieved by 2025 as articulated in the APSC/AEC/ASCC Blueprint 2025 (hereafter when referred to collectively, Blueprints 2025) that will be considered in ensuing sections of this chapter. What are the challenges and prospects for the realization of these lofty promises? This chapter focuses upon the rule of law in ASEAN as a key component for the rules-based community, good governance, and the protection of human rights.[2] It will argue that ASEAN has not yet put in place a structure capable of fulfilling the rule of law mandate of the ASEAN Charter and Blueprints and that such a structure is a necessity for the realization of the larger goals of the ASEAN Vision 2025. The chapter will begin with an assessment of the rule of law and human rights obligations ASEAN has assumed under the Charter and other instruments and then consider the way in which the Blueprints 2025 propose to implement these obligations. The discussion will conclude with consideration of the ASEAN bodies that may be tasked with responsibility for implementing rule of law and human rights principles and obligations.

Before beginning the discussion of the ASEAN Charter and other instruments, it may be useful to consider briefly why the rule of law is important. We must acknowledge, after all, that there are ASEAN Member States that appear to believe, though they might never publicly say so, that economic development

1 I would like to thank my colleague Tim Buehrer for his helpful comments and suggestions and my Stanford research assistant, Teo Zhi Ping, for her research on the secondary literature on the rule of law in ASEAN.

2 For a concise overview of the evolving ASEAN treatment of human rights, see Termsak Chalermpalanupap, "Promoting and Protecting Human Rights in ASEAN" (The Nation, December 18–19, 2008).

may be achieved without the rule of law and the protection of human rights.[3] Indeed, some may be convinced that the rule of law and human rights constitute impediments to rapid economic development. A full discussion of this issue would be a matter for a separate paper or monograph, but it is at least worth sketching out some of the reasons why the rule of law is important.

A key component to achieve the prosperity and development promised to the peoples of ASEAN is the ASEAN Economic Community (AEC), launched in 2016. Why is the rule of law important for the AEC? The importance of the rule of law for the realization of human rights is obvious, because without the rule of law and the political will to use the law to implement and enforce human rights, human rights remain paper promises – easily made and easily ignored. The track record of states that have ratified many if not all of the core human rights instruments but fail to provide the protections those instruments are supposed to guarantee testifies eloquently enough to such failures. To take but one example, ASEAN Member States are now in the process of ratifying the new ASEAN Convention on Trafficking in Persons (ACTIP). Human trafficking in a variety of forms and on a massive scale is widely recognized in ASEAN as one of its major human rights challenges. ASEAN Member States have adopted international instruments on trafficking, such as the Palermo Protocol to the Convention on Transnational Organized Crime and now ASEAN has chosen to affirm its commitment to combatting trafficking by the creation of its own regional convention. But conventions are not self-realizing and ASEAN will require political will, legislative action, capacity building on a very large scale, and robust enforcement to implement ACTIP in an effective manner. The track record on implementation and enforcement of the Palermo Protocol does not give rise to immediate optimism that this will be easily accomplished. Yet what is also required to effectively implement anti-trafficking obligations is the rule of law, one dimension of which is defeating the widespread corruption that undermines the rule of law and defeats effective enforcement of legal norms. Without such measures the promise of ACTIP will not be realized. The question raised above, however, is, why is the rule of law important for the AEC in particular as opposed to ASEAN societies in general?

The rule of law cuts across all three pillars of ASEAN and although the ASEAN Blueprints 2025 largely relegate the rule of law to the Political and Security pillar, the rule of law is essential for the realization of the potential of the AEC. The 2015 Blueprints commit ASEAN to a "rules-based community" and the rule of law is a central constitutive element of such a community. A glance at the AEC Blueprint 2025 indicates the wide range of legislative and regulatory action that will be required to implement the 2015–2025 agenda. Without an effective rule

3 The ASEAN Human Rights Declaration addresses this issue in part in Article 35: "the lack of development may not be invoked to justify the violations of internationally recognized human rights". The reference to "internationally recognized human rights" rather than to rights enumerated in the Declaration is curious in a regional human rights instrument that has in previous articles indicated that human rights are universal and indivisible.

of law regime at the national level in every ASEAN Member State, this broad framework designed to enable cross border transaction, increase foreign investment, and permit the free flow of goods, capital, services, and skilled labor within ASEAN cannot be fully realized. The regulatory regime, to be effective, will have to be implemented and enforced in a transparent and predictable manner, and legal disputes will have to resolved through a judicial process that is fair, impartial, independent, and substantially free from corruption.

The greater the impingement of the rule of law through corruption, political interference, lack of judicial independence, influence peddling, and many other factors, the greater will be the drag that impedes and holds back the implementation of the goals of the AEC. Predictability and certainty in legal transactions, litigation, and judicial decision-making are prerequisites for maximizing investment and economic development.

Predictability and certainty in the judicial sphere can only be accomplished through the rule of law and that is why it, and its intimate counterpart, anti-corruption initiatives, must be an absolute priority for development of the AEC. All of the Blueprints 2025 and their overall incorporation into the document Forging Ahead Together, adopted by the ASEAN heads of state in the 2015 Summit, promise the citizens of ASEAN a rules-based, people-oriented, people-centered community. The development of an ASEAN economic order that truly benefits the citizens of ASEAN as a whole, rather than the political and economic elites that dominate some ASEAN Member States, will require the political will to tackle the many impediments to the rule of law that make the promise of a rules-based community that provides prosperity to, and promotes and protects the rights of its citizens, an ASEAN vision rather than a reality.

The ASEAN Charter, the Declaration, and the Blueprints 2025

The ASEAN Charter, as other chapters have discussed, marks the transition of ASEAN from a political association to a regional organization with a legal identity. The Charter is a legally binding instrument and the rule of law features in a number of places, beginning with the Preamble, which provides that in adopting the Charter the Member States are "adhering to the principles of democracy, the rule of law and good governance". Article 1 of the Charter identifies the Purposes of the Charter and includes these same principles among those purposes: "To strengthen democracy, enhance good governance and the rule of law, and protect human rights and fundamental freedoms."[4] Article 2, Principles, clearly commits ASEAN Member States to adherence to the rule of law: "ASEAN and its Member States shall act in accordance with the following principles: … (h) adherence to the rule of law, good governance, the principles of democracy and constitutional government".[5]

4 ASEAN Charter 1.7. Article 1.11 includes access to justice, an element of the rule of law, among the purposes it enumerates.

5 Article 2.(i) also provides for the: "respect for fundamental freedoms, the promotion and protection of human rights, and the promotion of social justice".

On the one hand, the commitment to the rule of law in the Charter could not be clearer. On the other hand, however, other Charter principles give Member States considerable leeway in how to interpret and implement the rule of law within their borders. Article 2(e), for example, sets out what has been one of ASEAN's most fundamental principles since its foundation in 1967: "(e) non-interference in the internal affairs of ASEAN Member States".[6] Article 2(l) also provides for: "respect for the different cultures, languages, and religions of the peoples of ASEAN, while emphasising their common values in the spirit of unity in diversity". Along with Article 20.1, which institutes decision-making by consensus, these provisions represent key elements of the "ASEAN way". In application, these principles ensure that ASEAN can, on the one hand, commit itself to democracy, good governance, the rule of law, and protection for human rights, while in fact none of these obtain in some Member States. These principles, as will be seen in the ensuing discussion of the ASEAN Human Rights Declaration (2013), allow Member States to maintain that their particular form of democracy, the rule of law, and human rights is an expression of their individual cultures, histories, and national traditions, all encompassed within the "unity in diversity" of ASEAN.

The ASEAN Human Rights Declaration (AHRD) reaffirms the commitment of ASEAN to the Charter principles.[7] Its Preamble asserts that the ASEAN heads of state reaffirm "their adherence to the purposes and principles of ASEAN as enshrined in the Charter, in particular the respect for and promotion and protection of human rights and fundamental freedoms, as well as the principles of democracy, the rule of law and good governance". These commitments of the Preamble were reiterated in the Phnom Penh Statement of the ASEAN heads of state at the Phnom Penh Summit (2013) when the AHRD was adopted: "Reaffirming ASEAN's commitment to ... the purposes and principles as enshrined in the ASEAN Charter, including the principles of democracy, rule of law and good governance." It is interesting to note, however, that despite the Preamble and the Phnom Penh Statement the AHRD nowhere explicitly refers to the rule of law. The term does not appear in the body of the AHRD. How, then, is ASEAN's commitment to the rule of law reflected in the AHRD?

Since the rule of law has been identified in the ASEAN Charter and the Preamble to the Declaration as a core principle that, like democracy and good governance, undergirds the protection of human rights, and since the rule of law is a general category that encompasses many key civil, political rights, social, and economic rights, one would have expected a section or subsection of the AHRD to deal explicitly with the rule of law. What we find instead is that many of the rights that make up components of the rule of law are enumerated in a somewhat piecemeal fashion in the Declaration. Thus, the AHRD, in the sections "General Principles" and "Civil and Political Rights", recognizes many of the most important elements of the rule of law. For example, among the "General Principles" one finds the principles, albeit not explicitly referenced as rights, of

6 That principle is reiterated in subsection (f).
7 "ASEAN Human Rights Declaration" (2013) p. 3.

equality before the law and equal protection of the law.[8] Another section of the General Principles guarantees the right to an effective and enforceable remedy for violations of legal or constitutional rights.[9] In the section on Civil and Political Rights one finds a series of rights associated with the rule of law intermixed, in no particular order, with a variety of other rights. The rights commonly associated with the rule of law include the right to be protected from arbitrary arrest, detention, search, or deprivation of liberty (Art. 12), fair trial rights such as the presumption of innocence, the right to be tried by a fair, independent, and impartial tribunal, the right to a defense, and the principles of ***nullem crimen sine lege*** double jeopardy.[10] This is an impressive panoply of rights, embodying many, though by no means all, of the components of an effective rule of law regime that would appear to be guaranteed by the Charter's broad recognition of the central importance of the rule of law for the realization of the larger aspirations for the peoples of ASEAN.

The problem with the AHRD, however, is that what one principle appears to guarantee another one appears to qualify, relativize, or undermine. Thus, for example, the AHRD provides on the one hand that "All human rights are universal, indivisible, interdependent, and interrelated."[11] On the other hand, the very same paragraph also provides that the realization of those rights, "must be considered in the regional and national context, bearing in mind different political, economic, legal, social, cultural, historical and religious backgrounds".[12] What this apparently means in plain language is that although the Declaration recognizes the existence of these rights in the abstract, the implementation of them is at the discretion of the Member State that considers how implementation is to be qualified by the contextual contingencies of culture, society, politics, and so on.

Article 8 also provides, on the one hand, that the exercise of human rights shall only be limited by law "solely for the purpose of securing due recognition for the human rights and fundamental freedom of others". On the other hand, that sentence continues to state that human rights may also be limited "to meet the just requirements of national security, public order, public health, public safety, public morality, as well as the general welfare of the peoples in a democratic society". One can hardly imagine a broader saving clause that would enable states to justify, as many ASEAN Member States do, laws, regulations, and practices that render nugatory many of the broad guarantees of the "universal" and "inalienable" rights guaranteed by other provisions.

One would imagine that the development of a rules-based community would require elaboration of just how the Charter's guarantee of the principle of the rule

8 AHRD, Art. 3.

9 AHRD, Art. 5.

10 AHRD, Art. 20.

11 Art. 4 also provides that the rights of women, children, migrant workers, disabled persons, and other vulnerable and marginalized groups are "an inalienable, integral, and indivisible part of human rights and fundamental freedoms".

12 Ibid. pp. 4–5.

of law is to be implemented in light of these qualifications. Given the broad range of relative realization of the rule of law amongst the ten ASEAN Member States, as well as the equally broad range of implementation of and respect for human rights principles and obligations, the qualifications just noted would appear to be designed to secure and sustain those divergences rather than harmonize them.

The implications for the AEC are very real, however, for respect for, and instantiation of, the rule of law across ASEAN would appear to be a pre-requisite for fulfillment of the promise of the AEC. As noted above, only the rule of law provides the predictability and certainty in legal affairs necessary to attract foreign investment and secure economic development and prosperity as promised by the Charter and other instruments. Indeed, one must ask, what would it mean to have a "rules- based community" without the rule of law?

Although the phrase "rules-based community" appears to avoid the terminology of the rule of law, surely the rule of law is a constitutive requirement for a substantive rather than purely formal rules-based community. The question thus remains whether one can develop the rule of law or a rules-based community at the ASEAN level when so many of the ASEAN Member States are so far from realizing the rule of law within their own borders? How does ASEAN propose to proceed to create the "rules-based community" that has become the mantra of ASEAN discourse? To answer this question, we must turn to the Blueprints 2025 that articulate the ASEAN Vision for the realization of the ASEAN Community over the next decade.

In 2015, with the launch of the AEC on December 31 of that year, ASEAN prepared Blueprints for the next decade of the process of community building. As other chapters have explained in detail, the process of developing a body of ASEAN "laws" and regulations is most advanced in the Economic pillar, as one would expect given both the traditional priority of economic cooperation as well as the exigencies of launching the AEC. The Blueprints for all three pillars were promulgated together in the document entitled "ASEAN 2025: Forging Ahead Together" and endorsed by the ASEAN Summit in the "Kuala Lumpur Declaration on ASEAN 2025".[13]

Since the Economic Community has come into being, and because there is a far greater number of ASEAN instruments in the Economic pillar than in others, the AEC Blueprint 2025 contains a far more detailed and comprehensive scheme for implementation than the Political-Security or Social-Cultural Blueprints.[14] What it does not contain, however, is an outline for how the rule of law, or a rules-based community will provide the necessary foundation for the effective implementation of the goals of the Blueprint. This, of course, is in part due to the "silo" mentality that informs the three-pillar ASEAN structure, confining the rule of law to the Political-Security Pillar, and inhibits proper treatment of issues such as the rule of law and human rights that actually cut across all three pillars.

13 Adopted in November 2015.
14 ASEAN Economic Community Blueprint 2025 (2015).

Like the other Blueprints, the AEC document emphasizes the principle of ASEAN as a "people-oriented and people-centered" community.[15] None of the Blueprints elaborate exactly what is meant by a "people-oriented and people-centered" ASEAN, though one might assume that the Charter principles of democracy, good governance, and the rule of law would be important enabling elements. Indeed, the AEC Blueprint 2025 does set the goal of developing, among other things, good governance and transparency, but, notably, does not mention the rule of law or democracy as among the articulated goals.[16]

The AEC Blueprint addresses the development of good governance, but this is in one of its least detailed sections, standing in considerable contrast to the very detailed prescriptions on trade, investment, regulation of competition, and so on. The section on Good Governance consists in its entirety of the following:

> B.6. Good Governance
>
> 36. ASEAN recognises the need to continue engaging the various stakeholders to build a more dynamic AEC 2025. Strategic measures include the following:
>
> i. Promote a more responsive ASEAN by strengthening governance through greater transparency in the public sector and in engaging with the private sector; and
> ii. Enhance engagement with the private sector as well as other stakeholders to improve the transparency and synergies of government policies and business actions across industries and sectors in the ASEAN region.[17]

While good governance has been treated as an interrelated principle with the rule of law and democracy in the instruments examined above, here the only connection adduced is with "transparency". While one might argue that there is no need to consider democracy as a constituent element of the AEC (despite it being "people-oriented and people-centered"), promoting the "inter-related principle" of the rule of law along with good governance would seem to be essential to the success of the regional legal and regulatory framework proposed in the Blueprint. Also noticeably absent are commitments to what is vaguely implied by the phrase "greater transparency in the public sector": an effective regional regime to combat corruption and to promote the development of a competent, impartial, and independent judiciary across ASEAN to implement and enforce the legal and regulatory regimes prescribed by the Blueprint.[18] Neither the term "the rule of law" nor the word "corruption" appears in the AEC Blueprint 2025.

To find an indication of the role of the rule of law in the scheme for community building over the next decade we must turn to the Political-Security

15 AEC Blueprint p. 1.
16 Ibid., p. 2.
17 Id. at footnote 15, at para. B.6.
18 AEC Blueprint (2015) 18 and see also Par. 38.

Blueprint 2025. Before doing so, however, it is worthwhile to provide a comparative framework by examining the 2009 ASEAN Political-Security (APSC) Blueprint.[19] Strikingly, unlike the AEC Blueprint, the 2009 APSC Blueprint does recognize the Charter's principles related to the rule of law:

> "7. The APSC shall promote political development in adherence to the principles of democracy, the rule of law and good governance, respect for and promotion and protection of human rights ..."[19] Indeed, the Blueprint accords centrality to the concept of a "rules based community," a concept which would appear to follow from the principles just articulated: "10. Based on the above, the ASEAN Political-Security Community envisages the following three key characteristics: a) A Rules-based Community of shared values and norms."[20]

The intimate relation of the concept of a rules-based community to the rule of law is fleshed out in the ensuing section A, "A Rules-based Community of Shared Values and Norms." This section begins by asserting the dependence of ASEAN's political development upon achievement of the rule of law and associated principles:

> ASEAN's cooperation in political development aims to strengthen democracy, enhance good governance and the rule of law, and to promote and protect human rights and fundamental freedoms, with due regard to the rights and responsibilities of the Member States of ASEAN, so as to ultimately create a Rules-based Community of shared values and norms. In the shaping and sharing of norms, ASEAN aims to achieve a standard of common adherence to norms of good conduct.[21]

A subsequent paragraph in this section recognizes the importance of "combatting corruption; and cooperation to strengthen the rule of law, judiciary systems and legal infrastructure, and good governance".[22] The same paragraph references the impending establishment and role of an ASEAN human rights mechanism and would thus appear to suggest that the principles just articulated should be encompassed in the work of such a mechanism. As we will see below, that has not been the case.

What appears clear in this section is that democracy, good governance, and the rule of law are requirements for securing the political development of ASEAN Member States and for securing the promotion and protection of the "human rights and fundamental freedoms" of the citizens of ASEAN.[23] Given

19 ASEAN Political-Security Community Blueprint (2009) [hereafter, "APSC Blueprint"].
20 APSC Blueprint p. 1.
21 Ibid., p. 2.
22 Ibid., p. 3.
23 Ibid., p. 3.

the foregoing, however, it is striking that when the 2009 Blueprint articulates the seven objectives of the AICHR there is no mention of the rule of law or of democracy, transparency, or good governance.[24]

When one turns to the APSC Blueprint 2025 there appear significant differences in emphasis from the 2009 Blueprint. Both Blueprints contain a Section II that delineates the "characteristics and elements" of the APSC. As noted above, the 2009 Blueprint identified the Charter's principles of democracy, the rule of law, and good governance as central elements and characteristics of the APSC necessary for the development of shared norms and enhancement of the political cooperation necessary to achieve ASEAN's shared goals. In the Blueprint 2025, on the other hand, the corresponding section (II at paras. 5.1-4) has eliminated all references to democracy, good governance, and the rule of law, substituting more general references to the creation of a "rules- based, people-oriented, people-centered community bound by fundamental principles"[25] and shared values and norms. Unlike the 2009 Blueprint there is no specification of which "fundamental principles" are meant. Even more striking is the fact that whereas Blueprint 2009 referenced the rule of law and related principles as stemming from the Charter, this corresponding section in the APSC Blueprint 2025 omits all reference to the Charter.

APSC Blueprint 2025 goes on to specify the "key elements" of an ASEAN "rules-based, people-oriented, people-centered community" (Sections A.1.1–7), the first element of which (A.1) is adherence to and promotion of ASEAN fundamental principles and shared norms and values. None of the seven ensuing subsections, including one on full implementation of the ASEAN Charter (A.1.1), mentions the rule of law, good governance, democracy, or human rights as fundamental principles of ASEAN, as did the 2009 Blueprint. What some of the subsections do encompass, however, is the creation of a pool of experts to promote *understanding of the diversity of ASEAN Member States* (A.1.6.ii, my emphasis)[26] and promoting respect for the "principles of independence, sovereignty, equality, territorial integrity, non-interference and national identity" in ASEAN. Neither of such concerns was reflected in the corresponding section of Blueprint 2009. One must ask why reference to the rule of law, good governance, and democracy as key elements of the APSC have disappeared and why there appears to now be a greater emphasis on diversity and non-interference. These latter principles would appear to be ill-suited to developing a "rules-based" ASEAN political community of shared values and norms that is also "people-oriented and people-centered".

24 Ibid., p. 5. While Section A.1.7 takes up the issue of combatting corruption it does not designate specific mechanisms to address this issue, nor does it make any connection between combatting corruption and the rule of law, good governance, or human rights.

25 APSC 2016 Blueprint, p. 2.

26 Section A.1.1 of the 2009 Blueprint aims to promote understanding of ASEAN political systems and culture, and does reference their "diversity" as does Blueprint 2016.

When, in Section A.2, Blueprint 2025 does turn to good governance, democracy, and the rule of law as elements of the rules-based community, they are not identified as among the fundamental ASEAN principles and shared values and norms encompassed in Section A.1. Moreover, whereas the active development of the rule of law and good governance was identified in Blueprint 2009 as a core constitutive element of the rules-based community, in Blueprint 2025 the emphasis is far different. As noted above, the section of Blueprint 2009 defining the rules-based community began with the sentence: "ASEAN's cooperation on political development aims to strengthen democracy, enhance good governance and the rule of law, and to promote human rights and fundamental freedoms."

In Blueprint 2025, on the other hand, where the rule of law and good governance are no longer characterized as fundamental Charter-based principles, they are instead relegated to an aspirational status of *values* that are to be the subject of dialogue, discussion, education, and promotion. There is little indication that they are fundamental principles of a legally binding Charter, let alone that they are necessary elements for the development of a rules-based ASEAN Political and Security Community.

As regards democracy for example, the Blueprint exhorts Member States to "convene seminars" and "share experiences" on democracy. The recent "shared experiences" of Thailand, Cambodia, Lao PDR, and Vietnam on democracy would indeed make for interesting dialogue. With respect to good governance, the Blueprint advises the inclusion of the culture of good governance "in educational curricula" and the promotion of "dialogue" and the fostering of partnerships and "new ideas". In other words, from their former status as fundamental structural elements these Charter principles appear now to be up for grabs as the subjects of discussion, education, and dialogue.

As regards the rule of law, the 2025 Blueprint's treatment of this principle stands in even more striking contrast to the Charter and the 2009 Blueprint. Indeed, the only specific reference in the entire APSC Blueprint 2025 to the rule of law is in a section (A.2.4) entitled "Establishing programmes for mutual support and assistance among ASEAN Member States in the development of strategies for strengthening the rule of law, judicial systems, and legal infrastructure." The sole subsection (A.2.4.1) that specifies what is actually to be accomplished merely entrusts the ASEAN Law Ministers Meeting with developing cooperation programs "to strengthen the rule of law, judicial systems, and legal infrastructure".[27] From being a fundamental Charter principle, the rule of law now appears to have devolved to a matter of technical cooperation such as developing case management systems and other elements of legal infrastructure. The close link of the rule of law with good governance, democracy, and the protection of human rights has now been broken.

The bifurcation of the rule of law from the core concept of a rules-based community finds confirmation in the document "ASEAN 2025: Forging Ahead Together" in which the ASEAN leaders adopted the three Blueprints 2025 and

27 APSC Blueprint 2016 p. 7.

committed themselves to the integrative vision they encompass.[28] A rules-based, people-oriented, people-centered community is a fundamental goal articulated by "Forging Ahead Together" but the rule of law, democracy, and good governance are no longer directly incorporated into that concept of community. Thus, in "Forging Ahead Together 2025" the ASEAN leaders commit themselves to a rules-based community as follows: "8. We, therefore, undertake to realise: 8.1. A rules-based community that fully adheres to ASEAN fundamental principles, shared values and norms as well as principles of international law governing the peaceful conduct of relations among states." The rules-based community is now structured around "ASEAN fundamental principles", left undefined, with no reference to democracy, the rule of law and good governance as key principles set out in the Charter. The rules-based community is also based upon "shared values and norms", similarly undefined, but presumably encompassing non-interference and other elements of the "ASEAN way". The rule of law and good governance are noticeably absent here and appear only in the next paragraph: "8.2. An inclusive and responsive community that ensures our peoples enjoy human rights and fundamental freedoms as well as thrive in a just, democratic, harmonious and gender-sensitive environment in accordance with the principles of democracy, good governance and the rule of law." Here the rule of law, democracy, and good governance are principles that will contribute to an environment that is just, harmonious, and so on, but they are no longer pillars of the core rules-based community articulated in paragraph 8.1.

What explains the retreat from the robust treatment and prominence accorded democracy, the rule of law, and good governance in Blueprint 2009? Some insight may be provided by the positive inclusion of a subject that was referenced in the 2009 Blueprint but granted far greater weight and prominence in 2016: corruption. Unlike the 2009 Blueprint, in APSC Blueprint 2025 the drafters devoted a prominent and substantive section to combatting corruption. Unlike the vague references to promoting dialogue and discussion on democracy and good governance, this section mandates ASEAN Member States to fully implement the 2004 MOU on cooperation in combatting corruption (A.2.3.i) and to take other concrete steps in implementing anti-corruption measures. It appears that, with the advent of the AEC on December 31, 2015, there was a recognition that combatting corruption is essential to achievement of key elements of the economic agenda specified in the AEC Blueprint. While the issue of corruption remains a sensitive one in ASEAN, there is apparently consensus that it must be addressed if the AEC is to function as envisaged.

As for the rule of law and the related principles of democracy and good governance, developments in certain ASEAN Member States have made these issues even more sensitive than they were in 2009. Or perhaps a better way to put it is that Member States such as Thailand, Malaysia, and Indonesia might have been more disposed to advocate strongly for the centrality of the rule of law,

28 "ASEAN 2025: Forging Ahead Together" (2015).

democracy, and good governance in the political development of ASEAN than they were in 2009. The irony of course is that the rule of law and anti-corruption initiatives are two sides of the same coin. The rule of law is necessary to effectively combat corruption and corruption is the corrosive force that undermines the rule of law and defeats good governance.

A rules-based community and the rule of law

The goal of a rules-based community articulated in ASEAN Vision 2025 and the APSC Blueprint 2025 envisages changes at both the regional and the national levels. At the regional level the structural elements of the rules-based community involve the implementation of ASEAN's legally binding instruments, identified in Section A.1 Thus, three key elements of the rules-based community are identified as: implementation of the ASEAN Charter (A.1.1), the implementation of ASEAN Agreements (A.1.2), and upholding principles of international law "governing the peaceful conduct of relations (A.1.3)".[29] The remaining four elements identified in this section (A.1) are less directly related to the development of a regional legal structure that would constitute a rules-based community and instead have more to do with the political culture of ASEAN and how understanding of that culture should be promoted.

The ensuing section of the APSC Blueprint 2025 (A.2) turns to the strengthening of the rule of law, good governance, democracy, human rights, and the fight against corruption. This, of course, is an agenda that is to be pursued at the national level. As noted above, while the goal of combatting corruption is treated in a fairly concrete and robust manner, the measures for strengthening democracy, good governance, and the rule of law are largely general and vacuous. Indeed, the phrase "the rule of law" is mentioned only once in 43 paragraphs of this section. When it is mentioned (A.2.4.i), as noted above, it is only one of the three technical areas in which the ASEAN Law Ministers are entrusted "to develop cooperation programmes to strengthen the rule of law, judicial systems and legal infrastructure".[30] It is also striking that when this section (A.2) of the Blueprint turns, in its longest and most detailed section, to the promotion and protection of human rights and to the role and mandate of the AICHR, the rule of law is nowhere mentioned.

What this overview of the APSC Blueprint 2025 indicates is that at the regional level there is a recognition of the necessity of implementation of legally binding ASEAN instruments in order to create a rules-based community. It also indicates an awareness that the state of the rule of law, democracy, good governance, and human rights at the national level is also somehow related to an ASEAN rules-based community. What is missing at the regional level is a structure for moving beyond a mere call for implementation of existing obligations. What is missing at

29 APSC 2025, p. 3.
30 Ibid., p. 7.

the national level is any indication of how the rule of law is to be achieved and of the relationship of achieving the rule of law and good governance to the effective protection of human rights. At the core of this latter gap is the role of the AICHR and the other ASEAN human rights bodies.

The identification of these gaps raises two questions. At the regional level, can ASEAN develop a rules-based community without institutions to promulgate, interpret, and enforce a coherent body of rules, that is, a coherent body of ASEAN Law? As Walter Woon has eloquently argued, ASEAN almost entirely lacks the institutional infrastructure for a regional rules-based community. As he notes, "It is impossible to create a rules-based ASEAN Community without some means of drafting, interpreting, and enforcing rules."[31] While ASEAN does have an Enhanced Dispute Resolution Mechanism (2004)[32] as well as Charter provisions (Articles 22–27) and other dispute resolution mechanisms that have been discussed in other chapters, the nature of these mechanisms reveals that absence of enforcement mechanisms that would genuinely instantiate the rule of law at the regional level.[33] The general lack of resort to these more limited existing mechanisms also indicates the lack of political will to create or utilize a genuine enforcement structure as well as the widely noted preference for ASEAN to resolve internal disputes through political rather than legal channels.

ASEAN at the moment even lacks an adequate mechanism to track the national implementation of the plethora of ASEAN conventions, agreements, declarations and various other kinds of documents and to authoritatively determine which are "hard law" as opposed to "soft law". In the AEC the ASEAN Integration Monitoring Directorate monitors the execution of the AEC. Although it does not have an enforcement mechanism, it could provide the basis for a more robust monitoring and implementation-enforcement mechanism. Yet despite the acknowledged need for such monitoring in the economic sphere, ASEAN Member States appear to remain resistant to developing any centralized institutions with a more general and robust monitoring mandate. Apart from other considerations, the budget and chronic understaffing of the ASEAN Secretariat do not allow it to fulfill such functions. In other words, although the term "rules-based community" has become the mantra of the moment, it will remain a vision until an adequate institutional infrastructure to fulfill interpretative, adjudicative, implementation, and enforcement requirements are met. Even farther from sight is how such a rules-based community will become genuinely people-oriented and people-centered.

At the national level the question is: Can ASEAN ever be a "rules-based community" without a far greater realization of the rule of law in its Member States? This question presents itself with equal force in regard to the realization of basic human rights guaranteed by the ASEAN Charter and recognized in the AHRD

31 Piris and Woon, Towards a Rules-Based Community: An ASEAN Legal Service p. 184. See also Ewing-Chow and Tan, "The Role of the Rule of Law in ASEAN Integration" pp. 15–27.

32 See also the "Protocol to the ASEAN Charter on Dispute Resolution Mechanisms" (2010).

33 See e.g. AEC Blueprint 2025, Art. 82 (iv).

and in "ASEAN 2025: Forging Ahead Together" because without the rule of law the protection of human rights will likewise remain largely aspirational. What then is the state of the rule of law across ASEAN?

It would be the subject of a monographic undertaking to discuss the state of the rule of law in the ten ASEAN Member States. The most comprehensive country-by-country survey, conducted by the Human Rights Resource Center headquartered at the University of Indonesia, has shown how far many ASEAN Member States were fulfilling the requirements of a robust rule of law regime. Their more recent follow-on study brings that survey up to date and indicates how in some ASEAN Member States the situation has deteriorated rather than improved.

While there are serious questions surrounding the accuracy of global rule of law and transparency/corruption rankings, it may be nonetheless useful as a rough indicator to reference some of the more widely cited rankings. The following table shows the ranking of ASEAN Member States in regard to the rule of law in the left-hand column (World Justice Project 2015, 102 countries ranked) and the rankings in regard to the rule of law in the middle column (Transparency International Corruption Index 2015, 168 ranked). The far-right column indicates the World Bank Ease of Doing Business 2015 rankings (189 surveyed).

Singapore	9	8	1
Malaysia	39	54	18
Philippines	51	95	103
Indonesia	52	88	109
Thailand	56	76	49
Vietnam	64	112	90
Myanmar	92	147	167
Cambodia	99	150	127
Laos		139[34]	134

These figures give a rough idea of the range of rule of law realization across ASEAN, as well as the relation between the rule of law and ease of doing business rankings. The Baseline Surveys of the Human Rights Resource Center provide a far more nuanced and detailed account but the overall conclusion as to the distance ASEAN has to travel in order to achieve the rule of law at the national level remains the same. Such shortcomings are widely recognized in ASEAN Member States where democracy and freedom of expression permit legitimate surveys, as, for example, in Indonesia, where the National Police and the Attorney General's Office are consistently ranked by the public as among the most corrupt and least trusted institutions in the country. The question thus presents itself with renewed force of how can ASEAN as a regional organization achieve the rule of law promised in the Charter and the AHRD when, with few exceptions, it is so far from being achieved at the national level across ASEAN?

34 Brunei and Lao PDR were not ranked in the World Justice Project.

The AICHR and achieving the rule of law as the foundation for a rules-based community in ASEAN

What institution in ASEAN should take responsibility for implementing the rule of law agenda? It should not be the ASEAN Law Ministers Meeting because it should be judiciary led and because the ALMM does not meet often enough. The institution that would appear to have a mandate to develop the rule of law is the AICHR because the rule of law cuts across all human rights concerns and provides the indispensable foundation for their realization. The rule of law is not just about fair trial rights, judicial independence, and impartiality, and so on. It is the bedrock required for the realization of almost all human rights, as well as for the development of a rules-based community that encompasses human rights and fundamental freedoms.

The mandate of the AICHR is the promotion and protection of human rights, and human rights cannot be protected without a system of law and the administration of justice that is free from corruption, interference, and manipulation by political, governmental, economic, and private interests. Civil and political rights, economic and social rights, environmental rights, and all the rest depend upon a coherent, fair, accessible, and authoritative legal order that can enforce the laws and provide punishment for criminal conduct and redress for violations of the rights of citizens. How then, has the AICHR, designated as the ASEAN human rights body with an overarching mandate, dealt with the rule of law?

The Terms of Reference of the AICHR (TOR) make clear the relevance of the rule of law to its human rights mandate: "The AICHR shall be guided by the following principles: ... d) adherence to the rule of law, good governance, the principles of democracy and constitutional government".[35] The 2012–2015 Workplan of the AICHR also provides that "AICHR is guided by the ASEAN Charter, the TOR of AICHR, and the purposes and principles contained therein".[36] Despite the language of the TOR just cited, the phrase the "rule of law" does not appear in this Workplan, nor do the terms good governance, democracy, or constitutional government.

The 2016–2020 AICHR Workplan reaffirms AICHR's commitment to the promotion and protection of human rights in even broader language than did its predecessor:

> The AICHR desires that the ASEAN community shall be free from fear, war, aggression and poverty. The peoples of ASEAN shall enjoy the right to live in peace, dignity and prosperity. There shall be a balance between rights, duties and responsibilities of individuals in the context of the ASEAN Community. The Member States of ASEAN and all sectors of their respective societies

35 AICHR, "Terms of Reference" (ASEAN Secretariat 2009), p. 5.
36 "Five Year Workplan of the AICHR (2012–2015)", p. 1.

> have the shared responsibility to ensure the promotion and protection of these rights and duties.[37]

Again, there is no reference anywhere in the new Workplan to the rule of law. What then do the two AICHR Workplans envisage as the areas of key human rights concern in ASEAN?

The AICHR 2012–2015 Workplan includes a mandate to "Identify the current and potential human rights matters of interest to ASEAN."[38] Neither that Workplan nor the subsequent 2016–2020 Workplan explicitly identify such areas, though AICHR activities have included a broad range of workshops on human rights issues such as human trafficking, persons with disabilities, and so on, which reflect AICHR's conviction that they are of "interest to ASEAN". To date it appears that AICHR activities have not focused on the rule of law or core civil and political rights, including the rule of law, as contained in the ICCPR.[39]

A clear indication of what AICHR considers to be human rights issues of interest to ASEAN is found in both Workplans in the enumeration of topics on which the AICHR will undertake thematic studies. In the AICHR 2012–2015 Workplan these issues encompass, in apparent order of priority: "Corporate Social Responsibility, Migration, Trafficking in person particularly women and children, Child soldiers, Women and children in conflicts and disasters, Juvenile justice, Right to information in criminal justice, Rights to health, Rights to education, Right to life, Right to Peace."[40] In the AICHR Workplan 2016–2020 Corporate Social Responsibility has been removed, as it was the subject of AICHR's first baseline study. The topic of "child soldiers" has been removed as well and in its stead, the topics of "Legal Aid" and "Freedom of Religion and Belief" have been added. While the category of "legal aid" reflects a concern for access to justice, a key component of the rule of law, as does the "right to information in criminal justice", the overarching category of the rule of law is notably absent. Other key components of the rule of law, including rights provided for in the ICCPR, such as judicial independence and core fair trial rights, are also absent. The same is true of many core rights guaranteed in the AHRD such as freedom from arbitrary or extra-legal detention, torture, and so on.

The inclusion of topics such as "the right to information in criminal justice" indicates an awareness in the AICHR that the rule of law, and in particular, the corpus of fair trial rights, are an issue in ASEAN. On the other hand, the right to information and legal aid are perhaps the least politically "sensitive" fair trial rights and their inclusion seems to indicate that despite the awareness of the

37 Ibid.

38 Workplan 2012–2015, Section 4.11.1.

39 Review of the "Activities" section of the AICHR website reveals no activities dedicated to the rule of law in ASEAN. It should be noted, however, that the activities archive on the website does not appear to have a complete listing of all AICHR activities.

40 Ibid., pp. 4–5.

absence of basic fair trial rights in a number of ASEAN Member States, the general categories of the rule of law and fair trial rights are thought too sensitive to include. In other words, although the AICHR's TOR creates a plain mandate for dealing with the rule of law and associated Charter principles, to date the AICHR has not chosen to take up this topic among its thematic studies or core activities.

As noted above, the AICHR's Workplan includes the completion of thematic studies on key human rights issues. The AICHR has completed one such thematic study, on Corporate Social Responsibility (CSR), and it merits inquiring as to whether issues related to the rule of law found their way into their research.

The AICHR Baseline Study on CSR acknowledges the importance of corruption to increasing business performance. Interestingly, the Study also includes the weakness of civil and political rights in this assessment:

> Aside from the fact that there is not yet an agreed upon definition of CSR and no authoritative assessment of the performance of CSR in ASEAN, the high tendencies towards high level of corruption, weak civil and political rights, and constrained media would likely increase the risks of poor business practices in the region. Accordingly, the ineffectiveness of the "voluntary" CSR approach reinforces the need for strong, enforceable and comprehensive corporate accountability standards at national and regional levels (Middleton and Pritchard, 2013: 61).[41]

One can easily infer the crucial importance of the rule of law from this passage, which makes its absence from the AICHR agenda even more problematic. The CSR Baseline Study recognizes, for example, Singapore's unique status in ASEAN in regard to the achievement of the rule of law and anti-corruption success. Under the rubric of "Characteristics of an ASEAN approach to corporate sustainability" the Study indicates that anti-corruption and transparency must be "high on the agenda." In this regard they cite Singapore's achievements:

> Singapore consistently ranks as one of the most corrupt-free countries in the world. Brunei is likewise recognized as an exception in ASEAN when it comes to corruption. It is clear that the governments of both countries intend to sustain such corrupt-free environment by enforcing strict regulations and tough penalties on offenders. Singapore's Corrupt Practices Investigation Bureau (CPIB), for example, has a wide and strong mandate to investigate corruption-related offenses in both the public and private sectors.

The AICHR Baseline Study thus recognizes the importance of transparency, anti- corruption, and, implicitly, the rule of law for the success of the ASEAN Economic Community, indicating Singapore as the example of the benefits of such a regime. Although the title of this section of the CSR Study suggests that

41 AICHR, "Baseline Study on CSR and Human Rights" (2014) 9.

transparency and anti-corruption should be "high on the agenda", why do they, in fact, find no place in the AICHR Workplan?

It is also interesting that when the CSR Study turns from Singapore and Brunei to ASEAN's Middle-Income Countries, it notes the importance of strong and vocal civil society in these Member States but does not at all mention the important role that anti-corruption campaigns and mechanisms are playing in increasing economic performance in Indonesia and the Philippines. Turning to the CLMV countries the Study only discretely alludes to the importance of anti-corruption in attracting foreign direct investment, concluding that "this also presents the tangible risk of opening up its people and resources to exploitation, and that the tax money and other economic benefits will find their way to the pockets of only a handful".[42] In dealing with all of the ASEAN Member States other than Singapore and Brunei, it thus appears that corruption and the absence of the rule of law are issues too sensitive to mention directly.

What is also noticeably absent in these sections of the Baseline Study on CSR is the recognition that predictability and certainty in legal institutions are also key components, both of which are critically undermined by corruption. The absence of the rule of law and strong anti-corruption institutions enables the kind of corruption alluded to by the Study in that such a situation compels investors either to engage in corrupt practices in order to secure licenses, contracts, and generally function effectively in a massively corrupt environment or to abstain from investment altogether. The reluctance to recognize the key role that corruption plays in such a dynamic is indicated by the Study's conclusion

> that, "With high government control, uncompetitive corporate landscape and weak civil societies, CSR has simply not thrived in ASEAN's lower income countries."[43]

Surely what is missing amongst these factors are the weak and corrupt legal regimes, the general context of corrupt practices, and the lack of a stable and predictable legal environment that would encourage responsible firms to invest and enable them to conduct their enterprises in a manner consistent with international standards.

Conclusion

The lack of institutional mechanisms to instantiate the ASEAN Charter's principles of the rule of law and good governance appears clearly from a survey of the treatment of such issues in the ASEAN Blueprints and in the Workplan of the AICHR. Equally apparent is the importance of developing the rule of law at the regional and national levels for the success of the AEC. Walter Woon's suggestion

42 Ibid., at p. 18.
43 Ibid.

of the creation of an independent institution, which he terms an ASEAN Legal Service, deserves careful consideration by relevant ASEAN bodies.[46] The pressing need for such a mechanism to make the goal of a rules-based ASEAN Community more than an empty phrase is clear.

It will no doubt take ASEAN a considerable amount of time to move towards the creation of such an institution because of the tradition of resistance to centralized authority independent of the ultimate political decision-making institution of the ASEAN Summit. At present, however, another possible path has recently opened that could also assist in developing consensus for the creation of a mechanism such as that envisaged by Woon. In default of the AICHR assuming its responsibility for the promotion and protection of human rights by prioritizing the implementation of the Charter's guarantee of the rule of law in its Workplan, it is the ASEAN judiciaries that are now best placed to take up this issue.

The new framework provided by the recent creation of a Council of ASEAN Supreme Court Chief Justices may be best suited for key elements of this role. The framework created by that Council includes judicial working groups drawn from the judiciaries of the Member States and functioning under thematic mandates provided by the Chief Justices. These working groups are tasked with issues concerning legal harmonization, dispute resolution, enhancing court performance and transparency, all of which contribute to the development of the rule of law at the national and regional levels. This represents only preliminary steps towards the fulfillment of the Charter principles and the promises of the AHRD, but ASEAN has always functioned at a "step by step" pace. Ultimately, however, it will require the political will and consensus of the Member States to create the kind of independent institution that is indispensable for the realization of the rules-based community envisioned in the ASEAN 2025 documents. In the end, the cooperation of all branches of ASEAN governments to implement the necessary legislative, executive, and judicial reforms will be required to make the rule of law a structural feature of the ASEAN Economic Community rather than an aspirational promise.

Index

Note: Page numbers in **bold** denote tables.

For Product Safety Concerns and Information please contact our EU representative GPSR@taylorandfrancis.com
Taylor & Francis Verlag GmbH, Kaufingerstraße 24, 80331 München, Germany

www.ingramcontent.com/pod-product-compliance
Ingram Content Group UK Ltd.
Pitfield, Milton Keynes, MK11 3LW, UK
UKHW022125190926
475702UK00013B/1657
9780367647650